Special Issues from the *Teachers College Record*

ELLEN CONDLIFFE LAGEMANN, Series Editor

# Brown v.
# Board of Education

## The Challenge for
## Today's Schools

Ellen Condliffe Lagemann and LaMar P. Miller, Editors

Teachers College
Columbia University
New York and London

Published by Teachers College Press, 1234 Amsterdam Avenue
New York, NY 10027

Copyright © 1996 by Teachers College, Columbia University

Originally published in *Teachers College Record,* v. 96, no. 4, Summer 1995.

*Library of Congress Cataloging-in-Publication Data*

Brown versus Board of Education : the challenge for today's schools / Ellen Condliffe
      Lagemann and LaMar P. Miller, editors.
            p.      cm.—(Special issues from the Teachers College record)
      Includes biliographical references and index.
      ISBN 0-8077-3524-8 (pbk.)
            1.  Segregation in education—Law and legislation—United States—History.
      2. Brown, Oliver, 1918—Trials, litigation, etc.—History.   3. Topeka (Kan.).
      Board of Education—Trials, litigation, etc.—History.   I. Lagemann, Ellen
      Condliffe, 1945 –      .   II. Miller, LaMar P.   III. Series.
      KF 4155.B76    1996
      344.73'0798—dc20
      [347.304798]                                                                    95-42631

ISBN 0-8077-3524-8

Printed on acid-free paper

Manufactured in the United States of America

03   02   01   00   99   98   97   96      8   7   6   5   4   3   2   1

# Contents

# An American Dilemma Still

ELLEN CONDLIFFE LAGEMANN
*New York University*

Today, it is difficult to write with hope about the prospects for racial justice and equality in the United States. Historically recurrent debates about race and intelligence have been reignited by Richard Herrnstein and Charles Murray's mean-spirited, pseudo-scientific treatise *The Bell Curve*.[1] Despite the findings of the federal Glass Ceiling Commission, indicating that women and minorities are still disproportionately underrepresented in upper-management jobs in most sectors of the economy, affirmative action is under attack in the U.S. Congress.[2] And relentless efforts are also underway in the Congress to cut back on the public assistance provided to those least able to fend for themselves, especially young, poor single mothers and their children.

Compounding these recent events is new evidence suggesting that continuing poverty and disadvantage among African Americans are in considerable measure a result of white indifference and prejudice. Certainly this is one of the conclusions reached by sociologists Douglas S. Massey and Nancy A. Denton in *American Apartheid: Segregation and the Making of the Underclass*.[3] Seeking to demonstrate the futility of further debate concerning the primacy of either race or social class in explanations of poverty, the two being integrally connected, Massey and Denton illustrate the ways in which residential segregation, intense poverty, and the emergence of what they describe as "an oppositional culture that devalues work, schooling, and marriage and that stresses attitudes and behaviors that are antithetical and often hostile to success in the larger economy" have interacted with one another to create a largely black underclass that is locked in poverty and alienation.[4]

According to Massey and Denton, residential segregation, which has played a catalytic role in this downward cycle, "continues to exist because white America has not had the political will or desire to dismantle it."[5] Private prejudice and discrimination, combined with the prejudicial policies of banks and real estate companies and reinforced by ineffective government action, have resulted in a situation where individuals, usually ones who have suffered discrimination, have been expected to fight on their own or through nongovernmental advocacy organizations to fulfill their right to equal, desegregated housing. This places an intolerable burden on the victims of discrimination and helps to ensure that the underlying systemic problems will not be addressed. White America could but to date has not been willing to support effective residential desegregation policies.

Massey and Denton's assertion that segregation persists as a result of a failure of political will is echoed by Stanford economist Martin Carnoy in *Faded Dreams: The Politics and Economics of Race in America.*[6] According to Carnoy, there are three prevalent explanations for continuing black poverty in the United States, these being individual failure, pervasive racism, and changing economic structures. The first explanation suggests that individual African Americans have not taken advantage of the opportunities open to them; the second explanation posits that white discrimination has stood in the way of African-American progress; and the third explanation claims that new demands for high levels of skill have compounded the historic and contemporary educational disadvantages of many African Americans. None of these explanations is sufficient, Carnoy maintains, however, without the addition of politics, for it is politics that translates individual attitudes into public policies and that sets the normative rules that structure markets as well as conceptions of what is appropriate in terms of public entitlements.

Basing his argument on correlations he has discerned between national leadership and black educational and economic progress, Carnoy believes that the way people view race and class is, on the one hand, shaped by prevalent ideas and images, and, on the other, constitutive of public willingness to support policies and programs that will help lessen black disadvantage. Having come of age in the 1960s when racial justice and equality were widely shared and very compelling ideals, he is puzzled by the problems that continue to plague this nation. "Why, with my generation's once ardent commitment to building a just nation and our talent for making such significant changes in other aspects of life," Carnoy asked, "were we not able to overcome our own social problems?"[7] Combined with Massey and Denton's analysis of the problem of residential segregation, that question underscores the importance of studying past failures and suggests the urgency of considering what might be done to reenergize public commitment to equality and social justice for all Americans.

Two documents that exercised powerful influence on American aspirations earlier in this century may be instructive in this regard. The first is Gunnar Myrdal's *An American Dilemma* and the second, *Brown* v. *Board of Education of Topeka, Kansas.*

Few books have framed public discourse as profoundly as *An American Dilemma* did. For fifty-one years, it has served as a standard point of reference in discussions of race and equality and it has also had a discernible impact on public policy.[8] Commissioned by the Carnegie Corporation of New York to inform its consideration of the feasibility of developing cultural and educational programs for African-American adults, *An American Dilemma* became a much larger, more broadly framed study than its sponsors had intended.[9] As Myrdal's daughter, Sissela Bok, has observed, this was because its Swedish economist author brought to it a keen interest in questions of values and objectivity and a lifelong commitment to developing the social sciences as means to practical social improvements.[10] In addition, as Gunnar Myrdal himself explained, the study's design reflected John Dewey's "conception of what a social problem really is."[11]

Agreeing with Dewey's argument in *Freedom and Culture*, which was published while Myrdal was working on *An American Dilemma*, Myrdal emphasized the moral aspects of racial problems. This meant that he tried to clarify the degree to which they were a result of individual and social choices. He also viewed such problems in terms of the impact of "culture" on "human nature," culture being defined as a continuous interaction among a great many variables—laws, customs, social and economic circumstances, history, and the arts among them.[12] In combination, these influences enabled Myrdal to produce a book that was richly complex in analysis and that spoke with a self-conscious (and self-consciously analyzed) moral grandeur that few, if any, subsequent works of social science have achieved. Though much else was also involved, no single attribute ever being sufficient to explain the impact of a book or idea, the power and forthrightness of Myrdal's appeal to the conscience of white America were essential factors in the book's capacity to shape public thinking about the kind of society the United States could and should be.

That a study that was expressly concerned with values and moral premises and their impact on actual behavior should have had such a wide and relatively long-lasting impact is not irrelevant to current problems of political will. In *Whose Keeper? Social Science and Moral Obligation*, Alan Wolfe, a sociologist now at Boston University, makes the interesting observation that in modern societies once-standard guides to morality tend to lose their authority. Hungry for new alternative sources of guidance concerning how to live wisely and well, people look, Wolfe believes, not to "religion, philosophy, literature, or politics," but rather to the social sciences, where they can find moral theories as well as empirical data about how people think and behave. "As the Kinsey Reports first illustrated," he stated, "when all are interested in how others behave but few are secure that they are behaving correctly, social scientists are the closest we have to savants."[13]

Wolfe's point, buttressed by evidence attesting to the influence of *An American Dilemma*, may suggest that because they satisfy deeply felt needs for moral guidance, explicitly moral works of social science are likely to have a greater impact on public values and aspiration than works that are more neutral, detached, and "objective." If that is correct, the declining commitments to racial integration and equality that have been evident since the 1960s may, in some measure, be attributable to increasingly narrow-gauged and technical styles of social research as well as to less overtly action-oriented styles of social reporting than Myrdal relied on.

*An American Dilemma* carried a message concerning the wisdom, prudence, and possibility of purposeful progress toward racial equality. By reminding its readers that social situations are constructed and can be reconstructed, it powerfully affirmed the fact that wrongs can be righted. Hopefulness and efficacy were essential to the message it preached. The importance of combining those qualities has been sadly illuminated by recent politics, a message of hope having played a role in President Clinton's electoral success in 1992, and a lack of strong and consistent leadership having played a role in the public's repudiation of the Democratic party two years later. If there is to be a renewed effort to build a just society in the United States, discussions of current events will have to be charged with a seasoned but unstoppable determination to eradicate bias and discrimination. Finding multiple and varied ways to do that is one of the most significant challenges facing this society.

Another closely related challenge has to do with the public's faith in the public purposes of the public schools. If the Myrdal study shows the power of speaking directly and forcefully about matters of race and equality, *Brown* v. *Board of Education* illustrates how vital the American faith in education has been to social progress. Although the *Brown* decision was important most immediately because it established that segregated schools could not be equal schools and were therefore in violation of the laws of the United States, it was also important because it confirmed America's long-standing reliance on education as a means for addressing its most urgent social challenges. Just as education had been counted on in the seventeenth century to shield people from "that old Deluder, Satan," and then, in the eighteenth century, to teach the civic virtues that would enable the new Republic to survive, and thereafter also to teach the attitudes and skills necessary for productive work, so now was it being called on to open equal opportunity to black Americans.

Of course, there is much about the American reliance on education that is problematic. However powerful it may be, education is not a panacea, the American tendency to treat it as such too often bespeaking a long-standing and deep distrust of the more directly intrusive powers of the state. That aside for the moment, by linking education to issues of race, *Brown* demonstrated the wisdom of the decision of the National Association for the

Advancement of Colored People to attack segregation via challenges to seg-regated schooling and, in so doing, reaffirmed the centrality of education as an instrument of public policy, a strategy for planned change.

The American faith in education that was confirmed by *Brown*, and there-after by some of the most important legislation of the Kennedy-Johnson War on Poverty, notably Title I of the Elementary and Secondary Education Act (ESEA) of 1965, seems frighteningly precarious today. Often forgetting the extraordinarily challenging context in which public schools now oper-ate, commentators seem more likely to report school failures than school triumphs. Often confusing measures of operational efficiency with evidence of educational excellence, they tend to ignore the full range of purposes schools have traditionally been asked to pursue. Today it is frequently assumed that schools should be primarily concerned with enhancing the future vocational competence of their students. It is too rarely also asserted that they should be equally concerned with creating environments that teach children tolerance, cooperation, empathy, altruism, and all the other orientations needed to live peaceably and well in a complex, pluralistic world. Even where the institutional arrangements for schooling have not been privatized, public expectations concerning what schools should do are narrowing the potential contribution schools can make to public life.

Were there alternative institutions that could advance public agenda via educational means, this situation might not be so worrisome. But to my knowledge, no such institution exists. Some might venture that families could and should assume more responsibility for youth instruction and socialization. However, there is much to be said for preserving the private rights of families, including their right to transmit their own idiosyncratic beliefs, values, and behavioral preferences, and for pursuing common, non-familial agenda elsewhere. The political philosopher Bruce Ackerman once claimed that in a liberal society families should have a right to control the primary education of their children, including their earliest and most for-mative education in values, while the state should have a right to control their secondary education, which, by offering exposure to ideas different from their parents' ideas, would help them realize their own individuality.[14] Even though his argument would not be likely to win favor today, it does help to show that even though families serve crucial primary educational functions, they cannot and should not be seen as an alternative to public schools, which have traditionally been regarded as an effective and pre-ferred means for advancing common social, economic, and political goals.

Without an alternative agency devoted to promoting the public's interest in having young people prepared to be responsible, productive, civically engaged, tolerant people, declining respect for public schools and declin-ing support for their once broad, public missions will result in a diminished capacity to seek purposeful, planned social change. Even though too much has frequently been asked of public schools, they have served as a powerful, popular, and effective focus for public aspirations for a very long time. Clearly, therefore, if the United States is to fulfill its too often ambivalent and vacillating allegiance to racial justice and equality for all, public faith in the public schools, and especially in the public purposes of the public schools, will have to be restored. Doing that represents a challenge no less significant than finding ways to express the fact that bias and discrimination cannot be tolerated in the United States.

By focusing on *Brown* v. *Board of Education,* this set of essays is designed to contribute in at least a small way to meeting both of these challenges. Most of the essays here were first presented as papers at a conference convened by LaMar P. Miller, director of the Metropolitan Center for Urban Education at New York University's School of Education. Subsequently, LaMar and I worked together to organize a set of revised essays that could illustrate not only the historic significance of *Brown,* but also the continuing promise and problems associated with its implementation.

Forty plus years after *Brown,* it is readily evident that desegregation will not easily or automatically produce integrated schools. It is also evident that integrated schools cannot alone produce an integrated society. The enforcement of residential desegregation, equity in hiring and promotion in the work place, and much else will also be required. However, as the research of Teachers College sociologist Robert Crain and others has shown, there is strong evidence indicating that people who have attended integrated schools are more likely to live and work in integrated settings.[15] Obviously, therefore, school integration can be instrumental to an integrated society. Although we have a very long way to go before the promise of such a society can be realized to the benefit of all people, the faith in education that was inherent in *Brown* was not misplaced. Reading about *Brown* can remind us of that. Perhaps it can even help us realize anew that contributing to the achievement of racial justice and equality is among the most important public purposes of the public schools.

## Notes

1   Richard J. Herrnstein and Charles Murray, *The Bell Curve: Intelligence and Class Structure in American Life* (New York: Free Press, 1994).

2   *New York Times,* 16 March 1995, pp. A1 and A22.

3   Douglas S. Massey and Nancy A. Denton, *American Apartheid: Segregation and the Making of the Underclass* (Cambridge: Harvard University Press, 1993).

4   Ibid., p. 8.

5   Ibid., p. 186.

6   Martin Carnoy, *Faded Dreams: The Politics and Economics of Race in America* (Cambridge: Cambridge University Press, 1994).

7    Ibid., p. 1.

8    David W. Southern, *Gunnar Myrdal and Black-White Relations: The Use and Abuse of "An American Dilemma," 1944–1969* (Baton Rouge: Louisiana State University Press, 1987).

9    Ellen Condliffe Lagemann, *The Politics of Knowledge: The Carnegie Corporation, Philanthropy, and Public Policy* (1989; Chicago: University of Chicago Press, 1992), chap 6.

10    Sissela Bok, "Introductory Remarks," October 1994 conference on *An American Dilemma*, subsequently published in *Daedalus*, Winter 1995, pp. 1–13.

11    Gunnar Myrdal, *An American Dilemma* (New York: Harper & Row, 1944), p. xlvii. A new addition will be published by Transaction Press in the fall of 1995.

12    The depth of Myrdal's indebtedness to Dewey is readily evident when one juxtaposes *An American Dilemma* with John Dewey, *Freedom and Culture* (1939), in *The Later Works of John Dewey*, Volume 13: 1938–1939, ed. Jo Ann Boydston (Carbondale: Southern Illinois University Press, 1988), pp. 63–188. See also Walter A. Jackson, *Gunnar Myrdal and Americas Conscious: Social Engineering and Racial Liberalism, 1938–87* (Chapel Hill: University of North Carolina Press, 1990), pp. 105–06.

13    Alan Wolfe, *Whose Keeper? Social Science and Moral Obligation* (Berkeley: University of California Press, 1989), pp. 6, 7.

14    Bruce A. Ackerman, *Social Justice in the Liberal State* (New Haven: Yale University Press, 1980), chap. 5.

15    Much of this research is summarized in Amy Stuart Wells and Robert L. Crain, "Perpetuation Theory and the Long-Term Effects of School Desegregation," *Review of Educational Research* 64 (Winter 1994): 531–55. See also James M. McPartland and Jomills Henry Braddock, "Going to College and Getting a Good Job: The Impact of Desegregation," in *Effective School Desegregation: Equality, Quality, and Feasibility*, ed. W. D. Hawley (Beverly Hills: Sage, 1981); and Jennifer Hochschild, *The New American Dilemma: Liberal Democracy and School Desegregation* (New Haven: Yale University Press, 1984).

# Tracking the Progress of *Brown*

LAMAR P. MILLER
*New York University*

*Since 1954, the force of law has been required to achieve much of the desegregation that has taken place. Although* Brown *was a great achievement, it has not solved the problems we had hoped it would. Hence, there are great similarities between the conditions in 1954 and those in 1994. Because we face a different and more complex set of problems than we have in the past, we cannot rely solely on the force of law to solve the problems of desegregation in general and the issues associated with racially isolated schools in particular. The education community must accept its leadership responsibility if we are to fulfill the mandate of* Brown.

The 1954 Supreme Court decision in the case of *Brown* v. *Board of Education of Topeka, Kansas,* provided the legal basis for equal educational opportunity. The Court ruled that "in the field of public education the doctrine of 'separate but equal' has no place. Separate education facilities are inherently unequal. . . . We hold that the plaintiffs and others similarly situated . . . are by reason of the segregation complained of, deprived of the equal protection of the laws guaranteed by the Fourteenth Amendment."[1]

Since 1954, the force of law has been required to achieve much of the desegregation that has taken place so far. The very integrity of the three branches of government has been severely tested by the controversy over desegregation. While many of the once dual school districts in the South have converted to a nonsegregated or unitary status, segregation of black students in the Northeast has increased, as has the segregation of Hispanic students in all regions of the country. Moreover, the quality of the educational experience received by minority students continues to be a major problem. Even the national reports on the need for excellence and restructuring education do not address directly issues related to quality education and equality of educational opportunity.

It is against this background that the staff of the Metropolitan Center for Urban Education at New York University has tracked the progress of desegregation through three national conferences: Brown Plus Twenty, in 1974; Brown Plus Thirty, in 1984; and Brown Plus Forty, in 1994. The 1994 conference provided the articles included in this book and the opportunity for me to highlight the circumstances we are in and the challenges we face.

The court ruling on the *Brown* case and the subsequent events over the last forty years changed the lives of most African Americans and altered the educational landscape for many students regardless of their ethnic, cultural, or racial background. In my own case, *Brown* has shaped and driven my career. However, I, like many African Americans, face a dilemma in that my experiences have at times left me disillusioned and pessimistic about the prospects of changing the system. On the other hand, I know that no matter how embedded intransigent racist practices may be, the record shows that great social and political change of the magnitude called for by the *Brown* decision has taken place; for example, witness changes in South Africa. We know that change is not only possible; it is inevitable. Given the conditions in 1954 and the circumstances of today, it is important to compare the challenges in education of 1954 with those facing us in 1994.

The circumstance in which most African Americans found themselves in 1954, simply put, was living in a segregated world in America both North and South. The entire society, in fact, until about 1960 was divided along racial lines, and the schools simply reflected the dual arrangement that was taken for granted. Of course, "school segregation differed from other forms of segregation because education is compulsory. Students spend many years in school, and these formative years determine the entire course of a person's life. One can say, therefore, that in very important and significant ways, for generations, the schools merely reflected the values, mores, and cultural norms found in the society at large with respect to race."[2] While segregation in the North did not have the sanction of law, the practice of separate but unequal was just as devastating for most black children. Discrimination was rampant throughout the country and minority children suffered the indignities of a generally racist society.

Like many black college graduates of 1954, I greeted the *Brown* decision with great enthusiasm as I began a career in teaching and in education. I believed I could help turn things around for black children and other children as well and that people would see the folly of unequal education and schools. I am sure many other graduates both black and white shared this view. That of course was a naive assumption on our part. We did not understand the depth of feelings and attitudes that separated black and white schools and we have spent the last forty years in litigation, in politics, and in demonstrations and persuasion trying to turn things around. To be sure we have had some success, but for most of us the progress has been far less than satisfactory.

Clearly *Brown* was a great achievement, but it is also clear that it has not solved the problems as we had hoped it would. When the *Brown* decision of 1954 called for the dismantling of segregated schools, the schools were placed in contraposition to the society. *Brown* called for a level of community in America that had been unknown and unaccepted in the larger society. The Court had spoken but the pace of change characterizing black–white relations defied court orders. What then was the impact of *Brown*? What was accomplished by the 1954 decision?

We did not understand at the time that *Brown* broke the back of apartheid in America, and set the stage for the civil rights movement, Martin Luther King, the women's movement, the *Lau* decision and Hispanics, Asian groups, the American Association of Retired Persons, and other groups concerned about equality in this country.

The Court's decision called for change in attitudes all across our country. Because the basic ingredients of change—acceptance, mutual respect, justice, and equality—are missing, the decision has had to depend almost entirely on the force of law for its implementation. And "there are some things the law cannot do. The law cannot compel one group to accept another as equal. The law has not been able to change society's stubborn resistance to the alteration of long-standing practices based on racial stereotypes or the naive expectations of persons of good will who are oblivious to the extent and pervasiveness of racism in America."[3] There are of course some things the law can and must do, but I believe the full and effective implementation of the *Brown* decision requires the commitment, involvement, and leadership of educators.

Why is it necessary to make this appeal in 1994, when in fact some political and educational leaders consider integration an idea whose time has passed, irrelevant to the current priorities for school reform—a point of view that always make headlines? First, we need to understand the striking similarities between the conditions in 1954 and those in 1994. For the first time since the Supreme Court's ruling in *Brown* v. *Board of Education* took effect, racial and ethnic segregation—between cities, suburbs, schools, and classrooms—is growing worse. Harvard University researcher Gary Orfield calls it "the beginning of a historic reversal" in school desegregation trends. Orfield's latest research, for example, found the schools in New York State to be among the most segregated in the country.[4] Commenting on this finding, the New York State Education Commissioner, Thomas Sobol, acknowledged the existence of two distinct school systems—one urban, minority, poor, and failing; the other suburban, white, affluent, and successful. As Sobol said, "This is not a healthy condition for society."[5] Second, segregation is associated with inequalities, including lower test scores and college attendance and completion rates among poor and minority students. The problems are most severe for the increasing number of students who attend schools in poor neighborhoods that are nearly all black or Hispanic. Efforts, further, to compensate for these inequalities have yielded no conclusive results. Most of today's segregation is different from the kind originally struck down by *Brown*. The Supreme Court outlawed segregation that was either sanctioned by state law or traceable to school board policies. The new segregation is usually blamed on demographic change: differential birth rates and patterns of migration and housing, including federal policies on the location of public housing projects. By the year 2000, nearly 40 percent of the nation's schoolchildren will be members of minority groups; within thirty years half the nation's public schools will be mainly black and Hispanic. Moreover, poverty and race in America are statistically inseparable: According to the U.S. Census Bureau, 43 percent of black children and 36 percent of Hispanic children live below the poverty line, as compared with 14 percent of white children.

Finally, school improvement for racially isolated poverty schools is no longer just a local or national imperative; it is an international imperative. If we intend this country to maintain its strong leadership role in the global community, we cannot continue to let 40 percent of our human resources go down the drain.

Given this brief analysis, what then are today's challenges for desegregation and education? In addition to differences, there are similarities between today's conditions and those of forty years ago. We need a new vision if we are to succeed in changing the outcomes of our efforts to provide a successful education for all children. We face a different and more complex set of problems than we have in the past—hence the need to pay attention to new realities, some which I have attempted to describe. The vision of school administrators must include education reform that directly addresses racial isolation and poverty without leaving it entirely to the courts. Our psychologists must address the effect of adult expectations for children, which are often based on a combination of negative socially defined symbols; our teachers and curriculum specialists must develop new methods for teaching poor children how to think critically; and our sociologists and philosophers must examine whether the traditional structure of our schools is the best structure for the future.

More importantly, we must fulfill our obligation to create a microcosm in the schools that manifests the best that we know. We must create an environment within school walls that enables teacher and pupil to be the best that they can be. This environment must be fostered by an atmosphere of mutual respect for all persons and encourage each student and teacher to become a part of a miniature world that, for six hours, functions differently by inviting everyone to rise to the full potential of his or her capacities. This means that teachers, administrators, and parents have to acquire the sensitivity to deal with their students' world, to understand their vernacular, their thought coinage, their metaphors, and their outlook. It means constructing a curriculum on what is known, felt, and understood by their students, then teaching them what they need to master in order to become full and self–reliant participants in a free society.

That was the mandate of *Brown*. The court deliberately called for major social change beginning with the schools. The schools were to become the innovators in the culture, the agents of transition, and the intermediary for the community. The time has come to uphold the clear mandate and spirit of the Constitution against the long-standing entrenchment of a racially segregated school system. That was our challenge in 1954, and that is the challenge in 1994.

## Notes

1  Brown v. Board of Education of Topeka, Kansas, 347 U.S. 483 (1954).

2  Samuel Proctor, "School Integration and the National Community," in *Brown Plus Thirty*, ed. LaMar P. Miller (New York: Metropolitan Center for Educational Research, Development and Training, 1986), p. 13.

3  Ibid., p. 14.

4  Gary Orfield, with the assistance of Sara Schley, Diane Glass, and Sear Reardon, *The Growth of Segregation in American Schools: Changing Patterns of Separation and Poverty since 1968* (Alexandria, Va.: National School Boards Association, 1993).

5  Thomas Sobol, "A Report to the Governor and the Legislature on Educational Status of the State's Schools: Statewide Profile of the Educational System" (Albany: The University of the State of New York/The State Educational Department, Office for Policy Analysis and Program Accountability, January 1, 1989).

# Dream Deferred but Not Defeated

ROGER WILKINS
*George Mason University*

*The decision in* Brown *v.* Board of Education of Topeka, Kansas, *may have been the seminal civil rights event of the twentieth century. It led to the dismantling of the systems of laws that kept blacks shackled as closely to slavery as possible. But the expectations of the lawyers and civil rights leaders that equality would follow such a decision were dashed because they had underestimated both the depth of American racism and the enormity of the remaining task of getting all of America's black agricultural workers into the mainstream economy. As the twentieth century ends, that task, left over from slavery, still faces the American people.*

When the Warren Court handed down the decision in *Brown* v. *Board of Education of Topeka, Kansas*, it set in motion a train of events that changed the country and affected every citizen. It destroyed American apartheid and enriched our society. It also brought the nation a sobering dose of racial reality that foreshadows a long, painful, and expensive struggle if we are ever to free ourselves of the enduring destruction and anguish flowing from what James Madison called our "original sin."

*Brown* was ultimately about much more than education. To understand its full impact, we have to remember what this country was like before the decision.

For all its ugliness, there was something almost innocent about the pre-*Brown* time. A few years after the decision had come down and the complexities it spawned had become apparent, Robert Carter, Thurgood Marshall's chief deputy at the National Association for the Advancement of Colored People (NAACP) Legal Defense Fund, was asked why more thought had not been given to what would happen next. Carter replied that all the forethought had gone into destroying the dual system of education because "we thought segregation was the box we were in."

In fact, segregation was so stifling and humiliating that it was very hard to see other evils. If instead of cardboard the walls of the "box we were in" had been made of glass, we could say that blacks looking out from the suffocating insults of segregation could see nothing wrong with the rest of America except that they were not in it.

In addition, I think many African Americans believed that there were millions of "good" white people whose souls were imbued with the spirit of America's highest expressed ideals. It is also fair to say that in the eyes of most sympathetic whites and of most activist blacks, the terrible racial wrong was that "worthy" blacks were injured. The great bulk of black poverty was hidden in the rural South or stuck off in barely visible corners of large cities.

But ultimately, the fate of poor blacks is at the heart of America's racial problem. From the beginning, the race question in America was about economics and psychology, and it still is. Blacks were not brought to the Western hemisphere to be civilized or converted to Christianity. They were brought here for economic reasons. Their labor was required to help tame a wild continent and to wrest profits from it. To accomplish that task, they were degraded, brutalized, and kept ignorant. That was the state in which the vast majority left slavery in 1865.

The task for America then and now has been to find a way for the economy to absorb that mass of unskilled and degraded workers. Millions of them were penned up on rural southern plantations until the middle of this century, when mechanization pushed them—peasants and semi-slaves—off the farms and into the cities by the millions.

That exodus was in full swing at the time of the *Brown* decision. The exodus, like the decision, was a part of the breakup of the pre–World War II, postslavery American world. After the war black soldiers had come home hungering for freedom, and many Americans had become aware of the irony of the country's having fought a war against fascism with a segregated army. The Soviet Union was competing with us throughout the Third World by pointing to our disgraceful treatment of black citizens. In 1947, Jackie Robinson had driven the black man's dignity and ability into the national consciousness with his great rookie season. The next year, President Truman issued an executive order desegregating the armed forces.

But blacks were still brutally held in place by an economic-legal-police-caste system that was undergirded by violence. A year after *Brown*, a black Chicago teenager was lynched in Mississippi for violating racial mores in greeting a white woman. In the North, blacks were submerged under a thick culture of smug, superior condescension that led to such ironies as blacks' being limited to janitorial and elevator operator jobs on newspapers that thundered editorially against southern racism. And in 1954, the black poverty rate, while heading down, was still close to 70 percent.

In that world, *Brown* proved to be a second Emancipation Day. Blacks read the decision to say "the Constitution really does apply to me!" It ended seven decades of disgraceful racist jurisprudence by the Supreme Court. And the forces it liberated—from the Montgomery bus boycott and the rest of the civil rights movement to the youth/anti–Vietnam War movement, the antipoverty movement, the women's movement, and the lesbian and gay rights movement—exposed fault lines in a society that had previously been obscured by the patriotism deployed to fight World War II.

The societal change caused by *Brown* was enormous. In the post-*Brown* world, much school desegregation was accomplished and virtually all the public spaces in the rest of society were desegregated as well. The civil rights movement forced the federal government to move both legislatively and administratively in its behalf. Blacks moved into positions undreamed of in the pre-*Brown* world—chairman of the Joint Chiefs of Staff, president of Planned Parenthood, quarterback in the National Football League, president of the National Education Association, mayors of major cities, bank tellers, police chiefs, and professionals in institutions ranging from newspapers to investment banking firms.

Most of the public and economic aspects of American life continue to be controlled by white men, but the changes wrought by *Brown* widened opportunities—particularly in government at all levels—so that a solid black middle and working class emerged. As the sociologist William Julius Wilson has noted, that working and middle class has used desegregation to escape the confines of the traditional ghetto, leaving the less skilled and poorest blacks behind in decimated Third World sections of cities all over the country.

Successful blacks are still forced to engage in soul-wrenching struggles from the halls of Congress to medical associations to corporate board rooms, where their own aspirations and their visions for the country are often challenged by people who range from out-and-out bigots to those who are well-intentioned but in deep denial about racism. But middle-class problems pale by comparison with those of the blacks left behind and left out. One of the things that hurts the poorest blacks is a conclusion often drawn from that comparison. Many white Americans seem to hold the view that the gates of opportunity were thrown wide open during and after the sixties and that the worthy blacks "moved on up" while the unworthy languished because of their own deficiencies.

In our innocence, we thought that after *Brown*, white Americans could be educated out of their individual prejudices. Many of us thought the civil rights movement, the strong moral declarations from the White House, and the legislative activity by Congress would serve as a great national teach-in about the irrationality and un-Americanness of racial prejudice, and that bigotry would be isolated in a few twisted souls and some unreconstructed regions of the South.

We were yet to learn that more than three centuries of racial subordination had shaped much of American institutional behavior as well as the personal psychology of vast numbers of white people. We had thought of racism as damaging only blacks. We were yet to learn that vast numbers of whites were physically dependent on—addicted to, one might say—their belief in their superiority over blacks.

Moreover, the great migration of peasants from the farms to the cities—as many as 3.5 million by some estimates—had laid the foundation for another kind of lesson. The migrants came in such numbers that they over-whelmed the job-generating capacities of the cities and most of the systems that help make the cities habitable.

Connected to the rest of America as they were by television, these migrants were stirred in their ghetto desperation—as we all were—by the daily scenes of civil rights struggles and triumphs. But as the rest of the country changed, they saw their sorrowful position at the bottom of society as irretrievably static and absolutely untouched by all the Sturm und Drang they saw on their television sets. So they revolted in city after city during the mid- and late sixties. The riots sent shock waves through the rest of the country and provided fuel for the racism that smoldered just below the unnatural racial civility of the civil rights years.

Though we had civilized ourselves enough so that politicians now had to refrain from yelling "nigger, nigger, nigger," they could surely shout "law and order" and "forced busing." In his presidential campaigns of 1968 and 1972, George Wallace showed northern politicians that there was much political gold to be mined in the racial fears and resentments harbored by white northerners. Subsequently, Richard Nixon, Ronald Reagan, George Bush, and finally Bill Clinton found ways to make exquisite use of that deep American political knowledge.

Rapid economic and cultural change ripped through the country and ravaged the ghettos. America became saturated with sexuality; the streams of drugs and guns coming into the country turned into torrential rivers; finally, and most devastatingly, the economy hit a wall in 1973.

Part of the optimism of the 1960s flowed from a deep belief in the power of the economy and from the hope that its manufacturing sector would suck the migrants up into the world of work. In fact, the economic changes in the 1970s that forced middle-class wives into the work force to maintain living standards overwhelmed the unskilled portion of the labor force. Unskilled black men who were employed lost 25 to 40 percent of real income. Many fell out of the economy entirely.

In office, the president has yet to spend an ounce of political capital on programs directly affecting the black poor. His precipitate dumping of his erstwhile friend Lani Guinier was a graphic demonstration of how skittish he is about appearing in any way to be sympathetic to strong advocacy on behalf of blacks.

Guinier has called for a national conversation about race. In today's environment, that is a radical proposal. There is little honest public dia-logue about race. There are political issues, framed by white politicians and designed for white voter consumption, that seek to give the impression of controlling blacks. The welfare debate, for example, ranges from urging that we end the program altogether to plans to train people for the jobs they will be forced to take after two years. There is no discussion of the scarcity of jobs, despite the fact that our official perpetual undercount of unemployment shows more than 8 million Americans out of work.

Racism thus joins two other enduring strands at the center of American culture: individualism and capitalism. Myths about them are intertwined and mutually reinforcing. Americans are led to believe that capitalism is efficient and just. All individuals who are energetic and disciplined can make it in our economy. Those who fail are unworthy. Therefore, there is nothing wrong with the system. Capitalism is just. Individual worthiness and effort are rewarded. Those who have reaped the most rewards are, of course, the most virtuous and worthy citizens of that society.

Those myths obscure many unpleasant truths about America. One of those truths is that we never did really promise forty acres and a mule to freed slaves and surely never tried to deliver them. As a matter of fact, no real effort has ever been made to incorporate the mass of unskilled blacks into the economy. If economic circumstances require their labor, they are tolerated, as during the nation's four big wars of the twentieth century. If not, tough; they and their skin, and all of the attributes ascribed to it, are blamed for their misfortune.

And so we watch helplessly the slow but sure destruction of our cities, the erosion of our Bill of Rights, and the shredding of much of the civility that makes life livable. Our best hope rests on the fact that there have been some dark days in the past and America has then seen some light and has forged racial progress. Our ideals really do count for something. At some level we really do think we are special and that we live by the ideals of the Declaration of Independence and the Gettysburg Address.

It took us most of the twentieth century to throw off the legal shackles that had bound blacks as closely as possible to slavery during the last half of the nineteenth. *Brown* was the key event in that struggle. Facing up to the enduring racism at the center of our culture and undertaking the substantial and sustained social and economic efforts required to undo the massive damage inflicted on the poorest blacks is an even bigger challenge than the one we have overcome. A strong hundred-year effort would be a modest estimate of the time required. After all, it took us 375 years to get into the hole we now occupy. It's been only forty years since *Brown*.

# The Unending Struggle for Equal Educational Opportunity

*U.S. District Court for the Southern District of New York*

*This article finds that* Brown *has not fulfilled its promise of securing equal educational opportunity for black children and that racial discrimination in the nation's public school systems is still the norm. In the great metropolitan areas of the country, demographic factors, segregated housing, neighborhood assignment policies, and school district configurations clustering poor and minority children in school districts separate from the largely white surrounding areas mean that a generation or more of blacks will be educated in racially isolated schools in many of the urban centers of the country. Thus our immediate concern must be to require those racially isolated schools to produce quality education for the black children who must attend them. Educators must take the lead in the fight to make* Brown's *promise a reality, evaluating and monitoring the educational offerings provided for minority children to determine their quality and sufficiency. Educators should define and conceptualize equal educational opportunity in terms of its educational methodology, form, and content.*

We are commemorating the fortieth anniversary of the decision by the U.S. Supreme Court in *Brown* v. *Board of Education of Topeka, Kansas.* Ten years ago, the Metropolitan Center held a similar commemoration. Indeed, since the decision was announced on May 17, 1954, almost every year a meeting or conference has been called to discuss or explore yet again the decision's meaning and implications. While these recurrent reexaminations attest to *Brown*'s perceived perdurable significance, thus far, they have served to underline what dismal progress has been made in achieving the equal educational opportunity for black children supposedly "guaranteed" by *Brown* under the Constitution of the United States. I am afraid that in this respect this year's retrospective will be no different.

Some forty years after our highest court struck down racial segregation in our nation's public schools on the grounds that a separate but equal school system denied black children their right to equal educational opportunity, racial discrimination in our public schools is alive and well and the outlawed dual school system is still with us. More black children are in all or virtually all black schools today than in 1954. These schools (called inner-city schools in urban areas) are unequal in terms of facilities, educational offerings—indeed in any measurement of educational quality—to predominantly white schools, and, with rare exceptions, lag in tests measuring achievement in reading, writing, and arithmetic.

In fact, few if any of the children from South Carolina, Virginia, and Kansas on whose behalf the *Brown* litigation was instituted have benefited from the decision by actually attending desegregated schools in their home communities. Finally, in 1979, seventeen African-American parents, including Linda Brown, whose father had brought suit in the 1954 case on her behalf, moved to reopen the *Brown* case on the grounds that vestiges of segregation were still extant in the Topeka public school system. Linda Brown was seeking to secure for her son and daughter the educational benefits she had won in the 1954 decision. Thirteen years later, in 1992, the Tenth Circuit vindicated the 1979 claim of continued segregation in the school system in finding an unconstitutional imbalance in student and teacher assignments at the district's three high schools, six middle schools, and twenty-five elementary schools. The court held that the Topeka school system had not fulfilled its duty to desegregate; that some schools were still regarded as "black schools" and others as "white schools"; and that the disproportionately black schools had the lowest test scores.[1]

Much of the reason for the failure to realize the promise of *Brown* has stemmed from the Supreme Court's refusal at the time of the decision to be as forthright about the remedy for racial segregation as it had been about diagnosing it. Before 1954, constitutional rights had always been defined as personal and present, requiring immediate vindication, but in *Brown*, the constitutional rights of the black children were ordered secured over time and only with "all deliberate speed." The Court sacrificed the immediate and individual vindication of the newly declared right to education without racial barriers in favor of a mass solution. Thereafter, the Court refused for more than a decade to take any steps to quicken the pace of *Brown*'s implementation. Litigation seeking a holding that the Constitution, in the light of the *Brown* decision, required the states to eliminate disparities between the poorer school districts—where minority children were concentrated—and those of the largely white affluent communities, caused by the means by which states funded their public school systems, was rejected by the Supreme Court, as was a lawsuit to require the breaching of school district lines to eliminate de facto school segregation. Thus, urban communities, with poor minority children comprising a large segment of their school population, have fewer financial resources to deal with their pressing educational problems than their more affluent neighboring white districts, and the composition of the school population in these urban areas makes meaningful desegregation virtually impossible to achieve.

Since I had primary responsibility for conceptualizing the litigation and drafting the court documents for *Brown*, as well as being trial counsel in the Kansas, South Carolina, and Virginia cases, I believe I accurately speak for the lawyers in saying that we believed the surest way for minority children to obtain their constitutional right to equal educational opportunity was to require the removal of all racial barriers in the public school system, with black and white children attending the same schools, intermingled in the same classrooms, and together exposed to the same educational offerings. Integration was viewed as the means to our ultimate objective, not as the objective itself. We sought to have the *Brown* decision viewed as mandating integration, but the lower court on remand in the South Carolina case held that *Brown* required only desegregation, and that interpretation, unfortunately, has prevailed.[2]

Dismantling a segregated school system to achieve desegregation is a less stringent requirement than one mandating integration. In the great metropolitan areas of the North, in particular, demographic factors, segregated housing, neighborhood school assignment policies, and school district configurations that cluster poor and minority children in districts separate from the largely white surrounding areas have created insurmountable barriers to any meaningful integration. If the *Brown* decision had been interpreted as requiring integration, and the states had been made responsible for maintaining an unsegregated school system, then perhaps today we might not face a situation where the vast majority of black children are attending schools with the school population ranging from 50 to 100 percent black.

There has been an ongoing debate in the black community since the *Brown* decision about strategy—whether blacks should push for integration or give up on integration and concentrate on securing quality education in predominantly black schools. Frankly, that debate has no relevance today. At least in the short run, a generation of black children is going to be educated in racially isolated schools in many of the urban centers of the country regardless of this debate, and so ways and means must be agreed on to help or force those schools to produce quality education.

Both sides see education as a ladder providing upward mobility for black children, and agree that there is a desperate need for black children to obtain a decent education, particularly now when one cannot obtain much in terms of employment other than low-level, dead-end jobs without basic educational skills. In January 1992, the unemployment rate was 7.1 percent overall, 6.2 percent for whites, and 13.7 percent for blacks. Whatever the figures are today, the black unemployment rate will be at least double the white rate. The black community seems to be regressing in its ability to escape poverty. In 1990, 32 percent of our black population lived below the poverty level, as compared with 10 percent of the white population. Between 1980 and 1990 there was a 19 percent increase in the number of blacks living in high-poverty areas, and according to the 1990 census 71 percent of poor blacks live in high-poverty areas. In 1989, 40 percent of black children under five lived in poverty, compared with 13.8 percent of white children, and current projections show that 45 percent of all black children grow up in poverty, while the figure for white children is 15 percent; 80 percent of all black children had received some welfare benefits before reaching age eighteen.

Still, there has been no concerted national effort to make *Brown*'s promise a reality. For most of the forty years since *Brown* was decided, the effort to secure implementation of the decision has been left in the hands of lawyers, principally the National Association for the Advancement of Colored People (NAACP) and the Legal Defense Fund, without, in my judgment, sufficient input from educators. The lawyers have focused primarily on the elimination of racial segregation in the South and racial isolation in the North. Litigation has dealt largely with school structure and organization, and sought to eliminate racial isolation by, for example, assigning all children in a district in grades 1–3 to a heretofore all-white elementary school and assigning all children in grades 4–6 to what had been an all-black elementary school; and also through busing, through merging school districts, and through strategic placement of new school buildings. The absence of educators in spearheading the implementation drive has been unfortunate. Indeed, even if the lawyers' efforts at combating segregation had been more successful, we would still face the problem of dealing with educational policies that effectively segregate students within schools.

Integration or the elimination of the racial isolation of the black child, that is, removing the all or virtually all black schools from the system, does not in and of itself produce equal educational opportunity. In a school system with no apparent racial bars, integration can still be undermined by use of tracking, which, based on placement on an achievement test, allocates children to learning tracks ranging from the most to the least rigorous academic exposure. This system usually results in white children being clustered on the college preparatory track and black children being grouped on the track with the least academic incentives. In such a system the black child is given little stimulus to strive to go higher. Yet, if the promise of America's egalitarianism means anything at all, poor minority children, if they are to climb out of the ghetto and join the mainstream, must be exposed to the most rigorous academic training available.

A method similar to tracking, with similar results, is homogenous grouping, which usually results in poor inner-city children being assigned to one classroom and white children being assigned to another. Classes for the gifted usually mean classes for whites; special education classes usually mean classes for black males—usually hyperactive children as well as those perceived to have learning disabilities. Unfortunately, decisions as to special class assignments are too often made by personnel who cannot see beyond the black skin, with the result that too many aggressive black youngsters get trapped in dead-end special education classes, and lose all prospects of future academic interest or achievement.

I believe that educators should be in the forefront of the effort to implement the *Brown* decision. We must do more than change school structures and school organization. We must do more than remove overt racial barriers. Educational offerings to which minority children are exposed should be evaluated and monitored. Is their content designed to provide equal educational opportunity for these children? Indeed, what form must the content of educational offerings take to constitute equal education? These are questions that only one trained in educational theory and practice can answer. We, the lawyers, thought in 1954 that all one had to do was to eliminate southern-style segregation, and a year later, when we became aware of northern-style segregation, eliminate that, and then equal education would result. It is not that easy. Although there are a number of desegregation success stories, the isolation of black children in our great metropolitan centers in poor-quality schools must continue to be the focus of attention. Whatever is accomplished in isolated areas of the country, the metropolitan centers are where a majority of blacks now resides, and the schools in these centers must provide equal education for minority children.

The justification for the appalling lack of quality education in inner-city schools is said to be beyond the control of school authorities. Gary Orfield of Harvard University, in his most recent report on school desegregation, has correlated racial school segregation and poverty, concluding that segregation by race is likely to mean segregation by poverty and educational inequality.[3] But black educators like Mary Hoover of Howard University, Asa Hilliard of Georgia State University, and Ogle Duff of the University of Pittsburgh take a more hopeful view, contending that educational inequality need not be a given for these children; that children can be given and absorb quality education despite living in poverty and residing in a drug-infested environment, or having parents who cannot read or who for whatever reason are not involved in school affairs. According to these activist scholars, school authorities have the methods to overcome such handicaps to learning, but refuse to utilize them.[4]

It seems clear enough that some schools segregated by race and poverty do produce quality education. Every so often, we read about the great success achieved by a particular school in a poor black neighborhood in turning out college-bound children and we regard it as a miracle. Indeed, the most recent such story I recall appeared in *New York Newsday* about a year or so ago. The school was in Harlem, located in a drug-infested neighborhood, and 40 percent of the families of the children attending the school were on welfare. Yet a majority of the school's graduates were said to be college-bound. I have not been able to understand why whatever is being done to produce such outstanding results does not become a model for the system. Yet it never seems to be replicated in the system. Hoover, Hilliard, and Duff, among others, contend that these successes would become commonplace if school authorities applied proven methods to bring quality education to inner-city schools.[5] I need not tell you that I am no educational expert, and I am certain that many if not most of you here know more about these people than I do. But it seems to me that their views deserve to be tested.

Orfield's study shows that we are moving in the direction of increased school segregation.[6] But, despite the odds, this result is not inevitable. School organization, funding, and educational offerings could be allocated to further school integration and desegregation. There is some encouraging legal strategy in state courts designed to put school funding for inner-city schools on parity with funding for schools in the state's wealthiest districts by requiring the state to shoulder full responsibility for financing the public schools and to eliminate property taxes as a primary source for school financing. These cases are aimed at eliminating interdistrict school funding disparities on state constitutional grounds, rejuvenating a contention the Supreme Court had rejected as a federal constitutional requirement. But even though court victories have been won in several states, a determination of how much has been accomplished for the cause of equal educational opportunity for minority children must await the form of remedy the courts will order.

A most interesting development is the recent Connecticut legislation designed to secure racial diversity in the state's public school system. To get the bill passed, however, its sponsors had to remove all references to race and integration, and the term *diversity* was left undefined. The state is divided into eleven regions, and the towns and cities in each of the regions are to devise plans to improve the quality of education in the schools and the performance of students, overcome barriers to equal educational opportunity, and enhance student diversity. The legislation recommends ways for the regions to meet these goals, but there is no compulsion. The project is to be accomplished voluntarily. I think Connecticut deserves a great deal of credit for officially acknowledging that the problem exists and seeking to have the whole state participate in the effort to find an effective solution.

We need a similar acknowledgement at the national level. We have no national plan or policy to make equal educational opportunity a reality for all of our children. Head Start programs are funded nationally, desegregation is sometimes furthered by civil rights enforcement, and federal funds do go into poverty areas for educational purposes, but these efforts and programs have not been coordinated. The Reagan and Bush administrations sought to end all desegregation activity by the civil rights division of the Department of Justice. As far as I know the Department of Education under those two administrations did nothing to further effectuate *Brown*'s promise of equal educational opportunity.

The present administration, after its shameful handling of Lani Guanier's nomination, named a candidate to head the Justice Department's civil rights division, but it will be some time before we know whether he will be effective and priority may well be given to enforcement of the voting rights law and not the right to equal educational opportunity in public schools. I am not aware of any action taken or policy announced by the Department of Education under the present administration concerning equal educational opportunity.

Further, we can anticipate no help from the Supreme Court. Its most recent decisions advised lower federal courts to relax their standards for compliance with desegregation decrees and disengage themselves from supervision of the dismantling of school segregation. The Court put it this way: "As the de jure violations become more remote in time and . . . demographic changes intervene, it becomes less likely that a current racial imbalance in a school district is the vestige of the prior de jure school system."[7] If the view of the Court becomes commonplace, integration and desegregation in our school systems will become less and less viable over time.

We are in dire need of a national program and policy to secure the benefits of the *Brown* decision for minority children, with the Departments of Education, Housing, and Justice jointly planning and executing coordinated programs designed to put equal educational opportunity within the reach of poor minority children. We also need our foremost educational authorities to mount a national campaign to achieve this result. We need them to speak out forcefully concerning the harmful effects of racial isolation of minority children not only to them, but to the country as well. Educators must agree on the methodology that best assures quality education in racially isolated schools and publish what has been agreed on as a guide for local school authorities. The methods used in the successful schools should be documented as proven models for success. By reference to the documentation, educators could then preserve these methods for use, and we would not have to rely on recurrent anecdotal evidence to know that some of these poor minority children can be saved through education and so go on to better things.

*Brown* has been hailed as one of the giants of American jurisprudence, but whatever claim it may have to that classification, it cannot be based on its success in providing equal educational opportunity for minority children. Thus far, for most black children the constitutional guarantee of equal educational opportunity that *Brown* held was secured to them has been an arid abstraction, having no effect whatsoever on the bleak educational offerings black children are given in the deteriorating schools they attend. Unless this issue is given national priority, the prospects for securing equal educational opportunity for black children will probably seem impossible to achieve when you convene for your next retrospective ten years from now. We must act now.

## Notes

1    Brown v. Board of Education, 975 F.2nd 585 (10th Cir. 1992).

2    Brigs v. Elliott, 132 F. Supp. 776 (D.S. C. 1955).

3    Gary Orfield, with the assistance of Sara Schley, Diane Glass, and Sean Reardon, *The Growth of Segregation in American Schools: Changing Patterns of Separation and Poverty since 1968* (Alexandria, Va.: National School Boards Association, 1993).

4    Mary Hoover, Asa Hilliard, and Ogle Duff, papers presented at the NAACP Summit Conference on Education, Little Rock, Arkansas, 1990.

5    Ibid.

6    Orfield, *The Growth of Segregation in American Schools,* p. 28.

7    Freeman v. Pitts, 112 S. Ct. 1430 (1992).

# The Federal Government and the Promise of *Brown*

BRIAN K. LANDSBERG

*University of the Pacific, Sacramento*

*The U.S. Department of Justice has played an important role in the development and enforcement of school desegregation law, by participating in* Brown *and later cases. From the Truman administration to the present, the thrust of government policy has been to promote unity and vindicate the unmet promise of the equal protection clause. The ambiguity of the Supreme Court's decision in* Brown *has allowed considerable flexibility in defining and remedying discrimination. Whether* Brown *failed or succeeded depends on which possible meaning of* Brown *one accepts. The department now should protect the gains under* Brown *from retrogressive attacks and should oppose resegregation.*

Ten years ago, former U.S. Assistant Attorney General David L. Norman spoke at an observance of *Brown*'s thirtieth anniversary. He asked "whether there is a growing subscription to an unwritten amendment to a familiar principle: 'The amount of affirmative action, such as busing, required to overcome the effects of past discrimination is inversely related to the length of time which has elapsed since *Brown*.' "[1] On this fortieth anniversary of *Brown* v. *Board of Education of Topeka, Kansas*, signs of weariness and forgetfulness persist, but neither the federal government nor the courts have yet succumbed. It is appropriate to retell the reasons for the federal role in the *Brown* decision and its enforcement. The retelling should make evident the importance of renewed vigor in federal support for the promise of *Brown*.

During the pre-*Brown* era the federal government participated in racial segregation in various ways, such as federal financial assistance for separate schools, segregated public housing, and segregated programs for farmers. However, President Truman recognized the harm that racial discrimination wreaked on the nation and began to take steps to combat it. He ordered the military to desegregate. He convened a conference on civil rights. He strengthened federal equal employment opportunity efforts. And he enlisted attorneys of the Department of Justice, who filed *amicus* briefs attacking racially restrictive covenants,[2] segregated railroad dining cars,[3] and segregated public graduate education.[4] The story is well known of their filing an *amicus* brief in *Brown* v. *Board of Education* in December 1952, when President Truman was a lame duck president.[5] However, it is worth recalling what the federal government was seeking in *Brown.*

The Department of Justice's first brief in *Brown* noted that the federal government has a "special responsibility for assuring vindication of the fundamental civil rights guaranteed by the Constitution."[6] The brief focused on official race discrimination, observing that it "inevitably tend[s] to undermine the foundations of a society dedicated to freedom, justice, and equality."[7] Finally, the brief expressed concern that "the existence of discrimination against minority groups in the United States has an adverse effect upon our relations with other countries."[8] Thus, the main concern of the federal government was not with private rights, but with national unity, enforcing constitutional norms, and the public interest. President Truman's actions reflected understanding that the racial caste system was shredding the fabric of national life.

We should recognize that these goals may not have been identical to the goals of others involved in the litigation. Some may have sought educational reform and understood that segregation was a fatal shortcoming of American education in 1954. Others may have simply wanted to equalize educational opportunities. The government's goals had to do with unity and vindication of the unmet promise of the equal protection clause.

The United States in *Brown* argued that the plaintiffs could win without overruling *Plessy* v. *Ferguson*, but that if the Court reached the issue, *Plessy* should be overruled. Children do not enjoy equality when they "know that because of their color the law sets them apart from others, and requires them to attend separate schools specially established for members of their race."[9] The government concluded that "the Fourteenth Amendment forbids the classification of students on the basis of race or color so as to deny one group educational advantages and opportunities afforded to another."[10] As to relief, the brief recommended that the Court remand to the lower courts "with directions to devise and execute such program for relief as appears most likely to achieve orderly and expeditious transition to a non-segregated system."[11] Relief need not occur "forthwith." As justification for this gradual approach, the brief argued that "[a] reasonable period of time will obviously be required to permit formulation of new provisions of law governing the administration of schools in areas affected by the Court's decision."[12]

After hearing initial arguments during its October 1952 term, the Court set the case down for reargument in order to seek the views of the parties as to questions propounded by the Court. It also requested a further brief from the Eisenhower administration. That brief addressed the questions the Court had asked and took no position on the outcome, but at oral argument Assistant Attorney General Rankin said "it is the position of the Department of Justice that segregation in public schools cannot be maintained under the Fourteenth Amendment, and we adhere to the views expressed in the original brief of the Department in that regard."[13] As to relief, the United States noted the success of New Jersey in desegregating its schools. It noted various issues of school administration that the state would have to address. It assumed that neighborhood schools would be permissible even if they were substantially of one race.[14] It argued that relief should be entered "as expeditiously as the particular circumstances permit."[15]

After *Brown I* ruled for the plaintiffs, the government filed a brief in *Brown II*. In arguing that "the vindication of the constitutional rights involved should be as prompt as feasible," the Department of Justice pointed out that "the 'personal and present' right . . . of a colored child not to be segregated while attending public school is one which, if not enforced while the child is of school age, loses its value."[16] The federal government argued that the "right of children not to be segregated because of race or color . . . is a fundamental human right, supported by considerations of morality as well as law," and that "racial segregation affects the hearts and minds of those who segregate as well as those who are segregated, and it is also detrimental to the community and the nation."[17]

Thus, in the *Brown* litigation before the Supreme Court the federal government took a uniform position through two administrations, with varying levels of enthusiasm. This pattern persists to the present day. All presidents since John F. Kennedy have supported the correctness of *Brown*, and positions taken by the Department of Justice in court have echoed that support. However, as is shown below, commitments to enforcement have fluctuated, as have positions as to the operational details, sometimes lessening the extent to which the promise of *Brown* would be kept.

Although the executive branch had participated in *Brown* as *amicus curiae*, Congress had bestowed no enforcement authority on the attorney general.[18] The executive branch did take action to enforce the order to desegregate the Little Rock, Arkansas, schools in the face of defiance by Governor Faubus.[19] Responding to acts of private violence against school desegregation, Congress did make obstruction of federal court orders a crime in 1960.[20] However, not until ten years after *Brown* did Congress authorize a strong federal enforcement role: "Congress decided that the time had come for a sweeping civil rights advance, including national legislation to speed up desegregation of public schools and to put teeth into enforcement of desegregation."[21] From the outset the congressional authorization was hedged. It authorized the attorney general to bring school desegregation suits, but only after receiving a meritorious complaint from a parent who is unable to maintain appropriate proceedings for relief and only if the attorney general finds that "the institution of an action will materially further the orderly achievement of desegregation in public education."[22] Moreover, the Civil Rights Act of 1964 specified that it did not empower any court or official to "issue any order seeking to achieve a racial balance in any school by requiring the transportation of pupils or students from one school to another or one school district to another in order to achieve such racial balance."[23] It also authorized the federal government to provide technical assistance for desegregation and banned discrimination in federally assisted programs. The 1964 act thus signaled Congress's desire to bring *de jure* segregation to an end, but to keep the federal government out of de facto segregation cases.

In the years that followed, the Department of Justice and the Department of Education (and its predecessor Department of Health, Education, and Welfare [HEW]) did take vigorous steps on three fronts. First, they contributed to the development of the legal standards governing desegregation. HEW promulgated guidelines for desegregation that laid the foundation for judging desegregation plans in terms of their success in actually eliminating racial segregation. The Department of Justice participated as a party or *amicus* in every Supreme Court school desegregation case and many lower court cases. Second, the Departments of Justice and Health, Education, and Welfare developed a joint strategy combining administrative enforcement of Title VI of the 1964 act with Justice Department litigation against large numbers of school systems. The Department of Justice developed the statewide suit as a device for quickly obtaining desegregation decrees of general applicability.[24] The Education Section of the Justice Department grew to over thirty attorneys by the mid-1970s. Third, the Department of Education provided a substantial carrot to help school systems desegregate: federal financial assistance for desegregation. The Emergency School Assistance Act, as Orfield has told us, "helped hundreds of districts in teacher training, human relations, and curriculum development work needed to make the transition from segregated to desegregated schools more effective."[25]

Although the federal government thus has done much to promote the promise of *Brown*, the path has wavered. The definition of that promise was advanced in the Department of Justice *amicus curiae* brief in *Green* v. *County School Board*.[26] There the United States argued that "so-called 'freedom of choice' plans satisfy the State's obligation only if they are part of a comprehensive program which actually achieves desegregation."[27] The government identified the continued existence of "all-Negro schools, attended by an overwhelming majority of the Negro children" as the mark of an ineffective desegregation plan. Quoting the Fifth Circuit Court of Appeals, the

United States argued: "Against the background of educational segregation long maintained by law, the duty of school authorities is to accomplish 'the conversion of a de jure segregated dual system to a unitary, nonracial (nondiscriminatory) system—lock, stock, and barrel.' "[28] Further, "the Fourteenth Amendment bars State action which unnecessarily creates opportunities for the play of private prejudice."[29]

The issue then arose whether the Court's approach in *Green* to desegregation of a rural county would apply as well to a densely populated urban school system in which residential segregation prevailed. In *Swann* v. *Charlotte-Mecklenburg Board of Education*, the brief of the United States struck a cautious note.[30] The brief did embrace *Green*, saying:

> We think the right of school children articulated in *Brown* is to attend school in a system where the school board exercises its decision-making powers so as to operate a non-racial unitary school system free from discrimination, and that where this has not been done there is a violation of the rights of such children requiring remedial adjustments which give proper weight to that which is feasible and that which is just. If choices exist which may have a racial impact, they cannot be exercised in a racially neutral manner where to do so is to perpetuate segregation.[31]

Thus, the courts should "require that the governmental decisions affecting racial segregation be so made and implemented, when feasible alternatives are available, as to disestablish the dual system and eliminate its vestiges."[32] However, echoing Congress's ambivalence on the matter, the United States also concluded that "the Fourteenth Amendment does not require . . . racial balance in all public schools or integration of every all-white or all-Negro school."[33] Thus, contrary to the prior norm, the government's position in a school desegregation case diverged substantially but not wholly from that of the black plaintiffs.[34]

In the years that followed *Swann* the government has continued its homage to *Brown*, while sometimes urging the Court to limit *Brown*'s applicability. Thus, on the one hand the government took the position that metropolitanwide remedies could be ordered only where a metropolitan violation has been found.[35] On the other hand the government argued that systemwide busing was appropriate in Columbus, Ohio, because the record reflected a systemwide violation. The government argued that a unitary school system is entitled to be released from a desegregation decree, while agreeing that eliminating the vestiges of discrimination is a prerequisite to a unitariness finding.[36] To some extent the fluctuations in the government's position have been due to political changes from one administration to the next. Thus, at the Brown Plus Thirty conference, the assistant attorney general for civil rights stressed cessation of busing and dissolution of desegregation decrees as central themes of the government's program for enforcing *Brown*.[37] This represents a change from the position of the Carter administration and one may expect the Clinton administration to reject these themes as well.

Two other changes diminished the role of the federal government in enforcing *Brown* in the 1980s and continue to affect the federal role today. First, the resources devoted to enforcement have been curtailed. Today, the Civil Rights Division's section responsible for enforcing *Brown* employs only thirteen attorneys. That shrunken crew is responsible not only for hundreds of continuing court decrees requiring desegregation of elementary and secondary education, but for higher education and sex and disability discrimination as well. Similarly, in the Department of Education today only 16 percent of the civil rights budget is spent on race discrimination issues.[38] Second, the Emergency School Assistance Act program was essentially dismantled and its funds were diverted to general grants, which need not be used for desegregation or heavily minority school districts.[39]

In considering the future role of the federal government, one may appropriately begin by asking what the successes and failures of *Brown* have been. What has *Brown* accomplished? The structure of official racial segregation in schools has been dismantled, though vestiges remain. States that once required segregation now have the most desegregated schools in the nation. *Brown* served as impetus for integration of public facilities and public accommodations and for nondiscrimination laws governing voting, housing, and employment. The official racial caste system is dead. *Brown* is firmly entrenched in our jurisprudence and our national life and its repudiation would be virtually inconceivable. There is massive consensus, on a very general level, that racial discrimination and segregation are wrong and that government should take steps to eradicate them. Thus, as Kenneth Clark has observed, *Brown* contributed "a simple, direct and eloquent statement of a moral truth."[40]

Set against these impressive gains is not so much failure as a shortfall in terms of racial justice. Thus, some of the gains under *Brown* are in danger of erosion. The statistics already reflect a modest erosion, and the Supreme Court's decision in *Freeman* v. *Pitts*[41] could lead additional school districts to seek release from their desegregation obligations.[42] Moreover, *Brown* has not brought to our children or society all the hoped-for benefits. "The generative power of *Brown* . . . in the realm of equal educational opportunity, has been limited primarily to its ban on racial segregation. Even there, the refusal in *Keyes* to extend the ban to de facto segregation and the refusal in *Milliken* to extend it to interdistrict racial imbalance further confined *Brown*'s reach."[43] We now know that law is an imperfect tool of educational reform. Yet early resistance to *Brown* meant that too great an emphasis had to be placed on litigation and too little on educational issues. This has led to another type of criticism, which I believe is misplaced: "*Brown's* failure . . . lay in its acceptance of a monolithic, color-blind society premised on the continued supremacy of white cultural norms, without regard to the role to be played by African-American cultural norms."[44] The fact is that while *Brown* referred at one point to education's role "in awakening the child to cultural values," neither the parties nor the Court had occasion to address the issue of cultural norms. Nothing in *Brown* forecloses a claim of discriminatory imposition of white cultural norms. Finally, one's analysis of whether *Brown* failed or succeeded depends on which possible meaning of *Brown* one accepts. "If equal opportunity means the end of racial isolation and the achievement of equal funding or outputs, the Court long ago gave a negative answer. . . . If equal opportunity means freedom from present intentional racial discrimination in the public schools, its future is secure. If it also means freedom from the lingering effects of past discrimination, its future hangs in the balance."[45]

What must be done for the future? We know from the myth of a vengeful and destructive Reconstruction that factual distortion can undermine responsible efforts to achieve racial justice.[46] A new myth has arisen, that busing is a failed and destructive remedy. As Orfield demonstrates in his remarks in this issue, this too is a false and destructive myth. It is imperative that we not allow the constant drumbeat of the failure of school desegregation to go unanswered. The federal interest in the unity of the country suggests that we should stress the benefits of desegregation for all races and for our society as a whole. A vigorous effort to retain the gains under *Brown* must be mounted both in local communities and in the courts. The federal government, especially the Departments of Justice and Education, should join in that effort. They should renew the carrot-and-stick approach: federal money to encourage voluntary desegregation and assistance to racially impacted school systems combined with more enforcement resources targeted on racial discrimination in elementary and secondary education. The cases leave open the question of whether a former dual system that has become unitary has further obligations with respect to neutralized but not eradicated effects of past discrimination. Stated in non-legalistic terms, may such a system adopt assignment techniques that cause resegregation? The civil rights bar should continue to litigate that issue. The Department of Justice should oppose resegregation. At the same time it should stress flexibility and restraint as to desegregation techniques. Litigants should recognize, as well, that a remedy forged in the political process is more likely to succeed. We should not allow past difficulties to entice us to renewed separatism. We must look to other measures to help with the goal of achieving racial justice and not rely solely on the equal protection clause and nondiscrimination laws. Efforts to achieve economic equity, fair housing, and educational excellence in all schools are essential components in the quest for equal educational opportunity. Finally, we must emphasize *Brown's* "big tent" affirmation of the Declaration of Independence and the Fourteenth Amendment and thereby maintain the public and legal support for the core values of *Brown*.[47] We should experiment within the confines of those core values and abjure solutions outside those confines. We should remember that compliance with *Brown* is a necessary condition for equal education, but it is not alone a sufficient condition to ensure equality.

After forty years, the regime of *Brown* has not brought about equal educational opportunity. Many one-race schools remain. Even where schools are integrated, inequalities remain. School finances are unequal. Graduation rates are unequal. Other inequalities persist. Do these facts indict *Brown*? Or do they signify that the magnitude of the task is greater than we thought in 1954? Should we give up on *Brown*'s promise? The question calls to mind that several millennia have passed since we received the Ten Commandments. "Thou shalt not kill" remains a worthy aspiration. I believe the aspirations of *Brown* are similarly correct, and that our task is to rededicate our efforts—which have flagged in recent years—to achieve equal educational opportunity. The federal government's role in those efforts is as important as ever and should also be rededicated.

## Notes

1   David L. Norman, "The Strange Career of the Civil Rights Division's Commitment to *Brown*," *Yale Law Journal* 93 (1984): 983.

2   Shelley v. Kraemer, 334 U.S. 1 (1948).

3   Henderson v. United States, 339 U.S. 816 (1950).

4   McLaurin v. Oklahoma State Regents, 339 U.S. 637 (1950); Sweatt v. Painter, 339 U.S. 629 (1950).

5   See Richard Kluger, *Simple Justice* (New York: Vintage Books, 1977), pp. 558–60; and Philip Elman, "The Solicitor General's Office, Justice Frankfurter, and Civil Rights Litigation, 1946–1960: An Oral History," *Harvard Law Review* 100 (1987): 817.

6   Brief of United States as amicus curiae, 2.

7   Id. at 3.

8   Id. at 6.

9   Id. at 18.

10   Ibid.

11   Id. at 27.

12   Id. at 29.

13   Kluger, supra at 675.

14   Brief of the United States on reargument, 184.

15   Id. at 188.

16   Brief of United States on Relief, 4–5.

17   Id. at 6.

18   Theoretically, the attorney general might have brought criminal prosecutions against school officials who willfully violated *Brown*. See 18 U.S.C. 242. However, the ambiguities of *Brown* might have made it difficult to prove the requisite specific intent to deny a constitutional right (see Screws v. United States, 325 U.S. 91 [1945]). Moreover, it was believed that the right to jury trial would have led to jury nullification even if adequate proof had been presented. Finally, the government had primarily used section 242 to prosecute crimes of violence and fraud. Thus, 242 was available but exceedingly awkward. See Norman, supra, at 984. Judge Norman notes that there is "only one reported case in which a public school official was prosecuted under [§242]. *See* United States v. Buntin, 10 F. 730 (C.C.S.D. Ohio 1882)." Id., note 4. Although the case preceded *Plessy* v. *Ferguson*, 163 U.S. 537 (1896), in *Buntin* the issue presented to the jury was whether the black school in an adjoining district was equal to the white school from which the defendant had excluded a black child.

19   Cooper v. Aaron, 358 U.S. 1 (1958). See Kluger, *Simple Justice*, p. 754.

20   18 U.S.C. 1509.

21   This characterization appears in Judge Wisdom's seminal panel opinion in United States v. Jefferson County Board of Education, 372 F.2d 836 (5th Cir. 1956). Although the opinion was later replaced by an *en banc* opinion, it laid the foundation for the later Supreme Court decision in Green v. County School Board, 391 U.S. 430 (1968). See, e.g., Andrew Kull, *The Color-Blind Constitution* (Cambridge: Harvard University Press, 1992), p. 181.

22   Civil Rights Act of 1964, Sec. 407 (a).

23   Ibid.

24   Norman, supra at 987.

25   Gary Orfield, with the assistance of Sara Schley, Diane Glass, and Sean Reardon, *The Growth of Segregation in American Schools: Changing Patterns of Separation and Poverty Since 1968* (Alexandria, Va.: National School Boards Association, 1993), p. 28.

26   391 U.S. 430 (1968).

27   Brief of the United States as amicus curiae, 3.

28   Id. at 4.

29   Id. at 15.

30   402 U.S. 1 (1971).

31   Brief of United States as amicus curiae, 7–8.

32   Id. at 16.

33   Id. at 17.

34   The first case of such disagreement was Alexander v. Holmes County Board of Education, 396 U.S. 19 (1969), where the government agreed that the doctrine of all deliberate speed should be abandoned, but argued that a delay of one semester in the desegregation of the defendant school districts was permissible. The Court gave short shrift to the government's position and ordered desegregation "forthwith."

35   School Board of City of Richmond v. State Board of Education, 412 U.S. 92 (1973); Milliken v. Bradley, 418 U.S. 717 (1974).

36   Board of Education of Oklahoma City Public Schools v. Dowell, 498 U.S. 237 (1991).

37   Wm. Bradford Reynolds, "The Role of the Federal Government in School Desegregation" in *Brown Plus Thirty*, ed. LaMar P. Miller (New York: Metropolitan Center for Urban Education, 1986).

38   This figure was supplied at the conference by Beverly P. Cole, Director of Education & Housing, National Association for the Advancement of Colored People, and confirmed by Judith A. Winston, General Counsel, United States Department of Education.

39   Orfield, at 28.

40   Kenneth B. Clark, "Racial Justice in Education: Continuing Struggle in a New Era," *Harvard Law Journal* 23 (1980): 93.

41    112 S.Ct. 1430 (1992).

42    See Brian K. Landsberg, "Equal Educational Opportunity: The Rehnquist Court Revisits *Green* and *Swann*," *Emory Law Journal* 42 (1993): 848–55.

43    Id. at 828.

44    Alex M. Johnson, Jr., "Why Integrationism Fails," *California Law Review* 1401 (1993): 1431.

45    Landsberg, supra at 861.

46    See Eric Foner, *Reconstruction: America's Unfinished Revolution, 1863–1877* (New York: Harper & Row, 1988).

47    I use the "big tent" metaphor to suggest that *Brown*'s core values are sufficiently general to win the allegiance of persons within a broad spectrum of opinion.

# The Legacy of *Brown* v. *Board of Education*

CONSTANCE BAKER MOTLEY

*U.S. District Judge, New York*

*In my view, the single most enduring effect of the* Brown *decision and its progeny has been to reverse the public policy of racial segregation that received Supreme Court approval in 1896 in* Plessy v. Ferguson. Plessy *was a case that involved segregation on intrastate railroad cars in the state of Louisiana. The effect of* Brown *was to reestablish, as a constitutional mandate, the right of every African American to enjoy the same rights, privileges, and immunities under the same conditions white persons enjoy. This reversal of national policy has an immediate, convulsive, and permanent effect on our society. This is because race has been the single most divisive issue in our country since its formation.*

May 17, 1994, marked the fortieth anniversary of the Supreme Court's historic decision in *Brown* v. *Board of Education of Topeka, Kansas.* In the *Brown* case the Supreme Court held state-enforced racial segregation in public elementary and high schools unconstitutional in that it violates the equal protection clause of the Fourteenth Amendment to the Constitution, which is binding on the states, and the due process clause of the Fifth Amendment to the Constitution, which is binding on the federal government's operation of schools in the District of Columbia. Although all other official segregation has been similarly held unconstitutional by the high Court, the struggle to integrate public schools and colleges continues. As a result, we Americans who are interested in the issue of equality of opportunity for African Americans have spent this year revisiting *Brown* and assessing its impact on twentieth-century American society. In my view, the single most enduring effect of the *Brown* decision and its progeny has been to reverse the public policy of racial segregation, which received Supreme Court approval in 1896 in *Plessy* v. *Ferguson. Plessy* was a case that involved segregation on intrastate railroad cars in the state of Louisiana. The effect of *Brown* was to reestablish, as a constitutional mandate, the right of every African American to enjoy the same rights, privileges, and immunities under the same conditions that white persons enjoy. This reversal of national policy had an immediate, convulsive, and permanent effect on our society. This is because race has been the single most divisive issue in our country since its formation.

I think the one thing we must remember about the debates leading up to the *Brown* decision and those that followed, culminating in the Civil Rights Acts of 1964, is that they were essentially a reargument of the debates of the last century that culminated in the Thirteenth, Fourteenth, and Fifteenth Amendments to the Constitution and the numerous laws enacted by the Reconstruction Congress to enforce those amendments. The amendments had been expressly designed to abolish slavery and peonage, to guarantee to the former slaves and the free African-American population in the country equal rights, privileges, and immunities against deprivation by state governments and private citizens and to protect their right to vote. There was no doubt in the minds of the leaders of the Reconstruction Congress that when they finished their work of reforming American society, there was no right, privilege, or immunity that white persons enjoyed that was not also the possession of African Americans. State-enforced racial segregation in public facilities and services had not yet emerged as a national issue. The issue then was simply exclusion of all African Americans, slave and free, from such facilities.

However, in 1896, after a century of agitation against slavery, a particularly violent civil war, and debate surrounding the race question, the Supreme Court sought to end the bitter controversy that simply would not go away. Compromising on the constitutional rights of the former slaves and free "Negroes," as we were then called, to the equal protection of the laws seemed to be the answer. The southern states had refused to allow former slaves and free persons of color equal access to schools, railroad cars, cemeteries, and other public facilities and services. To justify their clearly unconstitutional action, southern theoreticians invented the theory that the constitutional mandate of equality of access could be met by providing separate facilities, like schools, for the two races. The Supreme Court, apparently seeking to relieve the nation of its most divisive domestic issue so we could get on with nation building, agreed. However, the effect of this state-sanctioned racism was to legally divide the country into two societies—one black and one white. Segregation affected all blacks—rich or poor, educated or uneducated, northern or southern, light-skinned or dark-skinned, foreign born or native born. It took sixty years to get the Supreme Court to reject the southern compromise and to reestablish equal access to public facilities and services for the descendants of slaves, the descendants of free persons of color, and persons of mixed race who were defined by state law as "Negro."

Race has proved to be as divisive and as convulsive in this century as it was in the last. The good news is that, although great progress was made in the last century in eliminating slavery and securing equal rights, privileges, and immunities for African Americans, that progress has been equalled, if not surpassed, in this century, notwithstanding a continuing legacy of racial segregation and discrimination.

The next century promises to be so different in terms of our racial, ethnic, socioeconomic, and demographic makeup that it is difficult to even discern what the various dimensions and shades of this problem will be. The only thing we can glean now is the fact that there is no longer any single public policy affecting all blacks and only blacks in the way that the so-called separate but equal policy did.

The violence that accompanied desegregation following the *Brown* case presented this nation with the most critical challenge to national supremacy since secession in the last century. In the last century the issue was whether a state could elect to leave the Union because of its disagreement with national policy. It took a civil war to establish the fact that a state could not secede from the newly formed United States of America and to establish the supremacy of the national government and the national Constitution. Thereafter it took three amendments to the national Constitution to abolish slavery, to guarantee African Americans equal rights with white citizens, and to secure their right to vote. The amendments not only resulted in a new Constitution but established a new national policy of racial and ethnic equality.

We had, of course, anticipated that there would be resistance to implementation of the Supreme Court's decision in the *Brown* case. We had contemplated that opposition to the end of segregation would be felt, particularly in 1954, in the Deep South states—that is, Mississippi, Louisiana, Georgia, Alabama, South Carolina, and parts of Florida. We thought that there would be some resistance in Virginia, but not to the extent to which resistance actually developed in that state during the period 1954–1964. The one thing we did not foresee was that federal troops would be utilized on more than one occasion to put down official resistance to the decision.

Starting with the case against the University of Alabama in 1956, a mob prevented the admission of a single black student, Autherine Lucy, to the University of Alabama. Significantly, this uncivilized mob response was against the backdrop of the wholly spontaneous Montgomery Bus Boycott. The nation was thus put on notice in 1956 that resistance to integration would be more than the usual southern politicians' electoral oratory, which it had been up to that juncture. However, neither the National Association for the Advancement of Colored People (NAACP) nor any of its allies in the struggle possessed the necessary political leverage in the country as a whole at that time to invoke strong federal intervention.

The first thing we civil rights lawyers learned about mob resistance to desegregation was that President Eisenhower was unenthusiastic about enforcing the *Brown* decision, particularly if it meant the mobilization of a state's national guard or sending in federal troops or marshals from outside the state. If the president, at that juncture, had made a strong statement endorsing the Supreme Court's decision or even declaring his duty as president to enforce it, the whole course of massive resistance might have been different.

The failure of the federal government to follow through, with force, to secure Autherine Lucy's admission to the university level of public education, two years after the *Brown* case, proved to be a major defeat for the civil rights forces. It led people in the Deep South to believe that if enough open resistance could be mustered, the federal government would back down with respect to enforcing the rights of even a single African American.

When Autherine Lucy withdrew from the lawsuit because of the lack of federal protection with respect to her bid to return, Alabama moved swiftly. It closed down the NAACP and barred its operation in the state.

In 1958, two years after the Alabama case, when a federal judge ordered the admission of nine African-American students to a high school in Little Rock, Arkansas, the governor of Arkansas decided that it was in his best political interests to prevent the arrival of desegregation in that state. Again, Eisenhower was not particularly enthusiastic about enforcing the *Brown* decision. Since Eisenhower was a president who apparently delegated all of his responsibility to his staff and other government officials, it became the problem of the attorney general at that time, William Rogers, to decide how Governor Faubus was to be dealt with. Faubus obviously made it clear to Rogers that he intended to avoid his responsibility as governor to enforce the federal court order. Faubus was up for reelection at that time and, apparently, his political intuition was to win reelection by siding with what he perceived to be the majority view in Arkansas.

Since Faubus could not be reasoned with, it became William Rogers's task to advise the president that the only way a federal court order could be enforced and the supremacy of the Supreme Court upheld would be to send federal troops to enforce the Court's order. Eisenhower was on a golf course in Rhode Island when the Arkansas crisis arose. It was the first time in this century that the governor of a state rejected the Supremacy Clause of the Constitution. As the documentary evidence shows, Rogers had to go to Rhode Island to talk to the president on the golf course, since he, apparently, declined to come back to Washington to discuss the crisis and take charge. Eisenhower saw no constitutional crisis whereas Rogers, the attorney general, did. The issue was clearly whether a governor of a state could elect to disregard the supreme law of the land on a critical constitutional issue as enunciated by the Supreme Court.

It was finally determined by Eisenhower that the Arkansas State Guard would be federalized and that it would accompany the nine children, the next day, who had been selected for the first integration effort in Arkansas at the lower school level since *Brown*. This use of federalized troops was perhaps the first time in this century that the federal government has been called on to use force to ensure the rights of African Americans. The presence of television cameras at Little Rock high school the next day sent a message around the world as to the status of race relations in our country. The cameras also sent a message about our respect for the law, which, of course, proved embarrassing to the Eisenhower Administration as well as to the people of the United States.

The next time it became necessary to use federal force to enforce the rights of African Americans was in the State of Mississippi. When it came time to enforce the judgment of the Court of Appeals for the Fifth Circuit, which had been upheld by the U.S. Supreme Court, providing for the admission of James Meredith to the University of Mississippi in Oxford, Mississippi, in 1962, we had our first statewide rebellion against the United States since the Civil War. By this time John Kennedy was the president of the United States. His brother, Robert Kennedy, was the attorney general.

President Kennedy and his attorney general brother faced their first major domestic crisis in Mississippi. Robert Kennedy thought that he had worked out an understanding with Ross Barnett, who was then the governor of Mississippi, with respect to how Meredith's admission would be effected. Robert Kennedy and his staff thought they had an understanding with Barnett that federal marshals would escort James Meredith to the campus to be registered and that the state guard would be present on the campus to maintain order. This agreement was reached after at least two failed attempts on the part of marshals to go onto the campus with Meredith. It was decided, therefore, that Meredith and the federal marshals would go on the campus at night under cover of darkness with the intention of misleading any antidesegregation protestors. However, the protestors were there that night when Meredith went on the campus with the marshals and found, to their chagrin, that Ross Barnett had not ordered state troopers to the campus to protect the marshals and Meredith. As a result, at least three newspaper reporters and a French photographer were killed on the campus by the anti-integration protestors. It was probably Robert Kennedy's lack of experience with Deep South politicians who had to run on pro-segregation platforms that led him to believe the governor of Mississippi when the governor said that he would perform his duty, as governor, to uphold the law, in effect, and enforce the Supreme Court decision. There could be no other reasonable explanation for what occurred.

We confronted in Mississippi, for the first time, resistance to desegregation in a state on a massive scale. The governor of Mississippi had, by proclamation, called on every elected or appointed official in the state to resist the end of segregation. Affirmative response to the governor's call was virtually unanimous. If there were people at the university who understood the real nature of the constitutional crisis, they feared speaking out, apparently because they were so greatly outnumbered. There were one or two professors on the campus who understood and tried to persuade the students to resist the chaos that would ensue if protestors continued their activity on the campus, but aside from these few professors, and perhaps one or two church people, everyone else was immobilized either by conviction or fear of loss of employment or mob violence.

President Kennedy certainly did not want to bring on a major domestic crisis by sending in federal troops, but he was convinced by his advisers, and his brother's advisers, that this was a constitutional crisis that could not be avoided, that it was the duty of the president of the United States to put down, with force, what amounted to rebellion against the national government. Since we had not encountered, in this century, open rebellion by a state against the national government, no one wanted to believe that it was actually occurring. A decision was made to send in troops from other states. Federal troops finally went onto the campus and secured James Meredith's admission.

U.S. marshals had to accompany Meredith every day to class during his attendance at the university, which fortunately was no more than a year. The situation was so perilous that the marshals had to sleep in the same room with Meredith lest he be killed. During this time that Meredith attended the university, we feared that the pressure on him was more than he could bear. During the Christmas recess, after his admission in September 1962, we arranged for Meredith to leave the university and be tutored by a group of volunteer professors. Arrangements were made for Meredith to stay near the campus at Yale and be aided by a rotating group of volunteer professors during that two-week holiday period.

We ourselves, as his lawyers and counselors, did not understand that the pressure was so great that Meredith could not really focus on anything. He had tried to explain to us that what he needed was an opportunity to return to Jackson, Mississippi, where he had been attending school awaiting his admission to the University of Mississippi, and spend his Christmas holidays relaxing with his friends in dance halls and private homes, as he had always done. He left Yale after a few days, went to Chicago to see Dick Gregory, the comedian, and then returned to Jackson, as he had wished, to dance at parties with his friends. He made his way back to the campus unescorted and miraculously unrecognized and unharmed at the end of the Christmas recess.

Although Governor Ross Barnett was held in contempt of court for interfering with Meredith's admission pursuant to court order, the Fifth Circuit Court of Appeals did not proceed with the contempt hearing once Meredith was admitted. The governor had been subjected to a daily fine rather than imprisonment until his compliance with the court order.

Notwithstanding this University of Mississippi crisis, we found it impossible to protect people like Medgar Evers, who was the NAACP's paid director in Mississippi, from the violence everyone knew would befall him. The government, of course, could not be required to afford Medgar Evers protection because there were people who might kill him. Up until the time he was actually shot, Evers had not received more than threatening telephone calls. The NAACP did not have the funds with which to employ private bodyguards. Medgar Evers was, of course, killed in 1963. It took thirty years to bring his killer to justice. His killer, Byron DeLa Beckwith, was convicted of Evers's murder after a third trial in January 1994. The first two trials resulted in hung juries. Medgar and I often spoke, when I was there, of this danger to his life, but Medgar, according to his wife, had made up his mind that he was ready to pay the price for ending the Jim Crow reign in his home state. The third trial produced witnesses who were apparently convinced that none of us was safe as long as Evers's murderer remained unconvicted.

Forty years after *Brown* the Supreme Court began its 1994–1995 session with several school desegregation cases on its docket, some of which have been around for more than a decade. School desegregation litigation has consumed much of the Court's time over the last forty years, but the one thing we can all be certain of is that separate but equal is no longer the law of the land. The controversy over that issue was resolved for all time in 1954. We, therefore, begin a new century with a new constitutional context, unlike the beginning of this century, which augurs well for the future.

# Revisiting the Supreme Court's Opinion in *Brown* v. *Board of Education* from a Multiculturalist Perspective

KEVIN BROWN

*Indiana University School of Law*

*This article looks back at the Supreme Court's school desegregation opinions, includ-ing* Brown *v.* Board of Education, *from the perspective of a multiculturalist. A multiculturalist prefers an American society that has learned to appreciate and value the existence of multiple racial and ethnic cultures. A prerequisite to accom-plishing this multicultural vision of a utopian American society is to bring diverse racial and ethnic students together in public schools. But for this appreciation to occur, more than the physical presence of a racially and ethnically diverse student body is required. Thus a multiculturalist also wants to foster meaningful cross-cultural understanding, though not necessarily cross-cultural agreement.*

*The Supreme Court's opinion in* Brown *produced significant positive changes in American society. Nevertheless, with the beginning of the termination of over 500 school desegregation decrees, the United States has entered a postdesegregation era. Racial and ethnic segregation in public schools is likely to increase. Thus the utopian vision of a multiculturalist is not where our society is currently headed. After reexamining the Supreme Court's school desegregation opinions, I conclude by stating the reason the multicultural vision is not the one our society is moving toward. This vision was simply not part of the vision of public schools articulated by the Supreme Court in the school desegregation cases. If local school systems decide to engage in further efforts to bring racially and ethnically diverse students together, it must not be on the ideological basis of the Supreme Court's school desegregation opinions. The very kind of thinking about the issues of cultural diversity that* Brown I *was based upon is the very kind of thinking that must be overcome in order for true multicultural education to occur.*

While I recognize that it is unusual to start an article with autobiographical information, bear with me for a moment because the relevance of such a beginning will be obvious by the end. I was born in 1956, the year that Mar-tin Luther King led the bus boycott in Montgomery, Alabama. Until the end of the fourth grade, I attended *de jure* segregated all-black schools in

Indianapolis, Indiana.[1] Before I started the fifth grade, however, my parents moved our family to a suburban area of Indianapolis. Even though our neighborhood was racially segregated, the schools were predominantly white. From the time I entered high school until I graduated from Yale Law School, less than 10 percent of the student body and faculties at the schools I attended were "Negroes" (later called "blacks" and still later "African Americans"). All of my significant employment has been at institutions—a local office of a national public accounting firm, a law firm, and two law schools—where I have been either the only one or one of two blacks or African Americans on the professional staff. Currently, I am one of two African-American law professors on a thirty-person faculty. I have two all-black children by my ex-wife. My current wife, however, is Caucasian and we have two biracial children. In short, I am—and my family is—a product of the desegregation of American society.

I have mentioned my personal history to show that I have long been a proponent of interracial harmony and cross-cultural understanding. By this I do not mean cultural homogeneity or domination, but individuals from diverse backgrounds appreciating and respecting—though not necessarily agreeing with—the beliefs embedded in different racial and ethnic cultures in our society. A prerequisite to accomplishing this multicultural vision of a utopian American society is to bring diverse racial and ethnic students together in public schools. I am, therefore, an avid supporter of true multicultural education in multiethnic and multiracial public schools. In order to have such an education, more than the physical presence of a racially and ethnically diverse student body is required. From my own personal experience, I know that it takes a considerable effort to understand views of the world embedded in cultures different from your own. Many times the beliefs of your native culture will consider such alien views to be products of ignorance, mistake, bias, or lack of understanding. In order to bring about appreciation of and respect for the culture of others, there must also be consistent and meaningful cultural interchanges that foster cross-cultural understanding, though not necessarily cross-cultural agreement.

Despite my personal predilections, however, I am forced to live with the current realities regarding race and ethnic relations in American society. A Harvard report published in December 1993 indicated that two-thirds of African-American students and over 70 percent of Latino students are currently attending majority-minority schools.[2] These percentages actually reflect increases in racial and ethnic separation from what existed in the late 1980s. Also, the U.S. Supreme Court in a 1991 opinion—*Dowell* v. *Board of Education*[3]—and a 1992 opinion—*Freeman* v. *Pitts*[4]—articulated what *de jure* segregated school systems must do in order to free themselves from the yoke of federal court supervision. At one time over 500 school systems were operating under some form of school desegregation decree.[5] With the termination of federal court supervision and the consequent dissolution of those decrees, large numbers of public school districts will regain plenary control over student school assignments. The goal of student assignments in those districts will no longer be motivated by the compelled need to maintain integrated student bodies. The foreseeable future for our nation's public schools is, therefore, one of increased racial and ethnic "separation." To state it bluntly, we have already seen the maximum amount of integrated public schools that we are likely to see in our lifetime.

As a supporter of multicultural education, I have had to reluctantly conclude that my utopian vision of public schools is not going to materialize. While the vision of true multicultural education in multiethnic and multiracial schools can exist for a minority of African Americans and Latinos, this kind of public education will be unattainable for the majority of these minority students. Because of this realization I am now willing to look back to the desegregation of America's public schools in order to assess what prevented this multicultural vision of public education from becoming our present-day reality. If local public school districts are going to engage in local efforts to racially and ethnically integrate their public schools, they must learn the lessons that were taught by court-ordered desegregation in the 1960s and 1970s. If not, such efforts to physically integrate public schools will run the risk of repeating an unnecessary mistake.

Though political and educational forces were also involved, the primary impetus for school desegregation was as a legal remedy for the violation of the constitutional rights of black school children. To find the blueprint for school desegregation, the place to look is to the Supreme Court's *de jure* segregation jurisprudence. In 1954, the Supreme Court struck down statutes that used race to segregate students in public school in *Brown* v. *Board of Education of Topeka, Kansas (Brown I)*.[6] The following year, in *Brown II*,[7] the Court addressed the remedy that was required in order to meet the constitutional obligations articulated in *Brown I*. In *Brown II* the Court required that public schools effectuate a transition to a racially nondiscriminatory school system.[8] The precise parameters of what was meant by a racially nondiscriminatory school system were originally left to the discretion of school authorities. Many of them and southern federal judges relied on the dictum from the District Court opinion on remand in the companion case with *Brown I* from South Carolina, *Briggs* v. *Elliot*.[9] In *Briggs* the District Court interpreted the meaning of *Brown I* as not requiring the mixing of persons of different races in the schools or of depriving parents of the right to choose the schools their children attended. "The Constitution, in other words, does not require integration. It merely forbids discrimination. It does not forbid such segregation as occurs as the result of voluntary action. It merely forbids the use of governmental power to enforce segregation."[10]

In its 1968 opinion in *Green* v. *New Kent County*, the Supreme Court moved beyond a possible interpretation of *Brown I* as merely forbidding discrimination.[11] Under a "freedom-of-choice" plan adopted by the New Kent County School Board, no whites had enrolled in the black schools, and only 15 percent of blacks had enrolled in the formerly all-white school.[12] In striking down the plan, the Court explicitly rejected the argument of the New Kent County School Board that the Fourteenth Amendment did not require compulsory integration.[13] The Court placed the obligation on public schools to dismantle their dual school systems and to do so immediately. The Court justified placing the obligation on school boards to achieve racial balancing by stating that "the constitutional rights of Negro school children articulated in *Brown I* required the desegregation of public schools."[14] To find the rationale articulated by the Supreme Court for court-ordered school desegregation we must do as the Court commanded in *Green* v. *New Kent County* and journey back to *Brown I*.

Before going back to *Brown I*, however, I want to emphasize that over forty years have elapsed since the Supreme Court rendered this opinion on that famous spring day in 1954. At the time the Court delivered that opinion, people of African descent were called "Negroes" out of respect, and were called "nigger," "darkie," and even "black" as an insult. America had not yet experienced the civil rights movement, the Black Consciousness Movement, or the Afrocentric Movement. Segregation and conscious racial discrimination were not only the explicit law of the land in many places, but also standard American business, educational, political, and social practice. To discriminate based on race in merchandising stores, eating facilities, places of entertainment, and hotels and motels was generally accepted as a fact of life. Negroes seldom occupied positions in American businesses and corporations above the most menial levels. Even lower-level management positions were for the most part unobtainable. What in the 1990s is referred to as the "glass ceiling," forty years ago was a firmly implanted outright concrete barrier. In 1954 only a handful of Negroes attended prestigious colleges and universities in this country and almost none of them taught there. A colored man had not been elected mayor of a major U.S. city in the twentieth century. And there were only four Negroes serving in Congress, none having been elected from the South since 1900. In 1954, many places in the country had separate water fountains, waiting rooms, transportation facilities, rest rooms, schools, hospitals, and cemeteries for whites and coloreds. The Court's opinion in *Brown I* preceded by ten years the Civil Rights Act of 1964, which was the single most sweeping piece of civil rights legislation in the country's history. It also preceded by eleven years the Voting Rights Act of 1965, which effectively secured the right to vote to most Negroes living in the South. This is where the majority of Negroes lived at the time and most had been disenfranchised since the 1890s.

In 1954, the collective history of race relations in North America—which had spanned almost 335 years—was primarily one of slavery and, after a period of Reconstruction following the Civil War, one of legally enforced and sanctioned segregation. It was a history of almost uninterrupted use of race as a means to classify people of African descent for purposes of subjugation.

According to the Court's opinion in *Brown I*, the harm of *de jure* segregation was not limited to intangible stigmatic harms, but also included tangible harms. In one of the most quoted phrases from *Brown I*, the Court said that "to separate [African-American youth] from others of similar age and qualifications solely because of their race generates a feeling of inferiority as to their status in the community that may affect their hearts and minds in a way unlikely ever to be undone."[15] The Court went on to quote approvingly from the district court in Kansas:

> Segregation of white and colored children in public schools has a detrimental effect upon the colored children. The impact is greater when it has the sanction of law; for the policy of separating the races is usually interpreted as denoting the inferiority of the negro group. A sense of inferiority affects the motivation of a child to learn. Segregation with the sanction of law, therefore, has a tendency to retard the educational and mental development of negro children and to deprive them of some of the benefits they would receive in a racial[ly] integrated school system.[16]

We must first understand the breadth of the Court's conclusions about the harm of segregation. Since the Court indicated that the harms suffered were unlikely ever to be undone, they presumably also affected those blacks who had attended segregated schools prior to 1954. As a result, it was not just black school childen who were psychologically damaged by segregation, but black adults as well. In an opinion that today may come close to group slander, the Supreme Court explicitly states that Negroes have had their educational and mental development stunted by segregation. Despite the presence of sociological testimony of the harm suffered by whites as a result of segregation, the Supreme Court's opinion is based on the fact that only African Americans were damaged by segregation.[17] It therefore implicitly assumes that the psychological and mental development of whites was unaffected by *de jure* segregation.

Let me first note that there is an important—critical—distinction to be drawn between segregation as being based on a false premise that African

Americans are not the equals of whites and believing that segregation actually distorted the cognitive, psychological, and emotional development of blacks. According to the former, the structure of education was based on the false premise. According to the latter, because of segregation blacks were actually inferior to whites. Under the former, racism was irrational because the premise it was based on was false. According to the latter, racism has a rational basis, but the inferiority of blacks is presumed to be curable. According to the former, since both blacks and whites were being indoctrinated with the false premise of black inferiority, both were victimized by *de jure* segregation—though in different ways. According to the latter, the harm of *de jure* segregation affected only blacks. According to the former, desegregation as a remedy for segregation would have benefited both blacks and whites. According to the latter version—and the Supreme Court—interracial exposure of Caucasians to African Americans was not beneficial to white students. In effect, the Supreme Court accepts the idea that blacks are inferior to whites, but simply changes how that inferiority should be treated. *Desegregation was needed because of—not in spite of—the fact that whites were thought by the Supreme Court to be superior to blacks.*

I do not wish to be perceived as voicing the proposition that the Supreme Court was wrong in striking down *de jure* segregation in 1954. It seems to me that only a fool would take such an outlandish position. It is obvious that had the Court not struck down *de jure* segregation in *Brown I*, I, an African-American law professor, would not be in the position to write this comment. I extol the valor that the Court exhibited in breathing life into the moral imperative of equality enshrined in America's most important legal documents. As a decision to strike down *de jure* segregation, *Brown I* should be looked on and revered as a fundamental effort by the Supreme Court that sparked a historic effort by American society to attempt to break with its racially oppressive past. Without question the opinion helped to open doors for African Americans that prior to it were permanently barred. Certainly there were extralegal implications for an opinion like *Brown I* that made it important for the Court to reach unanimity. And considerations about the inflammatory nature of the subject matter may have—quite correctly—caused the Court to write the opinion in the way that it did. I am therefore willing to concede that the Court delivered the best opinion that it possibly could have for the American society that existed in 1954.

But over forty years have passed since the Court's opinion in *Brown I*. This America is not the one that existed before the civil rights movement and the Black Consciousness Movement—more than twenty-five years have passed since those movements. Many of the people who were called "Negroes" as a term of respect in 1954 would be offended to be called a

Negro today. To call such a person "black" is not an insult, but a sign of respect. And in most circles the term used is "African American," making an explicit link with and showing respect for both past and present homelands. Americans no longer live with "white-only" and "colored-only" signs etched above water fountains, waiting rooms, transportation facilities, rest rooms, schools, hospitals, and cemeteries. This is not the America that existed before the Civil Rights Act of 1964, nor the America that existed before the 1965 Voting Rights Act. Even in contexts where it is not against the law to use race to consciously discriminate, the general American ethos makes it clear that it is at least considered wrong or in bad taste to discriminate against blacks solely on the basis of race. In brief, Americans today live in a society that has been altered by *Brown I* and not in the society that existed before it. American society is considerably different forty years later because of that opinion and many of those changes have been stunning.

I am not going back to the Court's opinion in *Brown I* for the purpose of criticizing an opinion written against the background of a 1954 American society. Rather, I am examining the legacy of that opinion to elucidate why the vision of public education as true multicultural education is not the reality our present society is moving toward.

Nineteen years after *Brown I*, the Supreme Court explicitly extended the *Brown I* presupposition about the effect of *de jure* segregation on the development on African Americans to Latinos in the Southwest. *Keyes* v. *School District No. 1* was the first Supreme Court opinion addressing *de jure* segregation in a city—Denver, Colorado—that was located in a state where in 1954 the public schools were not segregated pursuant to state statutory authority.[18] *Keyes* is noteworthy for three reasons: First, the Court accepts the *de jure*/*de facto* segregation distinction. Second, the Court also adopts a procedural rule that a finding of intentional school segregation in a meaningful part of a school district creates a strong presumption that segregated schooling throughout the district was similarly motivated. Finally, Denver was also a tri-ethnic as distinguished from a biracial community. Hence the Court had to address how Latinos should be treated for purposes of school desegregation lawsuits. The Court concluded that "in the Southwest Hispanos and Negroes have a great many things in common. . . . In fact, the District Court itself recognized that 'one of the things which the Hispano has in common with the Negro is economic and cultural deprivation and discrimination.' Although of different origins Negroes and Hispanos in Denver suffer identical discrimination in treatment when compared with the treatment afforded Anglo students."[19]

The Supreme Court's school desegregation opinions have operated as barriers to the institution of the kind of multicultural education in multiethnic and multiracial public schools that I spoke about earlier. Educational reform movements that arose in the wake of the Court's school desegregation opinions relied on the Court's explicit proposition that blacks were the only ones damaged by segregation. Hence these reforms not only perceived the assimilation premises and structures of American education as basically sound, but were also dominated by a "cultural deprivation paradigm" for African Americans.[20] As aptly stated by James M. Jones, "the popular notion of 'cultural deprivation' as a description of black children attests to the wholesale disregard of black life and culture."[21]

Given the Supreme Court's assertion that only blacks and Latinos in the Southwest were culturally damaged by segregation, it follows that their cultural beliefs are not worthy of being respected and appreciated. Just the opposite—those cultural beliefs reflect the distorting influence of segregation and need to be excised. The Court's school desegregation opinions were opinions directed at forcing black and brown people to accept the dominant American culture as their own. These were opinions based not on multicultural education, but on cultural homogeneity and the hegemony of the dominate culture.

I can now succinctly state the reason that my vision of public education as one of diverse racial and ethnic students learning to appreciate and respect each other's cultural beliefs is not the reality that our society is moving toward. This vision was simply not part of the vision of public schools articulated by the Supreme Court's school desegregation cases. If local school systems decide to engage in further efforts to bring the racially and ethnically diverse students together, it must not be on the ideological and structural basis of the Supreme Court's school desegregation opinions. The very kind of thinking about the issues of cultural diversity that *Brown I* was based on is the very kind of thinking that must be overcome in order for true multicultural education to occur.

## Notes

1    United States v. Board of School Comm'rs of Indianapolis, 332 F. Supp. 655 (S.D. Ind. 1971), *aff'd,* 474 F.2d 81 (7th Cir. 1973) *cert. denied,* 413 U.S. 920 (1973).

2    In 1991, 66 percent of African-American school children attended predominantly minority schools, up from 63 percent in 1986. The proportion of Latinos in minority-dominated schools has increased from 54 percent in 1968 to 73 percent in 1991 (William Eaton, "Segregation Creeping Back in U.S. Schools," *San Francisco Chronicle,* December 14, 1993, p. A15).

3    498 U.S. 237 (1991).

4    503 U.S. 467 (1992).

5    James S. Liebman, "Desegregating Politics: All-Out School Desegregation Explained," *Columbia Law Review* 90 (1990): 1463, 1465–66.

6    347 U.S. 483 (1954).

7    Brown v. Board of Educ. (Brown II) 349 U.S. 294 (1955).

8    349 U.S. at 301.

9    132 F. Supp. 776 (E.D.S.C. 1955).

10    132 F. Supp. at 777.

11    391 U.S., 430 (1968).

12    Green v. New Kent County 391 U.S. at 441. Id. The Court noted that "transition to a unitary, nonracial system of public education was and is the ultimate end to be brought about." *Id.* at 436. Prior to the Green opinion, freedom-of-choice plans were considered sufficient to meet the constitutional obligation imposed on school systems by Brown II. One of the provisions included in the Civil Rights Act of 1964 prohibited federal financial assistance from being given to programs or activities engaged in discrimination. The Department of Health, Education, and Welfare issued regulations addressing racial discrimination in federally aided school systems as directed by 42 U.S.C. § 2000d-1, and in the statement of policies or guidelines, the department's Office of Education established standards for eligibility for federal funds of school systems in the process of desegregation. 45 CFR §§ 80.1–80.13, 181.1–181.76 (1976). Freedom of choice plans were seen as acceptable under these regulations. See 391 U.S. at 433–34 n.2; see also Lino A. Graglia, *Disaster by Decree: The Supreme Court Decisions on Race and the Schools* (Ithaca: Cornell University Press, 1976).

13    Id at 437.

14    Id at 438.

15    *Brown I*, 347 U.S. at 494. The social science evidence cited by the Court (see note 11) was specifically intended to prove that segregation produced a psychological harm to African Americans. Doubt, however, has always been expressed as to whether the social science evidence cited in *Brown I* actually influenced the justices. See Edmond Cahn, "Jurisprudence," *New York University Law Review* 30: 150, 157–58 and note 16. In addition, the research by the psychologist purporting to show that African Americans in public schools had lower self-esteem has been the subject of criticism recently by (William Cross, *Shades of Black: Diversity in African-American Identity* [Philadelphia: Temple University Press, 1990]). He argues that in the 1950s psychologists assumed that racial group preference was closely correlated with self-esteem. But as psychologists developed methods of testing self-esteem directly, they discovered that African-American self-esteem tests out as high or higher than that of whites.

16    *Brown I*, 347 U.S. at 494 (quoting from the opinion of the District Court in the Kansas case) (emphasis added).

17    "Effects of Segregation and the Consequences of Desegregation: A Social Science Statement," reprinted in *Minnesota Law Review* 37 (1953): 427:

> With reference to the impact of segregation and its concomitant on children of the majority group, the report indicates that the effects are somewhat more obscure. Those children who learn the prejudices of our society are also being taught to gain personal status in an unrealistic and non-adaptive way. When comparing themselves to members of the minority group, they are not required to evaluate themselves in terms of the more basic standards of actual personal ability and achievement. The culture permits and at times, encourages them to direct their feelings of hostility and aggression against whole groups of people the members of which are perceived as weaker than themselves. They often develop patterns of guilt feelings, rationalizations and other mechanisms which they must use in an attempt to protect themselves from recognizing the essential injustice of their unrealistic fears and hatreds of the minority group. Id. at 431.

18    413 U.S. 189 (1973).

19   Id. at 197–8.

20   See, for example, James A. Banks, *Multiethnic Education: Theory and Practice*, 2nd ed. (Boston: Allyn & Bacon, 1988), p. 99; Myra Sadker et al., "Gender and Educational Equality," in *Multicultural Educational: Issues and Perspectives*, ed. James A. Banks and Cherry A. M. Banks (Boston: Allyn & Bacon, 1989), pp. 106–23; Geneva Gay, "Achieving Educational Equality through Curriculum Desegregation," *Phi Delta Kappan* 72 (1990): 56, 57; on the cultural deprivation paradigm, see Banks, *Muliethnic Education.*

21   James M. Jones, "The Concept of Racism and Its Changing Reality," in *Impacts of Racism on White Americans*, ed. Benjamin P. Bowser and Raymond G. Hunts (Beverly Hills: Sage Publications, 1981), pp. 40–41.

# Public Opinion and School Desegregation

GARY ORFIELD
*Harvard Graduate School of Education*

*Media reports and social commentators often assume that whites, African Americans, and Latinos are now uniformly disenchanted with racial integration. Meanwhile, recent Supreme Court rulings that allow for the termination of school desegregation plans may lead communities to consider entering a court battle to end such plans. It is therefore increasingly important that community leaders have the facts about what the public and parents and students affected by desegregation actually believe. Public opinion surveys reveal a reality of public opinion on desegregation far more nuanced and complicated and far more positive than media reports and common assumptions would have us believe.*

To hear most political leaders, commentators, and journalists tell it, it would seem that everyone knows, thoroughly and completely, that school busing is a failed social experiment, that even blacks have turned against the policy, and that people would like to return to "neighborhood" schools even when those schools are segregated by race. Relying solely on the press and the public statements of vocal political leaders for information on the issues of school desegregation and busing would lead most people to quickly accept such assumptions and generalizations. During the last year, for example, the views of several African-American mayors who have become disenchanted with desegregation and who favor neighborhood schools have been widely publicized.

Indeed, a number of African-American school officials and political leaders have been silent or critical concerning desegregation and some of those who do believe in the policy moved onto other concerns or were ignored by or invisible to the media, making the story of uniform disenchantment with desegregation—even uniform repudiation—seem more convincing. African-American statements in favor of desegregation or busing or surveys showing community attitudes supporting busing received far less attention than attacks by officials, which have been considered newsworthy breaks in what was presumed to be uniform African-American support for the civil rights orders.

Accurately understanding the experience with desegregation became much more important after the Supreme Court's 1990 decision in the *Dow-*

*ell* v. *Board of Education in Oklahoma City* case opened the door to the possibility of dismantling desegregation by allowing for the termination of plans under certain circumstances.[1] As *Dowell* and other rulings lead communities across the nation to consider the viability of their current desegregation plans and the educational, social, and political costs of undoing or continuing such plans, it is important that leaders have the facts about what the public and the parents and students affected by desegregation actually believe. The surveys reveal a reality of public opinion that is far more complex and far more positive than media reports and common assumptions about what "everyone thinks" would have us believe.

This summary of public opinion on the issues of desegregation, busing, and racial integration will consider the following questions.

1. Does the public support integrated education?
2. Does the public believe that integrated schools produce educational gains?
3. Does the public see school desegregation as a major disruption or problem?
4. Have attitudes toward busing and desegregation become increasingly negative or increasingly supportive over time?
5. What are the attitudes of parents and students who have actually experienced busing policies?
6. Have the African-American and Latino communities turned against school desegregation and busing?
7. What does public opinion suggest about policy directions?

## ATTITUDES ABOUT RACIAL INTEGRATION IN SCHOOLS

As part of their analysis of the fortieth anniversary of *Brown* v. *Board of Education of Topeka, Kansas, USA Today* and Cable News Network (CNN) sponsored a national Gallup poll on race. The survey found that by a huge majority—87 percent—Americans believe the Supreme Court's 1954 *Brown* decision that struck down southern school segregation was right, a sharp increase from the 63 percent support in the early 1960s. Change in the South was even more dramatic. In 1954, an overwhelming 81 percent of southerners thought the Supreme Court was wrong, according to Gallup polls at the time. Although the South has experienced far more integration—and far more coercion to achieve integration— than any other region, only 15 percent of southerners in 1994 said they thought the *Brown* decision was wrong. According to the *USA Today*/CNN Gallup poll, a large and growing majority, 65 percent of the public and 70 percent of blacks, said integration "improved the quality of education for blacks." This percentage of people who held such a view was up from 43 percent at the beginning of busing in 1971 and from 55 percent in 1988.[2] In contrast to those who say that there must be a choice between desegregation and educational improvement, most people thought that desegregation brought educational improvement.

There had also been a sharp increase in the belief that "integration has improved the quality of education for whites." Specifically, 23 percent thought this was true in 1971, 35 percent believed this was true in 1988, and by 1994, 42 percent agreed with the statement. This suggests a growing perception that white as well as minority students have something to gain from integrated schools that prepare students early to work and live in an increasingly interracial society.[3]

The public is also optimistic about the value of school desegregation in race relations. In the 1994 Gallup poll, 62 percent of whites and 75 percent of blacks said that integrated schools had improved race relations. A rapidly increasing fraction of the public believes that "more should be done to integrate schools." This number is up from 37 percent in 1988 to 56 percent in 1994. Among blacks, 84 percent support more efforts to achieve integrated schools.[4]

The kinds of hopes that are still strongly attached to integrated schools were evident in responses to a Gallup poll for *Phi Delta Kappan.* When asked in 1993 which values were most important to teach to "all students in the public schools of your community," one of the highest—supported by 93 percent of the public and 96 percent of public school parents—was "acceptance of people of different races and ethnic backgrounds."[5] A 1993 statewide poll by the University of Connecticut Institute for Social Inquiry showed that 63 percent of the public believed that "children who go to one race schools will be at a disadvantage when they grow up and must live and work in a multiracial society" and 68 percent believed that school desegregation reduced racial prejudice.[6] However, the only federal program that funded efforts to produce successful integration and educational gains in desegregated schools, the Emergency School Aid Act, was repealed in 1981.

The strong support for integration and belief in its educational value, however, was not matched by a strong preference for busing over other policies. Indeed, when asked whether integration or a decision to "increase funding to minority schools" would be the best way to "help minority students," blacks favored increased funding by a 60–25 percent margin. By a smaller (47–33 percent margin), whites also agreed that funding would be the best policy.[7]

When a 1994 Gallup poll asked the following complex question about neighborhood schools, the answers revealed some seemingly contradictory attitudes:

Which is better: Letting students go to local schools, even if it means that most of the students would be the same race, or transferring students to other schools to create more integration, even if it means travel out of the community?

Among whites, 88 percent said they favored local schools and 64 percent of blacks said they favored the local schools on this question.[8] In general, then, it seems the public holds a very strong and growing preference for integration but is seriously divided on how to get it and what its priority should be relative to other educational goals. The divisions and increasing complexities seem to arise when questions are asked about how to achieve integration.

It is very important to note, at the outset, that each of these questions contains assumptions and poses choices in a certain way. Inevitably, the questions tend to include part of the reality of the situation and to omit other parts. As the final portion of this analysis will show, most of the questions do not reflect the actual situation under contemporary desegregation plans and do not reflect the reality of the segregated schools in the neighborhoods where resegregation takes place. If this question were rephrased, for example, to ask whether the schools in the minority neighborhoods should be integrated and whether students there should be forced to attend schools almost totally segregated by race and poverty with much lower levels of achievement (which we found actually happened with the return of neighborhood schools in the first city to restore them under a federal court order), the responses would doubtless be dramatically different. If the question asked whether families should be allowed to choose among several integrated schools, there would be a different pattern of responses. In the final portion of the report, I will return to these issues.

## ARE INTEGRATED SCHOOLS BETTER?

Very often the debate over school desegregation is incorrectly posed as a choice between race mixing and educational improvement. Some survey questions ask people to choose between integration and spending money for educational problems in local schools. In formulating the question this way, they are asking for a choice between something that is clearly identified as an educational program and something that is identified only as desegregation. If the reality is that desegregation itself is an educational treatment, that it works better when pursued with certain other kinds of educational changes, and that there is little evidence that investment of small sums of money in segregated schools has significant effects, then the questions would pose misleading alternatives. Nonetheless, responses to these questions are important.

For example, the *Atlanta Constitution* in 1994 published a poll of south-erners and asked whether respondents agreed that integration was "not as important as making sure that each community or neighborhood school provides a good education." Blacks over age forty-five split evenly on this question, with half of those expressing an opinion saying that "integrated schools are necessary to ensure that all students have an equal chance at a good education." Younger African-American adults, age eighteen to forty-five, had a much higher majority, 60 percent to 40 percent, supporting the necessity of integration. Whites split quite differently. Only 22 percent of older whites thought that integration was necessary but 37 percent of younger whites believed that it was.[9] In contrast to the beliefs that experi-ence with integration produces skepticism and that integration was a goal of the last generation, this suggests that just the opposite may be true. The generation that has experienced the most integration of any region is con-siderably more likely than the previous generation to see it as a necessity for equal education.

Undoubtedly one reason whites were much less likely to see the necessity of desegregation was that they were also much less likely to believe that there was any educational discrimination against African Americans. Dur-ing the 1980s both African Americans and whites become more concerned about educational discrimination against African Americans but vast gaps of perception remained. Between 1981 and 1989 the percentage of blacks saying that "blacks generally are discriminated against in getting a quality education" rose from 27 to 37 percent and the percentage of whites agree-ing went from 6 to 11 percent. Even after this increase, however, almost nine-tenths of whites saw no educational discrimination.[10]

A 1988 *Newsweek* poll showed that among whites 39 percent said that blacks did better in desegregated schools, compared with 4 percent who said that they did worse. Among blacks the margin was 48 to 6 percent; most of the rest said that it made no difference.[11]

## GENERAL TRENDS IN ATTITUDES TOWARD BUSING

When the public is asked general questions about busing, the response is still generally unfavorable. In contrast to many commentaries, however, attitudes about busing have *not* grown increasingly negative over time. In fact, since the policy began, there has been increasing acceptance of bus-ing among both whites and African Americans.

Many of the questions about busing used in major surveys have limita-tions. For example, the questions usually offer little information about the goal of a hypothetical desegregation order. Respondents are often asked to give opinions on hypothetical busing plans—plans that would be much more far-reaching than those that would be approved by a court after the 1974 *Milliken* v. *Bradley* Supreme Court decision set up rigid barriers to busing across district lines.[12]

For example, the National Opinion Research Center's (NORC) General Social Survey, perhaps the nation's most important university-based survey of social attitudes, asked a basic question suggesting cross-district busing: "In general, do you favor or oppose the busing of black and white school children from one school district to another?" Among whites, opposition in 1977 was remarkably high at 87 percent but then the opposition began to decrease and by 1986, 75 percent of whites were opposed to the idea. Among southern whites, who experienced more busing than whites in other regions, opposition fell far more rapidly than it did among northerners. Specifically, 92 percent of white southerners in the eighteen to twenty-seven age group opposed busing according to this question in 1977 but the number opposed dropped to 63 percent nine years later in 1986.[13]

In their article "Young White Adults: Did Racial Attitudes Change in the 1980s?," Charlotte Steeh and Howard Shuman report on attitudes of a population primarily including whites in their twenties and thirties. In 1985, the year after President Reagan's reelection, 76.1 percent of whites in this age group said that they were opposed to busing based on the same NORC question. The level of opposition fell each time the question was asked and by 1990, only 65.9 percent said they were opposed.[14]

The Harris survey reported a similar moderation of white opinion that occurred during the Reagan years. Harris reported that "all through the 1970s" between 73 and 78 percent of those surveyed expressed opposition to busing. By 1986, however, "the number opposed to busing dropped by 25% so that 41% favored busing and the number opposed dropped to 53%."[15] Ironically, it was only after an intensely conservative administration came to power and began actively pressing to dismantle desegregation plans that public opinion on busing became substantially more moderate.

Opposition to busing among both whites and blacks actually reached its peak in the years following the initial Supreme Court order in the 1971 *Swann* decision that authorized busing as a desegregation remedy.[16] In 1971, a Gallup poll asked, "In general, do you favor or oppose the busing of Negro and white school children from one school district to another?" That year, only 18 percent overall said they favored the policy. According to the survey, 45 percent of blacks said they favored the policy, but only 17 percent of northern whites and 10 percent of southern whites said they favored it.[17] (Overall national samples during this period contained only about one-eighth African Americans.) Opinion remained intensely negative a decade later at the beginning of the Reagan administration. In a Gallup poll the month after President Reagan's election, "busing children to achieve a better racial balance in the schools" was opposed by a 72 to 22 percentage margin. Only 17 percent of whites supported it, compared with 59 percent of blacks, including 73 percent of sourthern blacks, the group who had experienced the most integration.[18]

Very few major policy changes have been undertaken in the face of such intense opposition as that shown to busing by whites in its early years. It was during this period that the perception of attitudes toward urban school desegregation became fixed in the minds of many observers. Little attention was paid to the trends that showed significant positive changes, first among African Americans and then among the general public. Nor did most survey researchers adjust their questions to reflect the newer kinds of desegregation plans, which put greater emphasis on choice and educational reforms and less on mandatory student assignments.

## AFRICAN-AMERICAN SKEPTICISM ABOUT DESEGREGATION

African Americans are often characterized in press reports as being increasingly skeptical of busing, a remedy that opinion makers presume that blacks once supported strongly in the early 1970s when large-scale busing began. Disappointment with the experience under the plans later seemed to trigger a new preference for educational reforms that would make racially separate schools "equal." Sometimes, survey questions seem to suggest that there is a known way to spend the money currently used for busing that would actually equalize opportunity in neighborhood schools, although the research of our project has identified no cases in which educational outcomes have been equalized in segregated schools.

Survey evidence does not support the story of growing disenchantment with busing and integration. It is true that there has always been divided opinion among African Americans on the question of busing. But the peak opposition to busing has not emerged in the 1990s—it came and passed in the mid-1970s. According to the NORC General Social Survey question, the high point of opposition among African Americans came in 1975 when 53 percent of blacks said they opposed the policy. But this opposition declined significantly by 1986, with just 38 percent saying they opposed the policy, in spite of the intense critiques by the Reagan administration.[19] Even in busing's earliest years, there was limited support from black elected and administrative officials. For example, local African-American leaders in Atlanta traded desegregation for winning more black leadership positions in that school district more than twenty years ago, near the beginning of the busing era.

The public opinion data suggest, then, that the well-publicized opinions of African-American politicians who reject integration clearly contrast with the majority views of the African-American public. This should not be surprising, since white political leaders often express preferences that differ from those of white constituents. No one would assume, if a white politician took a position on a racial issue, that this position necessarily represented "white opinion" and the assumption is equally questionable in the African-American community.

## AMERICANS' VIEW OF DESEGREGATION AS A LEADING PROBLEM FOR THE SCHOOLS

Although desegregation levels were highest during the 1980s and the Reagan administration during this time continually asserted that busing was unnecessary, ineffective, and disruptive, the share of Americans who saw desegregation as a negative, serious problem declined rapidly in the late 1970s and 1980s. It was only during busing's first few years that desegregation was viewed as a major, negative problem by the American public.

In recent years, a very small share of Americans put the issue of desegregation on their list of serious educational problems and, in fact, race-related issues have received very little public attention in recent years, with the exception of a brief period following the Los Angeles riot.

In the 1970s, for example, busing and race issues were placed near the top of the list of issues concerning schools in the annual Gallup polls of the American public for *Phi Delta Kappan*, a leading education policy journal. Busing and race, however, have been off that list for a long time. In other words, people do not consider this to be one of the serious problems affecting American schools. This also indicates that the issue of desegregation is much less volatile than it has been in the past. According to the Phi Delta Kappa Gallup polls, in 1969, the desegregation issue was among the leading concerns, cited by 13 percent of the public; in 1970 it was the second most important problem, cited by 17 percent; in 1971, at the peak of new busing orders, it nearly became the top issue, with 21 percent listing it as a leading local problem. Integration/segregation remained the second most serious problem, with 18 percent listing it during the next two years.[20] During the early Reagan administration, the urgency of the issue had declined dramatically even though greater acceptance of busing would occur only later. In 1982 only 6 percent of the public mentioned desegregation and busing as leading problems and the number was 5 percent in 1983.[21] Urban school desegregation was a very intense issue when it first emerged on the national scene. Twenty years later, little concern was expressed about its consequences.

When asked to identify "the biggest problems with which the public schools of this community must deal" in the 1993 Gallup survey, only 4 percent mentioned issues including integration, segregation, and racial discrimination. The number fell to 3 percent in 1994. Race ranked far behind the issues of money, drugs, discipline, violence, and academic standards. The percentage of those who believed that race-related issues were among the "biggest problems" in their communities was 5 percent in 1990 and 1991, dropping to 4 percent the next two years.[22]

When desegregation increased rapidly as a result of busing orders in the early 1970s, there was very intense concern and conflict. In the 1980s, desegregation continued to increase slightly and there was strong criticism by national leaders, including leaders in the Justice Department, but it never became a major public concern. Public concern over the issues of race and desegregation actually declined to a very low level. There has not been intense public concern about the busing issue for many years.

According to a 1981 ABC News/Washington Post Poll, a majority of public high school principals whose schools were involved with busing said they approved of the policy.[23] Specifically, 59 percent of principals involved with the policy said they approved of busing "for integration," and 27 percent said they disapproved of the policy.

When asked as part of the same poll whether busing "on the whole has improved education at your school, worked against education or not made much difference," 59 percent of these same principals said busing had "not made much difference" and 32 percent said they thought busing had "improved education." Only 9 percent of the principals said busing "worked against education."

The decline in attention to school desegregation was part of the much larger disappearance of most racial issues from overt political discussion. Race was a dominant national political issue in the mid-1960s and there were huge political and regional consequences to the great civil rights battles that changed the South. Since that time, however, "the fraction of Americans citing *any* explicitly racial problems declined gradually from 1964 through 1972, and then plummeted in the following years. By 1974, only 5 percent of blacks and 3 percent of whites, in both North and South named race as an important problem."[24] That low level of concern about racial issues remained for a decade.

Only in the latter part of the 1980s was concern about race revived—and then only among blacks. Concern about race among whites rose not at all: No more than 2 percent of whites, North or South, have mentioned race as a national problem since 1978. Among whites, and to a great extent among blacks as well, "explicit references to race as a national problem have all but vanished."[25] Although many argue that race continues to play a major role through indirect signals in campaigns and through attacks on welfare and crime, both of which have strong connections with big-city minority communities in the minds of many whites, the decline in explicit focus is, at least, a sign that there is no severe overt resistance to existing civil rights policies.

## ATTITUDES OF FAMILIES AND STUDENTS WHO EXPERIENCED BUSING

Some of the most revealing questions asked in surveys were posed to students and families who actually had experience with school desegregation policies. Responses to questions about busing and integration asked several times by the Harris surveys from the late 1970s through the late 1980s were far more positive than were the responses from the general public.

In 1978, the survey showed that 63 percent of black parents and 56 percent of whites said that their experience of being bused for integration had been "very satisfactory." Only 8 percent of blacks and 16 percent of whites said that the experience was "unsatisfactory."[26]

White parents' opinions became slightly less optimistic in the early years of the Reagan administration. Of the white parents, 48 percent of those surveyed in 1981 said that their experience had been "very satisfactory," another 37 percent said that it had been partly satisfactory, and just an eighth said that it was unsatisfactory. In 1981 the Harris survey reported that 19 percent of all families had had children bused for desegregation. Black families were more than twice as likely to have children who had been bused. Among those who had the experience, 74 percent of parents said it had been very satisfactory and 21 percent said it was partly satisfactory. Only one in twenty blacks said that the experience had been unsatisfactory.[27]

Another Harris survey, released in 1989, found that attitudes of families whose children had been bused had become more positive over eight years. Specifically, 64 percent of whites, 63 percent of blacks, and 70 percent of Asians whose children had been bused said that the experience was "very satisfactory." Only 4 percent of African Americans, 6 percent of whites, and 2 percent of Asians said that the experience was unsatisfactory.[28]

### LOUISVILLE SURVEY

One of the most interesting local surveys of the 1990s came in Louisville, Kentucky, after the school superintendent proposed returning to neighborhood elementary schools, with the support of his board's only black member. The superintendent said that this was necessary to implement key parts of the state's massive education reform law. Louisville had been desegregated across city-suburban boundary lines in a metropolitan busing plan in 1975. The federal court had released Louisville from its desegregation order in 1980 so the district was one of the few in the country where the school board could have simply ended busing without any legal battle. Connecting the termination of the plan for the early grades to the goal of educational reform seemed to make it politically untouchable. Since African Americans had always borne a disproportionate share of the busing, they were expected to welcome a return to neighborhood schools.

When busing was first implemented in Louisville–Jefferson County in 1975, more than nine-tenths of whites and two-fifths of African Americans were opposed.[29] When the *Louisville Courier-Journal* surveyed the community in 1992, however, it found that 36 percent of the overall community and 70 percent of African Americans opposed ending the plan. Among African Americans, 53 percent said that they thought that there would be stronger education in white than in black schools after return to the neighborhood system. Only 2 percent thought that the black schools would be superior. One of the reasons for the support was the experience of parents whose children were bused: 81 percent of African-American parents saw the experience as satisfactory, as did 53 percent of white parents.[30]

## VIEWS OF COLLEGE STUDENTS

Large-scale urban desegregation began in the early 1970s. A student entering first grade in the fall after the Supreme Court's first busing decision, in 1971, would have graduated from high school in June 1984, right in the middle of the Reagan administration's tenure. These were the students who entered school at the peak of a bitter and divisive struggle and came of political age in the most conservative era in American politics in sixty years. Students in this generation might be expected to be the most severe critics of busing policy.

Curiously, however, the massive annual survey of hundreds of thousands of college freshmen conducted by the American Council on Education and the University of California at Los Angeles (UCLA) shows that throughout the 1980s, a majority of students favoring busing, and this remains true in the 1990s. In fall 1989, after eight years of conservative government opposition to busing, 56.1 percent of college freshman favored the policy.[31] In fall 1992 the percent in favor was 55 percent and in fall 1993, the most recent survey, the question was not asked. However, 41.4 percent expressed their belief that "helping to promote racial understanding" was an essential or very important goal. Only 14 percent believed that "racial discrimination is no longer a major problem in America."[32]

## INDIANA: PUBLIC ATTITUDES AND ATTITUDES OF STUDENTS

Recent surveys of the general public in the Indianapolis area and of students from across the state of Indiana, where there are desegregation plans in most of the major urban communities, reflected different dimensions of the busing issue in a conservative state. Among the Indianapolis-area public there was an extremely powerful rejection of the idea of sending white and black students to racially separate schools. According to the survey, 90 percent of blacks and 89 percent of whites said that blacks and whites should attend school together. When asked whether they would object to sending their children to schools where their children would be in a racial minority, only 9 percent of blacks and 18 percent of whites said that they would object. However, when asked whether they would "favor the busing of black and white children from one district to another," African Americans divided closely—42 percent to 42 percent—while whites were opposed by a 68 to 19 percent margin.[33]

When students were questioned across Indiana, however, the results were quite different. Students who responded to statewide surveys report a consistently favorable view of their experience in the state's highly integrated schools. Two-thirds of recent graduates strongly support policies to continue integration, even if busing is necessary. White Indiana students questioned two years after high school not only support integration but also believe that students who attended interracial high schools have an advantage over those who did not. The views of minority and white students on these issues were very similar.[34] In a very conservative state, the opinions of those actually experiencing desegregation diverged strikingly from those of the general public.

## SEGREGATION OR BUSING?
## HOW THE PUBLIC DIVIDES ON DIFFICULT CHOICES

Throughout the past generation, the public has been critical of busing while simultaneously strongly favoring integrated schools. But, of course, when courts order busing, it is because they see it as the only means of achieving integration. Yet survey questions have seldom seriously explored the conflict between the desire for integration and the public's suspicion of busing.

One of the few exceptions was a January 1992 national poll conducted by the *Boston Globe*. The *Globe* asked Americans whether they would support busing if it were the only way to integrate schools. The question took seriously the conflict between the very strong commitment to integrated education and the opposition of whites to busing. In response to this question, whites supported busing by a 48–41 majority.[35]

A similar set of questions asked at the peak of the busing conflict in 1972 in a national survey by the Opinion Research Corporation for the U.S. Civil Rights Commission found similar results: Although only 21 percent said that they favored busing, another 15 percent said that they would support rerouting existing buses to increase integration and another 7 percent said that they would support busing if no other way could be found to integrate schools. Most whites and 71 percent of blacks expressing an opinion supported busing under these circumstances.[36]

Black and Latino support for busing when a question posed the choice between busing and segregation was overwhelming. This was true in both the early 1970s and the 1990s. Among African Americans, in the 1992 *Globe* poll, there was a 79–16 percent majority for busing if there was no other way to achieve desegregation, and the numbers were even higher among Latinos, who are often assumed to prefer linguistic and cultural homogeneity. The Latino preference was an astonishing 82–18 percent. When asked a more difficult question—"Would you be willing to have your own children go to school by bus so the schools would be integrated?"—whites split evenly, blacks said yes by a 76–21 ratio, and Latinos agreed by a 60–18 ratio.[37]

A 1989 Harris survey found that 67 percent of blacks and 38 percent of whites supported busing on a general question. When those opposed to busing were asked whether they would support busing if "white children were bused to top quality schools in the inner city and black children were bused to equally good schools," support for busing increased to 51 percent of whites and 79 percent of blacks.[38] These questions suggest both that the experience with busing is much more positive than is widely believed and that white opinion resisting busing is by no means monolithic or unchangeable. The goal of integration is a serious goal for many whites, even if it requires changes they otherwise would not prefer.

## QUESTIONS NOT ASKED

To at least some degree, questions about busing that are found in the current research literature are as relevant to the contemporary desegregation orders as questions abut the Cold War would be to contemporary international issues. In the early 1970s there were many orders that did little more than mandate the transfer of students of a specific race from one school to another. There have been only a handful of orders in the entire country that mandated transfer of students across school district boundary lines. Yet the most common questions are about these mandatory transfer and cross-district plans. Most of the information we get about public attitudes, in other words, taps reaction to an outdated set of alternatives.

In reality, actual desegregation plans for the past fifteen years have been combinations of mandatory desegregation, magnet schools, choice, and major elements of educational reform. Many cities have created wildly popular magnet schools that families fight to get into, even though they may be located in minority communities. Under the "controlled choice" plan, to cite another instance, families rank schools they think best for their children and are given the school closest to the top of the list that complies with desegregation requirements. Other plans are designed to encourage housing desegregation and to reward integrated neighborhoods with the restoration of neighborhood schools. Some pump hundreds of millions of dollars into minority schools that cannot feasibly be integrated to try to provide more equal opportunities. Integration itself is often no longer a question of blacks and whites but of multiracial schools.

But survey questions have not kept pace with the current reality. We do not, for example, see such survey questions as: "Would you be in favor of a desegregation plan that created excellent new schools and gave you one of your top choices among those schools while ensuring that all are desegregated?" Neither do the surveys ask whether families would prefer an effort to integrate neighborhoods and then restore naturally integrated neighborhood schools. There is, we know from other surveys, very strong support for choice policies of the kind often included in recent desegregation policies. For example, 65 percent of the public in 1993 favored "allowing students and parents to choose which public schools in this community, the students attend, regardless of where they live."[39] A 1994 U.S. Education Department report showed that most contemporary magnet and choice opportunities grew out of desegregation plans.[40] Questions better reflecting the educational reform and choice elements in the desegregation plans of the last fifteen years would almost certainly evoke a much more positive public reaction than the general questions about busing asked in most surveys that are testing response to the kinds of plans implemented in the 1970s.

## SUMMARY AND IMPLICATIONS

The busing issue shows a great deal about the profound American ambiguity about race. People believe strongly that it would be better if white and minority children went to school together but most, particularly most whites, do not see it as an urgent problem and are not prepared to pay any substantial cost to accomplish it. On the other hand, there is considerable evidence that we want the goal of school integration and that the means that have been adopted to accomplish it, including mandatory busing, have been much more successful than is commonly believed, particularly in the minds of those most directly affected, the parents and the students.

If policymakers took seriously the structure of public opinion, the choices would not be limited to mandatory busing or a return to segregated neighborhood schools. Since there is strong evidence that people think that school integration is valuable and beneficial but strong resistance, particularly among older whites, to busing, the survey evidence does not lead to a policy of neighborhood schools. The policies most congruent with the values expressed by the public are school desegregation with more choice and less mandatory student transportation. This is exactly the direction in which policy has evolved in the past fifteen years. The other policy that is very compatible with the structure of public preferences is an increased emphasis on housing desegregation to produce communities that are integrated and have neighborhood schools. President Clinton signed an executive order in January 1994 setting up a governmentwide process intended to increase housing desegregation.

This analysis is not, of course, an adequate basis for a new policy. Because a policy may be popular does not mean that it is effective and it is very important to examine direct measures of effectiveness. What the public opinion data do show, however, is that the public continues to value desegregation, that it does not see urgent problems with the existing plans, and that there is a developing white perception of benefits for white as well as minority children in interracial schools. One very important cautionary note that comes out of this summary is the need for much greater care by those expressing sweeping conclusions about the nature and direction of public opinion on sensitive racial issues. The basic data on African-American attitudes have been frequently reported in a fundamentally incorrect manner. Often news stories and commentaries are wrong both about what opinion was at earlier times and what it is now. There has been almost no attention by either those conducting polls or those using poll data to the fact that the questions no longer describe the actual range of alternatives before the courts or in operation in school districts with plans developed during the past fifteen years. As communities move toward decisions about the future of desegregation, it is very important to recognize and fully describe the desire and support for integration, the changing levels of opposition to busing, the positive experience of those actually affected by existing desegregation plans, and the kinds of desegregation plans now being implemented.

## Notes

1    Board of Education of Oklahoma City v. Dowell, 498 U.S. 237 (1991).
2    Patricia Edmonds, "Only Real Difference: How to Desegregate," *USA Today*, May 12, 1994, p. 8A.
3    Ibid.
4    Ibid.

5   Stanley M. Elam, Lowell C. Rose, and Alec M. Gallup, "The 25th Annual Phi Delta Kappa/Gallup Poll of the Public's Attitude toward the Public Schools," *Phi Delta Kappan*, October 1993, pp. 139, 145.

6   Robert Frahm, "Poll: Sharp Splits on School Integration," *Hartford Courant*, February 14, 1993, p. A1.

7   *USA Today*, May 12, 1994.

8   Ibid.

9   Atlanta Journal-Constitution University of North Carolina Southern Life Poll, "Integration and a Good Education," *Atlanta Constitution*, May 15, 1994, p. A9.

10   Washington Post-ABC News Poll, *Washington Post*, October 25, 1989, p. A16.

11   *Newsweek*, March 7, 1988, p. 23.

12   Milliken v. Bradley, 418 U.S. 717 (1974).

13   Gerald David Jaynes and Robin M. Williams, eds., *A Common Destiny: Blacks and American Society* (Washington, D. C.: National Academy Press, 1989), pp. 128–29.

14   Charlotte Steeh and Howard Schuman, "Young White Adults: Did Racial Attitudes Change in the 1980s," *American Journal of Sociology* 98 (September 1992): 340–67.

15   Harris and Associates, *The Unfinished Agenda on Race in America: Report to the NAACP Legal Defense and Educational Fund*, January 1989, pp. 22–23.

16   Swann v. Charlotte-Mecklenburg Board of Education, 402 U.S. 1 (1971).

17   George H. Gallup, *The Gallup Poll, Public Opinion 1935–1971*, vol. 3 (New York: Random House, 1972), p. 2323.

18   Gallup Report, February 1981, p. 29.

19   Jaynes and Williams, *A Common Destiny*, pp. 128–29.

20   Stanley Elam, *The Gallup Polls of Attitudes toward Education: 1969–1973* (Bloomington: Phi Delta Kappa, 1973), pp. 27, 66, 101, 135, 171.

21   Gallup data in *USA Today*, August 25, 1983.

22   Gallup surveys reported in *Phi Delta Kappan*, unpaginated insert; September 1991, p. 55; September 1992, p. 43; September 1993, unpaginated insert.

23   ABC/News/Washington Post Poll, The Roper Center for Public Opinion, Storrs, Conn., December 1981.

24   Michael G. Hagen, "Salience of Racial Issues," Harvard University Center for American Political Studies, Occasional Paper 93–11, May 1993, pp. 7–8.

25   Ibid.

26   Louis Harris and Associates, "A Study of Attitudes toward Racial and Religious Minorities and toward Women" (Report to the National Conference of Christian and Jews, November 1978, p. 38, New York).

27   Harris survey reported in *Boston Globe*, May 26, 1981, p. 2.

28   Harris and Associates, *The Unfinished Agenda on Race in America*, appendix B.

29   John B. McConahay and Willis D. Hawley, "Reaction to Busing in Louisville: Summary of Adult Opinions in 1976 and 1977," Duke University Center for Policy Analysis, 1979.

30   Stan McDonald and Scott Wade, "Whites Divided over Plan to End Forced Busing," *Louisville Courier-Journal*, October 27, 1991, p. A1.

31   Editors of the Chronicles of Higher Education, *Almanac of Higher Education*, (Chicago: University of Chicago Press, 1991), p. 39.

32   *Chronicle of Higher Education*, August 25, 1993, p. 15; and January 26, 1994, p. A31.

33   *Indianapolis Star*, February 28, 1993, pp. 4–5.

34   Indiana Youth Institute, "Race: How Equal Is Opportunity in Indiana Schools?" Report 7a in High Hopes, Long Odds series on Indiana Youth Opportunity Study, May 1994.

35   "Poll Shows Wide Support."

36    U.S. Commission on Civil Rights, *Public Knowledge and Business Opposition,* November 1972, p. 9 (au: text is difference from note).

37    "Poll Shows Wide Support across U.S. for Integration," *Boston Globe,* January 5, 1992, p. 15.

38    Harris and Associate, *The Unfinished Agenda on Race in America,* pp. 24–25.

39    Elam, Rose, and Gallup, "The 25th Annual Phi Delta Kappan/Gallup Poll," p. 151.

40    American Institutes for Research, *Magnet Schools and Issues of Desegregation, Quality, and Choice,* Phase I: The National Survey and In-Depth Survey of Selected Districts, February 1993, p. vii.

# Diversity and the New Immigrants

LAMAR P. MILLER AND LISA A. TANNERS
*New York University*

*New immigrants in the United States are enlivening the schools at the same time as they are overwhelming them. The waves of immigration have led to an increasingly diverse school population and have created a new set of problems. Today, with children from such diverse backgrounds, schools are inadequately prepared to serve the needs of the students who are arriving in increasing numbers. The challenges associated with the new immigrants are numerous. Problems now exist that are related to desegregation, multicultural education, higher-quality education, and bilingual education. As the population of our schools becomes more and more diverse, the most appropriate ways to educate this fascinating heterogeneous population must be sought.*

The mid-1900s marked a turning point in the history of segregated schools in the United States. The emergence of a number of black leaders, such as Roy Wilkins of the National Association for the Advancement of Colored People, A. Phillip Randolph of the Brotherhood of Sleeping Car Porters, Whitney Young of the Urban League, and Martin Luther King, Jr., of the Southern Christian Leadership Council, escalated the fight by African Americans for equal opportunities. Their leadership was supported by an unprecedented number of black and white Americans, and this persistent black initiative forced a reformulation of public policies in education. The most important result was the 1954 Supreme Court decision in *Brown* v. *Board of Education of Topeka, Kansas.*

The *Brown* decision struck down a kind of school segregation that is different from the type of segregation that exists today. The Warren Court of 1954 outlawed any segregation that was either sanctioned by state law or traceable to school board policies. Today, school segregation is usually blamed on demographic changes, differential birth rates, and patterns of immigration. The influx of new immigrants, in particular those who fit our outdated definition of "minority," has led to an increasingly diverse school population and created a new set of problems related to desegregation. This article will address some of these new concerns.

For most of the last forty years, the desegregation issue has been centered largely on the fight for equal opportunity by African Americans. The issue was race, and race was defined in terms of black and white. Now, with so many different ethnic groups, some with both black and white members, the issue can no longer be confined to a simple definition of race.

In this country, we have a unique way of describing and defining race. We ascribe to race characteristics that other cultures view very differently. For example, race and ethnicity appear to influence expectations and judgments at all levels of the spectrum of our society. Skin color has long been a factor that influences judgment and behavior.

In 1993, in a series of congressional hearings on the census, Congressman Tom Sawyer of Ohio pointed out that

> the country is in the midst of its most profound demographic shift since the 1890s, a time that opened a period of the greatest immigration we have ever seen, whose numbers have not been matched until right now. A deluge of new Americans from every part of the world is overwhelming our traditional distinctions. . . . The categories themselves inevitably reflect the temporal bias of every age and that becomes a problem when the nation itself is undergoing deep and historic diversification.[1]

Although we still have the black-versus-white issue, there is the question of the categories of racial groups as defined by government agencies. Do we look at groups on the basis of color or language or other categories?

Whether ethnic categories protect or divide us is a question that requires profound analysis, but clearly the growing heterogeneity of American society is having an impact on the educational system. What happens in our educational system may depend on our ability to address the issue of ethnic categories. We are being challenged to reexamine education in general, and more specifically, the way in which large numbers of youngsters in urban areas, who differ widely in their cultural backgrounds, are educated.

New patterns of immigration are also forcing us to examine the idea and concept of diversity or what we often call multiculturalism. The terms *multiculturalism* and *diversity* are often used interchangeably. They are sometimes not clearly differentiated, and are selected for their symbolic value rather than for their precise definition. Nevertheless, the idea of developing a concept of diversity, as opposed to a state of being, is the state we want to get to. Diversity has evolved from a concept of moral, social, legal, and educational responsibility to issues motivated by and linked with changes in the global economy and the makeup of our work force. Philosophically, it evolved from the concept of improving access to the work place for women and minorities in the 1960s and 1970s, adding the goal of valuing the diversity of groups in the work place in the 1980s. A definition of the concept recognizes the importance of "valuing diversity." This meaning provides us with a term that is broadly inclusive, embracing groups and differences not included in terms we have used before, and it views differences as valuable. Moreover, the term recognizes the importance of new strategies to respond to changes in our schools and our work force, and more flexible human resource policies to support differences and respond to a wider array of needs. Finally, it is linked with equal educational opportunity because it represents a new stage in the way we address the issues, problems, and futures of the many groups in our society.

The term *multiculturalism*, while similar to diversity in that it focuses on inclusion of groups of people, has encompassed a debate that goes far beyond educational circles. It has often been concerned with such things as culture, morality, political correctness, and the canons.

Donald Johnson has discussed the debate on multiculturalism and its subarguments over Eurocentrism and political correctness.[2] He pointed out how these issues have made the covers of major magazines, citing as an example the September 23, 1991, heading on the cover of *Newsweek*: "Was Cleopatra Black?" Johnson pointed out that these stories mask deeper societal disputes about our conceptions of history, who we are as a people, and what the future of a national culture is to be. Perhaps these issues are important and need to be addressed. The point is that it does not matter whether Cleopatra was black or white, but that she is in the schools and she will soon be in the American work force. To put it another way, the population of our schools is becoming more and more diverse, and we will have to find the most appropriate ways to educate this fascinating heterogeneous population.

The population of today's society is so diverse that it is predicted that within a decade, some 50 percent of elementary and secondary school children will belong to an ethnic minority. In some areas, such as California, white students are already a minority. Sustaining a truly multiracial society is unique to the United States. Most other countries maintain a distinct national identity, but these countries were not created and defined by voluntary immigration the way the United States has been. The influx of immigrants has caused Americans to ask what it means to become an American. White Americans can no longer think of themselves as the very picture of their nation. Becoming a multicultural society is bound to be a bumpy experience, but we must realize that a new world is here and it is the America to come.[3]

The nation as a whole and particularly the larger cities are already facing the issues associated with diversity. We use New York City as an example because the immigrant population in New York City has expanded enormously in recent years. In New York City today, about one out of every seven residents has arrived from a foreign country within the past ten years, and it is expected that another million immigrants will enter the city by the year 2000. Furthermore, statistics show that one out of every three New Yorkers is foreign-born.[4] This dramatic influx of immigrants has placed enormous stress on the educational system. A brief look at the history of immigration in New York, why these immigrants have come to New York, some demographics of the changing population, and some of the problems that plague schools will help us clarify the current situation.

Many different waves of immigration have influenced the educational system in New York City. The first wave of immigrants came over from Ireland and Germany from the 1830s to the 1880s. The second wave came in the 1880s and lasted until the 1920s. This group of immigrants was more diverse; Italians, Jews, Czechs, and Poles all began to settle in New York City. From the 1920s to the 1960s, large numbers of blacks migrated from the South. A growing number of Puerto Ricans began to reside in New York City between the 1940s and 1950s. Today's immigrants are tremendously diverse, and coming to New York City in vast numbers. In the past immigrants were primarily European; this is no longer the case. Today, Europeans make up 43 percent of New York City's immigrant population. The new immigrants include large numbers of people from South America, the Caribbean, Asia, the Middle East, and countries formerly a part of the U.S.S.R. It is estimated that about 800,000 to 900,000 immigrants came to New York in each of the past three decades. As David Reimers said, "New York is really a world city in terms of its population and [it is] becoming more so."[5]

As our population becomes more diverse, our identification and perception of who is to be educated constantly changes. Before the 1960s, educational standards were low. Most immigrants did not go to school and those who did rarely graduated from high school. Often families could not afford to send their children to school and made them work instead. Schools were expected to teach the rudiments of reading and writing as well as the elementary skills needed in the labor force. Schools taught Americanization; that is, they taught English and they taught patriotism. Differences in ethnic background were not addressed by the curriculum.

Today's immigrants represent a range of individuals, some of whom are skilled and educated and often replace poor and uneducated Americans, and others who are eager to develop skills and learn about technology quickly. In the schools, there is a need for education that is high quality, multicultural, and accommodating of language differences. The increasingly diverse population requires more bilingual teachers and teachers of English as a second languge. Hence, schools have more demands placed on them.

A recent study of immigrant education in New Jersey reflects the general trend and issues associated with immigrant education across the country.

The study concluded that immigrant education is not just an urban phenomenon; immigrant children are found in both urban and suburban districts throughout the state of New Jersey. We note that this is true throughout other states of the country as well.

> The distribution of immigrant students varies according to the relative property wealth of the districts. The immigrant children served by low property wealth urban districts are largely from Central and South America, the Caribbean and Vietnam. Immigrant children from India, Japan and Korea tend to attend school in high property wealth suburban districts. The challenges in serving immigrant students vary according to the districts' relative property wealth. The poor urban districts face a larger, more diverse population of immigrants, high student mobility, students with little or no prior schooling, and the need for adequately trained teachers.[6]

In the past few years, more than 120,000 immigrant children from over 167 countries have enrolled in the New York City schools.[7] To help immigrant students become acclimated to differences in culture, the schools must provide a wide array of services. The immigrant students have been through a lot of tumult, and some come from countries where the educational system is inferior to that found in New York City. They are often limited in their English proficiency and sometimes even illiterate in their own languages. This puts excessive demands on the school system because the schools are required to use such strategies as two-way bilingual programs, which helps students to make the transition from their own langue to English. The law requires the New York City Board of Education to teach English to the 117,000 public school students who have limited English proficiency.[8]

Not only are there many different ethnic groups in New York City, but there is also a great deal of diversity within each ethnic group. For example, Asians may be Chinese, Korean, Asian Indian, Vietnamese refugees, or Filipino. Immigrants from the Middle East may include Afghan refugees, Israelis, Palestinians, Lebanese, and Syrians. Some of the immigrants from the Caribbean are English-speaking, some are Spanish-speaking, and some speak Haitian-Creole. Twenty years ago, the Hispanic population was predominantly Puerto Rican. The 1990 census, however, showed that the New York City's 896,763 Puerto Ricans now account for only half of the city's Hispanic population. Increasing numbers of Hispanics come from Central and South America, and especially the Dominican Republic.[9] In fact, immigrants from the Dominican Republic are the fastest growing immigrant group in the city.

What has remained constant over the years is the reason families come to the United States: They come for freedom and economic prosperity.

Many immigrant families are fleeing poverty, unemployment, underemployment, inadequate living conditions (even for the elite), and political and social instability. New York City is appealing for a variety of reasons: There are employment opportunities; new immigrants do not stand out; established immigrant communities provide a sense of security; and the city is a place where families can reunite.[10]

The following facts and predictions about ethnic groups will have an impact on the social patterns that develop in New York City:

1.  One out of every four Americans defines himself or herself as African-American, Asian-American, Hispanic-American, or Native-American.[11]

2.  By the year 2000, the Hispanic-American population will increase by 21 percent; the Asian-American population, by 22 percent; the African-American population, by 12 percent.[12]

3.  By the year 2056, the "average" U.S. resident will be a person of color with a non-European origin.[13]

4.  Asian/Pacific Islander enrollments in the nation's public elementary/secondary schools are increasing more rapidly than those of any other group, more than 70 percent by 1995.[14]

5.  African Americans are still expected to be the second largest racial/ethnic group among elementary/secondary enrollments, but they are growing at a slower rate (13 percent, from less than 5.9 million in 1986 to almost 6.7 million in 1995) than Hispanic or Asian/Pacific Islander populations.[15]

6.  New immigrants have increased the New York City school population by 120,000 since 1990: 28,109 immigrants have come from the Dominican Republic, 11,206 from Jamaica, 9,731 from Russia, 8,144 from China, 7,863 from Guyana, 6,054 from Haiti, 5,131 from Trinidad and Tobago, 5,334 from Mexico, 4,103 from Columbia, 3,995 from Ecuador, and 3,755 from Korea.[16]

The challenges associated with new immigrants in the schools are numerous. We have made reference to instructional interventions such as programs in English as a second language, bilingual education, orientation classes, counseling, and tutoring services. The new immigrants that populate the city's public school system highlight problems associated with the changing urban scene. In the past, schools served mainly English-speaking children. Today, with children from such diverse backgrounds, schools are inadequately prepared to serve the needs of the students who are arriving in increasing numbers. One elementary school in Elmhurst, Queens, reports that less than half of its student body speaks English and that there are over thirty different languages spoken in the school.[17] Another school district in Queens has enough Spanish, Chinese, and Korean students to form bilingual classes of at least twenty students per grade.[18] In 1994, 150,000 students were enrolled in bilingual programs in the New York City public schools.[19]

In the New York City schools there are already more than 5,200 bilingual teachers, who constitute 8 percent of the staff.[20] Finding more teachers with bilingual certification is not easy, particularly for underrepresented groups. Immigrants who speak languages other than Spanish often must take all their classes in English, and educators fear that these students suffer in mathematics and science classes because they do not understand their teachers—not because they cannot grasp the material.[21] In addition, schools are having problems identifying immigrant students, and teachers often do not know when students speak a language other than English at home.[22]

Problems related to bilingual education are multifaceted. Economic factors accompany language diversity. Despite a shrinking budget, schools must find and pay for more bilingual teachers and teachers of English as a second language. Immigrant language programs cost the school $130.6 million a year, a steep bill to pay when there is a lack of state and federal funding.

The demand for new materials and new schools also has a profound economic impact on the schools. Schools lack materials in languages other than English and Spanish and tend to be extremely overcrowded. The teacher-pupil ratios are very high. For example, one New York City elementary school has 2,100 students from 45 different countries and is so crowded that it equals the size of a high school that typically draws from far larger geographical zones. In one district, classrooms are held on auditorium stages and in assistant principals' offices because more space is needed.[23] Further complicating the already large class sizes is the fact that so many students are academically delayed. Some immigrant students have had little or no learning in their original countries. In addition, other obstacles to school learning, such as language differences, low income, and low parental education, lead to lower achievement levels.[24] Emanuel Tobler fears that while hard-driving immigrants may find success among the city's employers, the children of those immigrants may lose their hunger to learn in schools that are overcrowded and underfinanced.[25]

There is political pressure on the schools to revamp their curriculum to take into account the cultural backgrounds of newcomers. Proponents of a multicultural curriculum think that teaching about different groups is important for raising students' self-esteem; multiculturalists are fighting for a more inclusive curriculum. The traditional history curriculum often gives very little attention to the contributions of some ethnic groups, if not ignoring them all together.[26] But whose stories should be told and how much time should be devoted to each? One proponent of multiculturalism thinks that the current curriculum is "too concerned with the European origins of American ideas, traditions and people. Multiculturalists claim that the number of non-European Americans is increasing and it is wrong to impose an alien European culture and heritage upon their children in the public schools. These children deserve a curriculum of their own culture and heritage."[27] Students will feel proud when their own cultures are positively reflected in the classroom. Some people believe that by learning about other groups and the importance of respecting differences, racial and ethnic tensions will be eased.

Critics of a multicultural curriculum argue that teaching some forms of multicultural education in the schools is divisive. For example, they see ethnocentric studies as promoting disunity in American society.[28] Furthermore, critics think that focusing on how we are different leads to increased tension among races and ethnic groups.

Aside from the difficulties already mentioned, schools must handle the frequent mobility of immigrant students, minimize conflicts between immigrant students and others, and get parents from different cultures to work with the schools.[29] The sharp rise in the number of immigrants in New York City and other places, and the change in immigrant patterns, has also exacerbated problems associated with desegregation. School districts throughout our region face increasingly complicated desegregation issues. Immigrant children often face a multitude of learning, adjustment, and social challenges, including becoming the targets of racial hostility.[30] Clearly, equal educational opportunities cannot exist if the obvious sources of information, skills, knowledge, and instruction are less accessible to some students than to others. Where that accessibility is limited because of a student's race, sex, national origin, or limited English proficiency, our mission is to eliminate all vestiges of whatever discriminatory practices have contributed to that denial of accessibility.

Intensifying the debate on issues of immigrant education are questions raised about illegal immigrants and their rights. Clearly, schools are faced with a mandate that goes beyond the *Brown* decision. Desegregation strategies must encompass a wide array of ethnic groups created by the influx of new immigrants, a large number of whom might well have been considered minorities according to old definitions. In this case, the question is how we provide equal access and equal educational opportunity, an issue that has been raised with the passing of Proposition 187 in California in the 1994 election year. Among other things, Proposition 187 deprives illegal immigrants of state services, including education. The proposition was immediately challenged in court by its opponents and a federal judge issued a restraining order against implementing most of the new law. A state judge had already barred enforcement of the provision to deny schooling to illegal immigrants. The restraining order came as no surprise, since a 1982 Supreme Court decision, *Plyer* v. *Doe*, granted illegal immigrants the right to a free public education. We believe that ultimately the state of California will have to provide education for immigrant children regardless of whether they are illegal aliens or have been legally admitted to the country. In any case, California, along with all other states, will have to address the challenge of immigrant education.

Despite all of its problems and challenges, the school system has the greatest role in serving New York City's immigrants. Schools offer the most common shared experience for most Americans. They are the key to the Americanization process. Immigrant parents have high expectations of the schools and rely on schools to help their children do better. As the schools adapt to the needs of the changing student body, we hope that immigrant students will perform better in school and make substantial gains every year. As demographics continue to shift in the direction of increased diversity, education must accommodate that shift.

## Notes

1   Quoted in Lawrence Wright, "One Drop of Blood," *The New Yorker*, July 1994, pp. 46–55.

2   Donald Johnson, *Multiculturalism: In the Curriculum, In the Disciplines, and In Society* (New York: The Metropolitan Center for Educational Research, Development and Training, 1992).

3   William A. Henry, III, "Beyond the Melting Pot," *Time*, April 9, 1990, pp. 28–31.

4   Robert Friedman, "Immigration Surge Accents New York Life," *New York Newsday*, June 24, 1990, pp. 14–20.

5   David Reimers, "Diversity: The Newcomer and Urban Education" (Transcript of symposium, New York University, May 8, 1992), p. 39.

6   Ana Maria Villegas, "Education of Immigrant Children," *Public Education Institute Quarterly*, Fall 1993, pp. 1–2.

7   Joseph Berger, "Schools Cope with Influx of Immigrants," *New York Times*, April 15, 1992, p. 6.

8   Friedman, "Immigration Surge Accents New York Life."

9   David Gonzalez, "Dominican Immigration Alters Hispanic New York," *New York Times*, September 1, 1992, Metro Section.

10   Nancy Foner, "Introduction: New Immigrants and Changing Patterns in New York City," in *New Immigrants in New York*, ed. Nancy Foner (New York: Columbia University Press, 1987), pp. 1–33.

11   "The Road to College: Educational Progress by Race and Ethnicity," Western Interstate Commission for Higher Education and the College Board, 1991.

12   Ibid, p. ii.

13   Ibid, p. vii.

14   Ibid, p. ix.

15   Ibid.

16   Emergency Immigrant Education Census: New York City Board of Education City-wide Version, April 14, 1993.

17   Foner, "Introduction."

18   Berger, "Schools Cope with Influx of Immigrants."

19   Telephone conversation with Dennis Sayers, director of the bilingual education program at New York University.

20   Berger, "Schools Cope with Influx of Immigrants."

21   Joseph Berger, "Immigrants Jam Schools, Invigorating a System," *New York Times*, April 26, 1992, Metro Section.

22   Peter Schmidt, "Asians Often Face Bigotry in Schools, Report Says," *Education Week*, March 11, 1992, p. 20.

23   Berger, "Schools Cope with Influx of Immigrants."

24   Bernadine J. Duran and Rafaela E. Weffer, "Immigrants' Aspirations, High School Process, and Academic Outcomes," *American Educational Research Journal* 29 (Spring 1992): 163–81.

25   Berger, "Schools Cope with Influx of Immigrants."

26   Debra Viadero, "Issue of Multiculturalism Dominates Standards Debate," *Education Week*, April 22, 1992, p. 18.

27   Willard L. Hogeboom, "America Has Shaped Us More Than We Have It," *Education Week*, December 4, 1991, p. 36.

28   Viadero, "Issue of Multiculturalism Dominates Standards Debate."

29   Ana Maria Villegas, "The Education of Immigrant Children in New Jersey: Programs and Issues" (Roundtable Meeting, Educational Testing Service, October 23, 1992).

30   Schmidt, "Asians Often Face Bigotry in Schools, Report Says," p. 20.

# Two Cities' Tracking and Within-school Segregation

JEANNIE OAKES

*University of California, Los Angeles*

*Evidence from two school systems whose ability grouping and tracking systems were subject to scrutiny in 1993 in conjunction with school desegregation cases demonstrates how grouping practices can create within-school segregation and discrimination against African-American and Latino students. In both school systems, tracking created racially imbalanced classes at all three levels—elementary, middle, and senior high, with African-American or Latino students consistently overrepresented and white and Asian students consistently underrepresented in low-ability tracks in all subjects. Neither district's placement practices created classrooms with a range of measured student ability and achievement in classrooms sufficiently narrow to be considered homogeneous "ability groups," and African-American and Latino students were much less likely than whites or Asians with comparable scores to be placed in high-track courses. These disproportionate lower-track placements worked to disadvantage minority students' achievement outcomes. Whether students began with relatively high or relatively low achievement, those who were placed in lower-level courses showed lesser gains over time than similarly situated students placed in higher-level courses. In both systems, grouping practices created a cycle of restricted opportunities and diminished outcomes, and exacerbated differences between African-American and Latino and white students.*

Since the 1920s, most elementary and secondary schools have tracked their students into separate "ability" groups designed for bright, average, and slow learners and into separate programs for students who are expected to follow different career routes after high school graduation. Tracking has seemed appropriate and fair, given the way psychologists have defined differences in students' intellectual abilities, motivation, and aspirations. Tracking has seemed logical because it supports a nearly century-old belief that a crucial job of schools is to ready students for an economy that requires workers with quite different knowledge and skills. According to this logic, demanding academic classes would prepare bright, motivated students heading for jobs that require college degrees, while more rudimentary academic classes and vocational programs would ready less able and less motivated students for less-skilled jobs or for post–high school technical training. With the development early in the century of standard-ized tests for placement, most people viewed a tracked curriculum with its "ability-grouped" academic classes as functional, scientific, and democra-tic—an educationally sound way to accomplish two important tasks: (1) providing students with the education that best suits their abilities, and (2) providing the nation with the array of workers it needs.

Despite its widespread legitimacy, there is no question that tracking, the assessment practices that support it, and the differences in educational opportunity that result from it limit many students' schooling opportuni-ties and life chances. These limits affect schoolchildren from all racial, eth-nic, and socioeconomic groups. However, schools far more often judge African-American and Latino students to have learning deficits and limited potential. Not surprisingly, then, schools place these students dispropor-tionately in low-track, remedial programs.

Educators justify these placements by pointing out that African-Ameri-can and Latino children typically perform less well on commonly accepted assessments of ability and achievement. Moreover, conventional school wis-dom holds that low-track, remedial, and special education classes help these students, since they permit teachers to target instruction to the par-ticular learning deficiencies of low-ability students. However, considerable research demonstrates that students do not profit from enrollment in low-track classes; they do not learn as much as comparably skilled students in heterogeneous classes; they have less access than other students to knowl-edge, engaging learning experiences, and resources.[1] Thus, school track-ing practices create racially separate programs that provide minority chil-dren with restricted educational opportunities and outcomes.

In what follows, I will illustrate these points with evidence from two school systems whose ability grouping and tracking systems have been sub-ject to scrutiny in the past year in conjunction with school desegregation cases. The first system, Rockford Public Schools, in Rockford, Illinois (pre-viously under an interim court order), was the target of a liability suit brought by a community group, The People Who Care. Among other com-plaints, the group charged the school system with within-school segrega-tion through ability grouping and discrimination against the district's nearly 30 percent African-American and Latino students. The second sys-tem, San Jose Unified School District, in San Jose, California, approached the court hoping to be released from its desegregation order of 1985. The plaintiffs in the San Jose case argued, among other things, that the district had used its ability-grouping system to create within-school segregation and, thereby, circumvented the intent of the court order with regard to its approximately 30 percent Latino student population. I analyzed data about the grouping practices in both these cities, prepared reports for the court, and testified. The San Jose system reached a settlement prior to the formal hearing date. The Rockford system was found liable by the court.

To shed light on the grouping practices in these two systems, I conducted analyses and reported my conclusions about tracking and ability-grouping practices around several questions:

1.  Does the school system employ tracking and/or ability grouping? If so, what is the specific nature of these practices?
2.  Does the system's use of tracking and/or ability grouping create racially imbalanced classrooms?
3.  Does the system's use of these grouping practices reflect sound, consistent, and educationally valid considerations?
4.  Are the racial disproportionalities created by the system's ability-grouping practices explained by valid educational considerations?
5.  What are the consequences of the system's grouping and tracking practices for the classroom instructional opportunities of Latino children?
6.  What are the consequences of the system's grouping and tracking practices for the educational outcomes of Latino children?
7.  Does the system have the necessary support and capacity to dismantle racially identifiable tracking and create heterogeneously grouped classrooms?

I addressed these questions with analyses using data specific to the two school systems. These data were gathered from a variety of sources: district and individual school curriculum documents (e.g., curriculum guides, course catalogs, course descriptions, etc.); school plans; computerized student enrollment and achievement data; prior reports prepared by court monitors; and depositions taken from school district employees in the course of the discovery process.[2]

Several analytic methods were applied to these data, all of which had been used in prior published research on tracking and ability grouping. In both systems, I used statistical methods to calculate the achievement range within each track; the distribution of students from various ethnic groups into various tracks; and the probability of placement of students from each ethnic group whose prior achievement "qualified" them for various tracks. In San Jose, but not in Rockford, I was also able to calculate rather precisely the impact of track placement on achievement gains of students with comparable prior achievement. I applied "content analysis" techniques to district and school curriculum documents in order to classify courses into various track levels, determine placement criteria and processes, and identify curricular goals, course content, and learning opportunities. These documents constitute official district policy statements about the levels and content of the districts' programs and courses, as well as the criteria and procedures by which students enroll in various programs and courses.

The scope of possible analyses was limited, more in Rockford than in San Jose, by a lack of some essential data. Even so, the available data permitted quite comprehensive analyses of many aspects of the district's grouping practices. They provided a clear picture of tracking and ability grouping in the two systems, and enabled me to place the district's practices in light of national research.

### Proliferation of Tracking

Grouping practices and their effects on minority children were remarkably similar in both systems. Both systems used tracking extensively. At most grade levels and in most academic subject areas at nearly all schools, educators assigned students to classes based on judgments about students' academic abilities. The schools then tailored the curriculum and instruction within classes to the students' perceived ability "levels." The districts' tracking "systems" were not only very comprehensive (in terms of the subject areas and grade levels that are tracked); they were also quite rigid and stable. That is, the districts tended to place students at the same "ability level" for classes in a variety of subject areas, and to lock students into the same or a lower ability-level placement from year to year.

### Racially Disproportionate Track Enrollments

In both school systems, tracking had created racially imbalanced classes at all three levels—elementary, middle, and senior high. This imbalance took two forms: (1) White (and Asian, in San Jose) students are consistently overrepresented, and African-American and Latino students are consistently underrepresented, in high-ability classes in all subjects; (2) in contrast, African-American or Latino students were consistently overrepresented, while white and Asian students were consistently underrepresented, in low-ability tracks in all subjects.

### Inconsistent Application of Placement Criteria

The criteria used to assign students to particular tracks were neither clearly specified nor consistently applied. Accordingly, neither district's tracking policies and practices could be construed as the enactment of valid educational purposes; neither did either district present an educational justification for the racial imbalance that results from tracking. Moreover, my analyses demonstrate quite clearly that neither district's placement practices—practices that result in racially imbalanced tracked classrooms— could be justified by a racially neutral policy of creating classrooms that are distinctly different from one another in terms of students' academic ability or achievement. To the contrary, neither district had enacted ability grouping and tracking in ways that narrow the range of measured student ability and achievement in classrooms sufficiently so that these classrooms can be considered bona fide ability groups.

Both school systems honored parent requests for students' initial track placements and for subsequent changes. This policy undermined the basis of student assignments in either "objective" measures of students' abilities or more subjective professional judgments. Making matters worse, not all parents were informed about tracking practices or about parents' right to influence their children's placements. Specifically, African-American and Latino parents had less access than others to this knowledge.

Additionally, teacher and counselor recommendations at the critical transitions between elementary and middle school and between middle and high school included a formal mechanism to take into account highly subjective judgments about students' personalities, behavior, and motivation. For example, the screening process for gifted programs usually began with a subjective teacher identification of potentially gifted children, who were then referred for formal testing. Such referrals were often based on subjective judgments about behavior, personality, and attitudes.

### Tracks Actually Heterogeneous Groups

The "theory" of tracking argues that, to facilitate learning, children should be separated into groups so that they may be taught together with peers of similar ability and apart from those with higher or lower abilities. But in both school systems, classes that were supposed to be designated for students at a *particular* ability level actually enrolled students who spanned *a very wide range* of measured ability. These ranges demonstrate quite dramatically that in both Rockford and San Jose racially imbalanced tracked classes have borne little resemblance to homogeneous ability groups—even though they have been labeled and treated as such by schools. While the mean scores in each of the tracks followed expected patterns—with average achievement score for students in the low track less than average score for students in the standard or accelerated tracks—the extraordinarily broad range of achievement in each of the three tracks makes clear how far these classes are from being homogenous ability groups. In sum, the district's practices do not represent what tracking advocates would claim is a trustworthy enactment of a "theory" of tracking and ability grouping.

For example, at one Rockford middle school, the range of eighth-grade reading scores in Honors English (31–99 National Percentile [NP])overlapped considerably with the range in Regular English (1–95 NP), which overlapped considerably with the range in Basic English (1–50 NP). At one of the senior highs, the math scores of tenth-graders in the normal progress college prep math track (26–99 NP) overlapped considerably with those in the slow progress college prep courses (1–99), and both overlapped considerably with the scores of those in non–college preparatory classes (1–99). I found similar patterns of large, overlapping ranges of qualifying scores throughout the system.

The same was true in San Jose. For example, sixth-graders placed in a low-track mathematics course demonstrated abilities that ranged all the way from rock-bottom Normal Curve Equivalent (NCE) achievement scores of 1 to extraordinarily high scores of 86. Even more striking, sixth-graders in standard-track math classes had achievement scores that spanned the entire range, from NCE scores of 1 to 99. And, while sixth-graders in accelerated courses had a somewhat more restricted ability range, they too scored all the way from 52 to 99 NCE scores. I found similar patterns in a number of other subjects in most middle and senior high school grades.

*Placements Racially Skewed beyond the Effects of Achievement*

As a group, African-American and Latino students scored lower on achievement tests than whites and Asians in Rockford and San Jose. However, African-American and Latino students were much less likely than white or Asian students *with the same test scores* to be placed in accelerated courses. For example, in San Jose, Latino eighth-graders with "average" scores in mathematics were three times less likely than whites with the same scores to be placed in an accelerated math course. Among ninth-graders, the results were similar. Latinos scoring between 40 and 49, 50 and 59, and 60 and 69 NCEs were less than half as likely as their white and Asian counterparts to be placed in accelerated tracks. The discrimination is even more striking among the highest scoring students. While only 56 percent of Latinos scoring between 90 and 99 NCEs were placed in accelerated classes, 93 percent of whites and 97 percent of Asians gained admission to these classes.

In Rockford's tracks and class ability levels, the groups of *higher* track students whose scores fell within a range that would qualify them for participation in either a higher or lower track (i.e., their scores were the same as students in the lower track) were consistently "whiter" than groups of students whose scores fell within that same range but were placed in the *lower* track. In a number of cases, Rockford's high-track classes included students with exceptionally low scores, but rarely were these students African Americans. Conversely, quite high scoring African Americans were enrolled in low-track classes; again, this was seldom the case for high-scoring whites. For example, in 1987, none of the African-American students who scored in the top quartile (75–99 NP) on the California Assessment Program (CAP) reading comprehension test at two of Rockford's large high schools were placed in high-track English, compared with about 40 percent of top-quartile whites who were enrolled in the high track at those schools. In contrast, at three of the system's senior high schools a small fraction of white students who scored in the bottom quartile (1–25 NP) were in high-track classes, while no similarly low-scoring African Americans were so placed. At two other senior highs, while some top-quartile African Americans were placed in Honors English, many more top-scoring African Americans were in the basic classes. No low-scoring whites were so placed. I found similar patterns in other subjects at the district's high schools.

I found other striking examples of racially skewed placements in Rockford's junior highs. For example, at one, the range of reading comprehension scores among eighth-graders enrolled in Basic English classes was from the first to the seventy-second national percentile. Of these, ten students scored above the national average of 50 NP. Six of the highest scoring, above-average students were African-American, including the highest achieving student in the class. One other of the above-average students was Latino.

In both San Jose and Rockford, placement practices skewed enrollments in favor of whites over and above that which can be explained by measured achievement.

*Low Tracks Providing Less Opportunity*

In both school systems, African-American and Latino students in lower-track classes had fewer learning opportunities. Teachers expected less of them and gave them less exposure to curriculum and instruction in essential knowledge and skills. Lower-track classes also provided African-American and Latino students with less access a whole range of resources and opportunities: To highly qualified teachers; to classroom environments conducive to learning; to opportunities to earn extra "grade points" that can bolster their grade point averages; and to courses that would qualify them for college entrance and a wide variety of careers as adults.

*Low Tracks and Lower Achievement*

Not only did African-American and Latino students receive a lower quality education as a result of tracking in San Jose and Rockford; their academic achievement suffered as well. In Rockford the initial average "achievement gap" (i.e., the difference in group mean achievement scores) between white and African-American and/or white and Latino students (i.e., that found on district-administered achievement tests in first grade) did not diminish in higher grades. To the contrary, eleventh-graders exhibited gaps somewhat larger than first graders. For example, on the 1992 Stanford Achievement Test in reading comprehension, the gap between African-American and white first-graders was 25 percent; that between African-American and white eleventh-graders was 30 percent. Undoubtedly more telling, at the time of the seventh-grade test—probably the last point before considerable numbers of lower-achieving minority students drop out of school—the achievement gap between African Americans and whites had grown considerably wider, to 36 percent. A similar pattern was found in students' raw scores in reading comprehension and mathematics for grades 1–6 on the 1992 Stanford Achievement Test. Here, the reading achievement gap between African-American and white students at first grade was .88 of a standard deviation and grew to .99 by grade 6. The Latino-white gap grew from .67 to .70 over the same grades. In math, the African American–white gap grew from .87 to 1.01; in contrast, the Latino-white gap dropped from .98 to .79. Clearly, the district's tracked programs failed to close the minority-white gap between average group scores. Neither did these practices correct the overrepresentation of black and Latino students in the group of lowest scoring students in the district. For example, in 1992, 37 percent of the first-grade children scoring between the first and the twenty-fifth national percentiles in reading comprehension on the Stanford Achievement Test were African-American; at seventh-grade, the percentage of African Americans in this low-scoring group had risen to 46 percent, and by grade 11 (following a disproportionately high incidence of dropping out by low-achieving African-American students), African-American students still made up 35 percent of this group. Neither did student placements in various instructional programs enable minority students to rise into the group of district's highest achievers. In fact, *the proportion of minority students in the highest achieving group of students dropped quite precipitously*. For example, in 1992, 10 percent of the first-grade children scoring between the seventy-fifth and the ninety-ninth national percentiles in reading comprehension on the Stanford Achievement Test were African-American; at seventh grade, the percentage of African Americans in this high-scoring group had dropped by half, to only 5 percent (28 in number); this low proportion was also found at grade 11 (even though the actual number of students, twenty, was smaller).

Rockford's grouping practices that created racially identifiable classrooms and provided unequal opportunities to learn (with fewer such opportunities provided to minority students) *did not serve a remedial function for minority students*. To the contrary, these practices did not even enable minority students to sustain their position, relative to white students, in the district's achievement hierarchy.

In San Jose, better data permitted me to analyze the impact of track placement on individual students over time. Students who were placed in lower-level courses—disproportionately Latino students—consistently demonstrate lesser gains in achievement over time than their peers placed in high-level courses. For example, among the students with pre-placement math achievement between 50 and 59 NCEs, those who were placed in a low-track course began with a mean of 54.4 NCEs, but lost an average of 2.2 NCEs after one year, and had lost a total of 1.9 NCEs after three years. Students who scored between 50 and 59 NCEs and were placed in a standard-track course, by contrast, began with a mean of 54.6 NCEs, gained 0.1 NCEs after one year, and had gained 3.5 NCEs after three years. The largest gains were experienced by students who were placed in an accelerated course, who began with a mean of 554 NCEs, gained 6.5 NCEs after one year, and had gained a total of 9.6 NCEs after three years.

These results are consistent across achievement levels: Whether students began with relatively high or relatively low achievement, those who were placed in lower-level courses showed lesser gains over time than similarly situated students who were placed in higher-level courses.

## In Sum, Considerable Harm

The findings from my analyses of San Jose and Rockford support disturbing conclusions about tracking and within-school segregation and discrimination. The districts' tracking system pervade their schools. The harm that accrues to African Americans and Latinos takes at least three demonstrable forms: (1) unjustifiable disproportionate and segregative assignment to low-track classes and exclusion from accelerated classes; (2) inferior opportunities to learn; and (3) lower achievement. In both systems, grouping practices have created a cycle of restricted opportunities and diminished outcomes, and exacerbated differences between African-American and Latino and white students. That these districts have not chosen to eliminate grouping practices that so clearly discriminate against its African-American and Latino children warrants serious concern and strong remedial action.

## Implications for Remedial Activities and School Reform

Is it technically possible or politically feasible to abandon these discriminatory practices in San Jose, Rockford, or other school systems that are like them? The two systems are currently charged with making significant progress toward that end.

Both Rockford and San Jose school systems have considerable technical capacity to reform their placement practices so that they teach all children in heterogeneous settings, including the gifted, for part or all of the school day in most or all core academic courses. Conspicuous examples of successful heterogeneous grouping exit currently in San Jose schools. Much of the professional expertise and some of the support structures needed to implement such practices districtwide are already in place. Moreover, in both systems administrative and teaching staff demonstrate considerable knowledge of the harms of tracking, and ample ability to implement educationally sound alternatives.

Further, both districts are situated in a national and state policy environment that encourages the development and use of such alternatives. For example, such national policy groups such as the National Governors' Association and federally supported efforts to create "national standards" in each of the curriculum areas all recommend against tracking. In California, the State Department of Education's major policy documents on the reform of K–12 schooling (*It's Elementary, Caught in the Middle,* and *Second to None*) and the state's subject matter frameworks caution schools about problems with tracking and strongly recommend that they not use it.[3] Similar state-led initiatives promote heterogeneity in Illinois—for example, the state's involvement in middle-school reform and its adoption of the Accelerated Schools model.

However, racially mixed school systems that have tackled this issue around the country have experienced considerable difficulty creating alternatives. Amy Stuart Wells and I are currently studying ten such schools.[4] While each has made considerable progress toward integrated classrooms and a more even distribution of educational opportunities, most have been the target of considerable fear and anger. As with the nation's experiences with between-school segregation, the pursuit of court sanctions against tracking and ability grouping may be critical to ensuring educational equality. However, like that earlier effort, remedies are neither easily specified nor readily accepted.

## Notes

1   For a comprehensive review of the literature, see Jeannie Oakes, Adam Gamoran, and Reba Page, "Curriculum Differentiation: Opportunities, Outcomes, and Meanings," in *Handbook of Research on Education,* ed. Philip Jackson (New York: Macmillan, 1992).

2   These previously unpublished analyses are available in the form of a 1993 report to the court in The People Who Care v. Rockford Board of Education School District no 205 and in my July 1993 deposition in conjunction with Jose B. Vasquez v. San Jose Unified School District et al.

3   California State Department of Education, *It's Elementary* (Sacramento: Author, 1993); idem, *Caught in the Middle* (Sacramento: Author, 1988); and idem, *Second to None* (Sacramento: Author, 1991).

4   The study in progress, "Beyond Sorting and Stratification: Creating Alternatives to Tracking in Racially Mixed Schools," is sponsored by the Lilly Endowment.

# Reexamining Social Science Research on School Desegregation: Long- versus Short-term Effects

AMY STUART WELLS

*University of California, Los Angeles*

*This article summarizes the role of social science research in examining the effects of school desegregation policies on African-American students. The author argues that much of the earliest research on the short-term effects of school desegregation on African-American students was not particularly helpful to policymakers because it tended to be simple input/output studies of standardized test scores after only one or two years of desegregation. Thus, this research tried to answer the question of whether school desegregation "works" to improve student achievement without contextualizing the experiences of African-American students in desegregated schools or considering that "school desegregation" implementation may look radically different in different schools and districts. On the other hand, research on the short-term effects of desegregation on intergroup relations, which was more focused on what was taking place within the schools, and the long-term-effects research, which emphasized that integrated institutions provide access to social mobility and powerful social networks, are more insightful and helpful to policymakers.*

Looking back over the forty years since the Supreme Court's *Brown* v. *Board of Education of Topeka, Kansas,* decision and the twenty-six years since the *Green* decision, when more forceful implementation of desegregation policy began, many Americans refer to school desegregation as a "failed social experiment"—one that resulted in massive white flight, resegregation within desegregated schools, loss of jobs for African-American educators, and a greater sense of alienation among African-American youth. While many of these conditions exist in cities and towns across the country, their causal relationship to desegregation court orders is not always clear. In fact, there is growing evidence of the more positive outcomes of school desegregation and a clearer understanding of the ways in which desegregation policy can be designed and implemented to assure that it fulfills the promise of *Brown.*

Educational researchers, policymakers, and educators must now reflect on the intended effects of school desegregation on students, critically examine mistakes made in the implementation process, and question whether the large body of research on school desegregation was helpful in making desegregation work. This article presents one attempt to tackle these issues.

The research literature on the effects of school desegregation on students is separated into two distinct bodies of work:

1.  A large collection of research on the *short-term effects* of school desegregation, especially achievement test scores and intergroup relations.[1]
2.  A smaller and less well known body of research on the *long-term effects* of school desegregation, which focuses on educational and occupational aspirations and attainment of African-American students into adulthood.

While both areas of research examine whether school desegregation policy provides African-American and Latino students equal educational opportunities, the short-term-effects research, conducted mostly in the 1970s, attempts to measure immediate achievement gains or losses and the more psychological aspects of desegregated experiences for children. Meanwhile, the long-term-effects literature, the bulk of which has been conducted since the late 1970s, has taken a more sociological bent with its emphasis on social mobility and social networks.

Both bodies of work are important, but I argue that the short-term-effects research, which received more attention and held greater sway in the policy arena, has traditionally been less informative. Until recently, this literature ignored key issues such as how school- and district-level policies and practices could make desegregation more effective and instead tried to draw broad, sweeping conclusions regarding whether desegregation "worked" based on narrow criteria that were difficult to measure.[2] Still, because researchers wanted quick results and because policymakers require instant feedback on program effects, the bulk of school desegregation research conducted during the late 1960s and early 1970s forcused on the short-term effects, especially achievement test scores.[3] As Prager and associates note, "desegregation research has suffered because it has come to stand as a kind of scholarship guided largely by public concerns and public issues, not by theoretically generated empirical questions."[4]

The long-term-effects research, on the other hand, despite its relative obscurity, has been more in line with the original intents and purposes of the constitutional and moral arguments for school desegregation: The idea that guaranteeing African-American students access to predominantly white institutions would enhance their opportunities for social mobility and thus improve their life chances. For instance, the National Association for the Advancement of Colored People (NAACP) desegregation cases preceding the landmark *Brown* ruling were predicated on the theory that degrees from prestigious, predominantly white universities were the key to high-status employment, social networks, and social institutions. Without access to these universities and the status of the degrees they conferred, African Americans, no matter what their level of educational achievement or attainment, would remain a separate and unequal segment of our society.[5] This is a structural argument aimed at addressing barriers to social mobility.

In order to assess the impact of school desegregation policy on the status attainment of African-American adults, researchers and policymakers must look beyond the older short-term-effects research, which simply compares standardized test scores, and pay more attention to long-term social and economic outcomes as well as a small but growing body of most recent short-term-effects research that focuses on second-generation desegregation issues such as resegregation within desegregated schools and multicultural curriculum.[6]

## RESEARCH ON THE SHORT-TERM EFFECTS OF SCHOOL DESEGREGATION: WHY MUCH OF IT FAILED TO BE USEFUL

By the mid-1970s, several social scientists, including sociologist Robert L. Crain and political scientist Gary Orfield, began lamenting that academic research on the effects of school desegregation failed to be useful. Crain notes, for instance, that virtually none of the research was concerned with how desegregation should be done to maximize student benefits but rather whether some desegregation was better than none. "When research has asked whether desegregation was good or bad, it has almost always asked the questions in the wrong way—namely, in terms of short-run achievement tests rather than long-run effects on students or the impact of desegregation on the whole community."[7]

### STUDENT ACHIEVEMENT

In a thoughtful late-1970s critique of school desegregation research and its relationship to policymaking, Orfield points out that *Brown* spoke not of test scores but of the damage to the "hearts and minds" of black children forced to attend segregated schools. Yet he argues that when social scientists were confronted with the problem of measuring whether desegregation "worked," they began to reshape the issue by turning to their most frequently used instruments—standardized achievement tests. According to

Orfield, researchers were quick to employ these tests in part because the technology was highly developed, familiar, and easy to use. Thus, these achievement tests set a standard for success and failure of desegregation even when they were measuring the change in the achievement gap *after only one year* of desegregation and ignoring important contextual variables such as school climate.[8]

In an earlier article, Orfield summarized the situation:

> Strange as it may seem, social scientists have produced little systematic, carefully controlled research on educational processes within desegregated schools. Most of the existing desegregation research merely measures achievement scores at the beginning and end of the first year of desegregation. And even this simple research effort is often done in a manner which, by aggregating all scores from a given school or a given grade level throughout a school system, obscures possible findings about ways the process facilitates or impedes effective integration.[9]

As more research on student achievement was conducted, it became increasingly clear that much of the earliest and politically most influential research on school desegregation was not getting at the issue of *how* desegregation was being implemented—that is, what form of resegregation was taking place, whose history and culture was reflected in the curriculum, and whether there were policy interventions and resources to help educators create more effective desegregated schools.[10]

For instance, in the first comprehensive review of research on the effects of school desegregation on children, Nancy St. John examined thirty-seven pre-test/post-test studies of black students' achievement. Twenty-five of these studies had measured the "impact" of desegregation on black student test scores over a one-year period, usually during the first year of desegregation. The range of the research designs varied dramatically across this literature, from national cross-sectional studies to local longitudinal studies. St. John noted the incompatibility of the different studies on such fundamental aspects as the independent variable considered: "In most studies school racial composition rather than classroom racial composition is the focus, and reports do not specify whether grouping practices resulted in within-school desegregation."[11] She also noted that researchers had not controlled for such variables as the level of "community controversy over desegregation, the friendliness of white parents and students, the flexibility or prejudice of the staff, the content of the curriculum, or the method of teaching."[12] Given these factors, it is not surprising that St. John was unable to draw any conclusions regarding the causal relationship between school desegregation and student achievement: "More than a decade of considerable research effort has produced no definite positive findings."[13]

The shortcomings in the literature on the short-term effects of desegregation—that it was comprised mostly of input-output studies simply comparing student characteristics and racial balance of the schools with test scores and did not provide much information on the nature of the desegregation experience—were echoed by sociologists Robert L. Crain and Rita Mahard in their review of the literature on black student achievement and school desegregation:

> Part of the confusion surrounding desegregation research arises because academics have frequently not viewed desegregation from a policy making viewpoint. They have been too fascinated by what is intellectually the most interesting question: All else being equal, will the mixing of races alone result in higher black achievement? That question cannot be answered because in the real world, desegregation is never an "all else being equal" situation.[14]

Crain and Mahard argue that because of the distinct situations in different desegregated settings, they were unable to draw any overarching conclusions about the effects of school racial balance on student achievement. They found, for example, that in forty of the seventy-three studies they examined, desegregation appeared to have a positive effect on black achievement; in twenty-one studies it showed little or no effect; and in twelve studies it seemed to have had a negative result. If anything, such results should have alerted policymakers to the fact that school desegregation means different things in different settings and thus more attention should be paid to the implementation processes in those schools that had more positive results in terms of test scores. Researchers have to conceptualize *how* desegregation might be implemented so that it could lead to better results. To understand how the implementation process differed at various schools, researchers had to ask different questions and employ different methodologies than input/output studies.

In the most recent and one of the most careful reviews of the literature on the effects of desegregation on student achievement, Schofield discusses methodological problems with the research but concludes that school desegregation does not appear to have any consistent negative effect on the academic achievement of African-American, Latino, or white students; furthermore, the research suggests that desegregation has had some consistently positive effect on the reading skills of African-American students. Schofield noted, however, that it is clear from her review that school desegregation can be implemented in very different ways and that these differences have "marked and often predictable effects."[15] Thus, Schofield, as others before her, finds no clear answers in the research literature to the question of whether "school desegregation policy"—as a vague, overgeneralized term used to describe school-level racial balance—has any causal effect on student achievement.

INTERGROUP RELATIONS

The second largest subset of the research on the short-term effects of school desegregation is that focusing on the impact of school desegregation on intergroup relations. This body of research is comprised of a decidedly smaller collection of studies than the literature on student achievement. Yet, this smaller body of research has in many ways been more helpful than the student-achievement research in that it has focused more carefully on school environment variables. Rather than relying on premeasured standardized test scores and using racial composition of the school as an independent variable, many of the researchers who sought to measure the effects of school desegregation on intergroup relations attempted to relate a wide range of school characteristics, politics, and practices to particular outcomes.[16]

Clearly some of the research on the impact of school desegregation on intergroup relations shares the same shortcomings as much of the research on student achievement. Schofield notes that the dependent measures used in the majority of studies are "zero-sum" measures that pick up only the changes in out-group acceptance, which occurs at the expense of in-group members.[17] But the group of researchers who were focused on variables such as intergroup relations within schools were more likely to question what policies and practice are most effective in creating good desegregated schools.

For instance, Patchen found that the racial composition of the classroom as opposed to the school as a whole is more likely to influence interracial interaction rates.[18] And yet we know that one of the most likely outcomes of a school desegregation plan is resegregation within schools, or the process of placing students of color into the low-track, remedial classes and white students into high-track or honors classes. Thus, despite Patchen's findings, which could help explain why school desegregation is more successful in some schools than others, policymakers have until recently paid little attention to within-school segregation issues.[19]

Findings such as this have pushed desegregation researchers in the last ten to fifteen years to think more carefully about the process of school desegregation—the lived experiences of students within desegregated schools—and the specific conditions that foster positive intergroup relations.[20] Paradoxically, this body of work is in many ways more helpful in understanding how and why students achieve academically in racially mixed schools than is the research focused on student achievement per se.

FUTURE DIRECTIONS FOR SHORT-TERM-EFFECTS RESEARCH

The obvious direction for new research on the short-term effects of school desegregation flows from the intersection of the more process-oriented work on intergroup relations within desegregated schools and the prior focus on student academic outcomes. Ironically, by the 1980s, when many of these process-oriented, "second-generation" desegregation issues—especially resegregation through rigid tracking practices, the culture reflected in the curriculum, and school climate issues—became the central focus for most desegregation researchers, the perceived importance of school desegregation as a policy and research topic had waned, as had government and private support for research in this area. And yet the need to connect the original research focus—the effect of desegregation on student achievement—to the more thoughtful process-oriented research on students' experiences in desegregated schools is perhaps greater than ever. Despite the fact that interest in school desegregation as a policy or a research topic has waned, hundreds of thousands of students attend racially mixed schools every day. This more focused, process-oriented research will help explain the inconsistent results of the early research on student achievement by demonstrating the ability of policymakers, educators, and parents to make desegregation work for all children in their schools and communities.

For instance, a recent case study of the St. Louis metropolitanwide desegregation plan attempts to link these process-oriented, second-generation issues with the different success rates of African-American students in various suburban school districts.[21] Thus, by documenting the different policies and practices employed by four of the sixteen different suburban school districts participating in the desegregation program, which allows African-American students to transfer to predominantly white suburban schools, we show the crucial linkages between the culture and politics of a given district and its success in creating effective desegregated schools in which all students achieve.

Similarly, in a study that Jeannie Oakes and I are conducting of ten racially mixed secondary schools across the country that are in the process of "detracking," or desegregating students within the schools, we are focusing on the overlap between students' experiences in schools and the process-oriented, intergroup relations issues. Drawing on the prior research in school desegregation, especially the work on the politics of desegregation and the intergroup relations research, we have identified the normative, technical, and political dimensions of change within schools undergoing this reform.[22]

Educational researchers interested in the short-term effects of school desegregation must continue to move toward conducting more thoughtful studies that address the uniqueness of each desegregated school and the societal and political context that shapes its policies and practices.

## LONG-TERM EFFECTS OF SCHOOL DESEGREGATION: THE SOCIOLOGICAL EXPLANATION

Though there may be overwhelming evidence that schools have not equalized life chances . . . such equalization remains a criterion worth using in asking the value of school desegregation. The research question that arises directly from this criterion is whether the life chances of blacks who attend desegregated schools are significantly improved over those of comparable blacks who do not. Because there is ample evidence that test scores and grades in school do not explain much of the variance in later income or status . . . these latter results must be studied directly.[23]

Despite the tendency for researchers and policymakers to focus on the short-term effects of school desegregation, the more recent literature on the long-term effects demonstrates some of the subtle sociological effects of desegregated educational experiences on the social mobility and life chances of African Americans in particular.

Because educational achievement alone does not solve economic inequality, school desegregation must do more than raise black students' test scores; it must also break the cycle of racial segregation that leaves blacks and whites worlds apart. This is not to say that educational outcomes are not important or that higher achievement levels for African-American students should not be a national goal. But these outcomes do not necessarily hinge on the racial makeup of a school. Black children do not need to sit next to white children to learn, although they are generally more likely to have access to high-status knowledge if they do.

Still, the research on and theory of network analysis as applied to the long-term effects of school desegregation inspire the old adage that *who* you know is as important (or even more important) in social mobility as *what* you know. The social network advantage of desegregated schools for African-American students is real, even though it could not be measured in time to satisfy policymakers who lost sight of the original goals of desegregation by the 1970s.

In an attempt to refocus the policy debate on the effects of school desegregation on more theoretical and sociological arguments, Robert L. Crain and I reviewed twenty-one of the most substantial studies on the long-term effects of school desegregation.[24] This body of literature remains significantly smaller than research on short-term effects, but most of it is more recent. Much of this work was published in the last ten years as the long-term effects of desegregation plans implemented in the late 1960s and early 1970s became more apparent. Meanwhile, due to the ambiguous findings of the research on the short-term effects and the ongoing resistance of many white Americans to desegregation policies, school desegregation had already been declared a failure in many policy circles by the time much of this long-term-effects literature was available. Thus, the more positive findings in these studies were virtually ignored, and ours is the first attempt to bring them all together and examine them as a whole through the lens of perpetuation theory—a micro-macro sociological theory of racial segregation originally developed by sociologist Jomills Braddock.[25]

Perpetuation theory, as it has been developed by Braddock and furthured in his work with James McPartland, states that segregation tends to repeat itself "across the stages of the life cycle and across institutions when individuals have not had sustained experiences in desegregated settings earlier in life."[26] Drawing on Pettigrew's research on social inertia and avoidance learning, Braddock derived perpetuation theory by focusing on the tendency of Americans, particularly blacks, to self-perpetuate racial segregation. He notes that minority students who have not regularly experienced the realities of desegregation may overestimate the degree of overt hostility they will encounter or underestimate their skill at coping with strains in interracial situations.[27] These segregated students will, in most instances, make choices that maintain physical segregation when they become adults because they have never tested their racial beliefs. While Braddock's perpetuation theory does not preclude the existence of real structural constraints to racial integration, his focus is on how individual agents adjust their behavior to accommodate, and thus perpetuate, these constraints and how exposure to integrated settings can change this behavior.

Expanding on Braddock's theory of perpetual segregation, we have added network analysis, or the more structural argument that segregation is perpetuated across generations because African Americans and Latinos lack access to informal networks that provide information about and entrance to desegregated institutions or employment. This structural explanation of perpetual segregation complements Braddock's writing on blacks' lack of information on which to test their racial beliefs.

In applying network analysis to perpetuation theory, we draw from Granovetter's work, which shows the strong impact of "weak ties," or less formal interpersonal networks—that is, acquaintances or friends of friends—on the diffusion of influence, information, and mobility opportunities.[28] These weak ties, Granovetter argues, are the channels through which ideas that are socially distant from an individual may reach him.[29]

In linking his work to the research of Braddock and others who study the effects of school desegregation, Granovetter notes the importance of even the weakest ties in bridging the often separate cliques of white and nonwhite teenagers:

> School desegregation studies frequently show that cross-racial ties formed are not very strong. But even such weak ties may significantly affect later economic success. Because employers at all levels of work prefer to recruit by word-of-mouth, typically using recommendations of current employees, segregation of friendship and acquaintance means that workplaces that start out all white will remain so.[30]

Other network analysts have argued that people on the bottom of the social structure, including African-American students from low-income families, have more to gain than white and wealthy students through the use of weak ties because these ties will invariably connect them to more affluent and better connected people, whereas strong ties usually connect them to family and close friends who are also poor.[31] For instance, sociologist Nan Lin has found that "the advantage of using weaker ties over the use of stronger ties decreases as the position of origin approaches the top of the hierarchy."[32] As William Julius Wilson and other social scientists have noted, the greatest barrier to social and economic mobility for inner-city blacks is the degree to which they remain isolated from the opportunities and networks of the mostly white and middle-class society.[33]

There are obvious and not-so-obvious ways in which social organizations, especially schools, filled with white and wealthy students provide greater access to information about colleges and careers than schools serving mostly low-income minority students. For instance, our research on black students from inner-city St. Louis who attend predominantly white and middle-class high schools in the suburbs demonstrates that these students benefit from access to informants and well-connected acquaintances that they would not have in all-black urban schools, where less than 20 percent of the students go on to college. In their suburban schools they attend college fairs, are constantly reminded by their counselors and peers about college opportunities and deadlines, have access to a wealth of information on the college application process, and are assigned to college counselors with strong ties to college admissions offices across the country. Students have told us that their level of awareness about the college application process is heightened in suburban schools in which virtually all students are going through these steps and applying to college is a schoolwide norm.[34]

Similarly, two sociologists, Julie Kaufman and James Rosenbaum, found that African-American students from inner-city Chicago who moved to predominantly white suburbs through the Gautreaux housing desegregation program were more likely to finish high school and go on to four-year colleges because suburban teachers and counselors helped prepare the children for postsecondary education and were "in touch" with colleges. Parents and students spoke of the advantages of attending a high school where there was a constant flow of information about scholarships and college visits and where classmates' older brothers and sisters had gone to college and could offer help and advice to their younger siblings.[35]

Given these obvious links between network analysis and school desegregation, perpetuation theory must encompass not only Braddock's micro-level acknowledgement of racial fear and distrust on the part of isolated minorities, but also the micro-macro connections inherent in the flow of information and opportunities as they are carried through interpersonal networks. Findings from the twenty-one long-term-effects studies reviewed in our article strongly suggest that interracial exposure in school can indeed reduce blacks' tendency to avoid whites while penetrating barriers between African-American students and networks of information and sponsorship. In our review of the long-term-effects research, we divided the literature into three sections, the conclusions of which are summarized briefly below.

## OCCUPATIONAL ASPIRATIONS AND EXPECTATIONS

Two main conclusions can be drawn from the research on African-American students' aspirations: (1) Desegregated black students set their occupational aspirations higher than segregated blacks, and (2) desegregated black students' occupational aspirations are more "realistically" related to their educational background and aspirations than those of segregated black students.

The first finding, however, is not as strongly supported because only three of the four studies found this, while the fourth study found the opposite. Also, Dawkins found significantly higher occupational aspirations for only one of four gender-region groups—black males from the south.[36] Still, these studies challenge what Kaufman and Rosenbaum refer to as the "Relative Disadvantage Hypothesis"—that higher standards and a greater degree of academic competition within desegregated schools will place black students at a disadvantage and possibly lessen their self-confidence and lower their aspirations.[37]

The second finding, concerning the rationality of aspirations, is more clearly supported, with all three of the studies that raise the issue concurring. Each of these studies bolsters Granovetter's theory of the impact of weak ties on the diffusion of influence, information, and mobility opportunities.[38] The finding that African-American students who attend desegregated schools have more "realistic" expectations supports the idea that access to the information networks used by white students in planning for postsecondary education is helpful to students who might not find those same networks in a more racially segregated setting. This finding, however, could be perceived negatively if students' so-called realistic expectations are lower than those of black students who attend all-black schools, but the main focus of this work is the relationship between students' performance in schools and their postsecondary school plans. Thus, the emphasis is on students' understanding of the requirements for particular occupations and their articulation of a plan of action for how to attain their goals. This information is more readily available for students in schools in which most of the other students are making similar plans and in communities in which adults have had access to a wide range of occupations in the past.

## CHOICE OF COLLEGE AND EDUCATIONAL ATTAINMENT

The major conclusion to be drawn from the eight studies concerned with college choice and educational attainment is that black graduates of desegregated schools are more likely than those of segregated schools to attend desegregated colleges. This section, therefore, provides support for Braddock's view of perpetuation, which depicts the tendency of blacks to self-perpetuate racial segregation—that is, choosing a predominantly black college over a predominantly white one—when they have not experienced desegregated situations.[39]

While I am aware of the many potential benefits that African Americans derive from attending historically black universities, the reality is that in our society, predominantly white universities are considered the most prestigious and therefore the highest-status institutions. Access to and acceptance at prestigious and high-status universities pays off for African-American students in later life—as they apply to graduate schools, search for jobs, and attempt to advance in their careers. Graduates of these high-status institutions use their affiliation with these institutions for professional advancement through personal networking. African Americans who are shut out of these quite powerful networks are at a disadvantage in a white-dominated society.

As for evidence on the educational attainment of desegregated blacks, the research, for the most part (with the obvious exception of Crain and Mahard's findings on Southern students[40]) supports the conclusion that blacks from desegregated schools will have greater educational attainment. Still, the findings of Braddock and McPartland and Braddock concerning the greater tendency of desegregated blacks to attend two-year as opposed to four-year colleges, especially in the North, are disturbing. Issues of classmates' social class and the quality of education available at two-year colleges in this country, which are not addressed in this literature, make these findings more tenuous. At the same time, Braddock's findings on college majors—that black graduates of majority white high schools are five times as likely to major in architecture and nearly four times as likely to major in computer and information sciences as black graduates of segregated schools—are promising and underscore the need for more research on the different educational experiences of blacks in two- and four-year colleges.[41]

## OCCUPATIONAL ATTAINMENT AND ADULT SOCIAL NETWORKS

Three major conclusions can be drawn from the studies we reviewed on occupational attainment and adult social networks: (1) African-American students who attend desegregated schools (K–12) are more likely to have desegregated social and professional networks in later life; (2) these desegregated black students are also more likely to find themselves in desegregated employment; and (3) African-American students who attended desegregated schools are more likely to be working in white-collar and professional jobs in the private sector and students from segregated schools are more likely to be in government and blue-collar jobs, although there is less consistent evidence for this last finding.

This last set of findings brings all the elements of perpetuation theory and the long-term effects of school desegregation together. Not only is there evidence in this literature that African Americans (and whites, for that matter) who experience desegregated situations early in life are less likely to avoid desegregated settings in the future, but this research also suggests that once social and informational networks are opened to blacks, they are likely to take advantage of them, using personal contacts in the same way that whites do—to glean greater information about occupational and social opportunities.

In our review of this less-well-known literature on the long-term effects of school desegregation, we do not deny that much of this research suffers from some of the same shortcomings as did the early short-term-effects research. For instance, all but four of the studies examined here are based on national longitudinal data sets, which provide a valuable cross-regional viewpoint but do not allow for differentiation between various types of school desegregation policies—voluntary versus mandatory, intradistrict versus interdistrict—or the degree of socioeconomic class desegregation that black students experience. In terms of perpetuation theory and its relevance to the long-term effects of school desegregation on blacks, information on the socioeconomic status of the white students in the desegregated schools would be helpful.

Despite these shortcomings, the long-term-effects research, with its broader focus on student mobility as opposed to test scores, presents some meaningful findings. Also, because the studies focus on different stages in the lives of blacks, the work as a whole provides substantial evidence that desegregated schooling can help blacks end perpetual segregation at different stages in their life cycle.

## CONCLUSION

On this fortieth anniversary of the *Brown* decision, it is worth noting that the research on the effects of school desegregation on students has improved tremendously, especially in the last fifteen years. We find fewer researchers concentrating their efforts on simple input/output studies and more focusing on the processes of school desegregation. We now know more about what policies and practices make for more effective desegregated schools, and we have a clearer understanding of the long-term effects of school desegregation on the life chances of African-American students. More specifically, we also now have evidence of how access to higher-status institutions can open doors and opportunities.

Unfortunately, this higher-quality research with its profound policy implications may be too little too late. Policymakers, lawyers, and judges must not ignore this more recent evidence. They need to reevaluate what educational research has taught us about the social benefits of school desegregation as well as ways in which we can create better desegregation policies. Now that the more meaningful research is available, those with the power to make policy changes must give these findings as much attention and consideration as their predecessors once gave to less informative research on student test scores.

*Notes*

1   There is a sizable amount of research on white flight from desegregating school districts that is also considered part of the short-term-effects literature. That work is not discussed in this article, which focuses on student effects more directly.

2   Robert L. Crain, "Why Academic Research Fails to Be Useful," *School Review* 84 (May 1976): 337–51.

3   See Jomills Henry Braddock and James M. McPartland, *Assessing School Desegregation Effects: New Directions in Research* (Greenwich, Conn.: JAI Press, 1982); and Henry M. Levin, "Education, Life Chances, and the Courts: The Role of Social Science Evidence," *Law and Contemporary Problems* 39 (Spring 1975): 217–40.

4   Jeffrey Prager, Douglas Longshore, and Melvin Seeman, "The Desegregation Situation," in *School Desegregation Research: New Directions in Situational Analysis,* ed. J. Prager, D. Longshore, and M. Seeman (New York: Plenum Press, 1986), p. 4.

5   See Richard Kluger, *Simple Justice* (New York: Vintage Books, 1976).

6   See Willis D. Hawley, "Equity and Quality in Education: Characteristics of Effective Desegregation," in *Effective School Desegregation: Equity, Quality, and Feasibility,* ed. W. D. Haw-

ley (Beverly Hills: Sage Publications, 1981), pp. 266–96; John B. McConahay, "Reducing Racial Prejudice in Desegregated Schools," in ibid., pp. 35–54; Jeannie Oakes and Amy Stuart Wells, "Beyond Sorting and Stratification: A Study of Racially Mixed Schools That Are Detracking" (Research proposal) (Los Angeles: UCLA, Center for the Study of Democratic School Communities, 1991); Janet W. Schofield, "School Desegregation and Intergroup Relations: A Review of the Literature," *Review of Research in Education* 17 (1991): 335–409; and Amy Stuart Wells, Robert L. Crain, and Susan Uchitelle, "When School Desegregation Fuels Educational Reform: Lessons from Suburban St. Louis," *Educational Policy* 8 (Spring 1994): 68–87.

7    Crain, "Why Academic Research Fails to Be Useful," p. 337.

8    Gary Orfield, "Research, Politics and the Antibusing Debate," *Law and Contemporary Problems* 42 (Summer 1978): 141–73.

9    Gary Orfield, "How to Make Desegregation Work: The Adaptation of Schools to Their Newly-Integrated Student Bodies," *Law and Contemporary Problems* 39 (Spring 1975): 314–40; extract from p. 316.

10    Willis D. Hawley, "The New Mythodology of School Desegregation," *Law and Contemporary Problems* 42 (Autumn 1978): 214–33.

11    Nancy St. John, *School Desegregation: Outcomes for Children* (New York: John Wiley, 1975), p. 37.

12    Ibid, p. 39.

13    Ibid, p. 36.

14    Robert L. Crain and Rita E. Mahard, "Desegregation and Black Achievement: A Review of the Research," *Law and Contemporary Problems* 42 (Summer 1978): 17–56, extract from p. 49.

15    Janet W. Schofield, "Review of Research on School Desegregation's Impact on Elementary and Secondary School Students" (Paper commissioned by the Connecticut State Department of Education, 1989), p. 36.

16    See, for instance, Schofield, "School Desegregation and Intergroup Relations"; M. Patchen, *Black-white Contact in Schools: Its Social and Academic Effects* (West Lafayette, Ind.: Purdue University Press, 1982); Maureen Hallinan, "Classroom Racial Composition and Children's Friendships," *Social Forces* 61 (1982): 56–72; and idem and R. Teixeria, "Students Interracial Friendships: Individual Characteristics, Structural Effects and Racial Differences," *American Journal of Education* 93 (1987): 563–83.

17    Schofield, "Review of Research on School Desegregation's Impact on Elementary and Secondary School Students."

18    Patchen, *Black-white Contact in Schools.*

19    Oakes and Wells, "Beyond Sorting and Stratification."

20    See Janet Schofield, "Promoting Positive Peer Relations in Desegregated Schools," *Educational Policy* 7 (September 1993): 297–317.

21    Amy Stuart Wells, Robert L. Crain, and Susan Uchetelle, *Steppin Over the Color Line: African-American Students in White Suburban Schools* (New Haven: Yale University Press, forthcoming).

22    Oakes and Wells, "Beyond Sorting and Stratification."

23    Mark Granovetter, "The Micro-Structure of School Desegregation," in *School Desegregation Research: New Directions in Situational Analysis*, ed. J. Prager, D. Longshore, and M. Seeman (New York: Plenum Press, 1986), pp. 81–111, extract from p. 103.

24    Amy Stuart Wells and Robert L. Crain, "Perpetuation Theory and the Long-Term Effects of School Desegregation," *Review of Educational Research* 64 (Winter 1994): 531–55.

25    Jomills Henry Braddock, "The Perpetuation of Segregation across Levels of Education: A Behavioral Assessment of the Contact-Hypothesis," *Sociology of Education* 53 (July 1980): 178–86.

26    James M. McPartland and Jomills Henry Braddock, "Going to College and Getting a Good Job: The Impact of Desegregation," in *Effective School Desegregation,* ed. Hawley, p. 149.

27    Braddock, "The Perpetuation of Segregation across Levels of Education," p. 181.

28    See Mark Granovetter, "The Strength of Weak Ties," *American Journal of Sociology* 78 (1973): 1360–80; idem, "The Strength of Weak Ties: A Network Theory Revisited," in *Sociological Theory,* ed. R. Collins (Vol. I) (San Francisco: Jossey-Bass, 1983), pp. 201–33; and idem, "The Micro-Structure of School Desegregation: New Directions in Situational Analysis (New York: Plenum Press, 1986), pp. 81–110.

29    Granovetter, "The Strength of Weak Ties."

30    Granovetter, "The Micro-Structure of School Desegregation," pp. 102–03.

31    See Nan Lin, "Social Resources and Instrumental Action," in *Social Mobility and Social Structure,* ed. R. Breiger (Cambridge: Cambridge University Press, 1990), pp. 247–71; and James Montgomery, "Job Search and Network Composition: Implications for the Strength-of-Weak-Ties Hypothesis," *American Sociological Review* 57 (1992): 586–96.

32    Lin, "Social Resources and Instrumental Action," p. 251.

33    William Julius Wilson, *The Truly Disadvantaged: The Inner City, the Underclass, and Public Policy* (Chicago: University of Chicago Press, 1987).

34    Wells, Crain, and Uchitelle, *Steppin Over the Color Line.*

35    Julie E. Kaufman and James Rosenbaum, "The Education and Employment of Low-Income Black Youth in White Suburbs," *Education Evaluation and Policy Analysis* 14 (Fall 1992): 229–40, extract from p. 238.

36    Marvin P. Dawkins, "Black Students' Occupational Expectations: A National Study of the Impact of School Desegregation," *Urban Education* 18 (1983): 98–113.

37    Kaufman and Rosenbaum, "The Education and Employment of Low-Income Black Youth in White Suburbs," p. 230. For evidence of the inaccuracy of this hypothesis in the long-term effects of desegregation literature, see William W. Falk, "Mobility Attitudes of Segregated and Desegregated Black Youths," *Journal of Negro Education,* 1978, pp. 132–42.

38    Granovetter, "The Strength of Weak Ties."

39    Braddock, "The Perpetuation of Segregation across Levels of Education."

40    Robert L. Crain and Rita Mahard, "School Racial Compositions and Black College Attendance and Achievement Test Performance," *Sociology of Education* 51 (April 1978): 81–101.

41    See Braddock and McPartland, *Assessing School Desegregation Effects;* and Jomills Henry Braddock, "Segregated High School Experiences and Black Students' College and Major Field Choices" (Paper presented at the National Conference on School Desegregation, Chicago, June 1987).

# Reflections on the Promise of *Brown* and Multicultural Education

CARL A. GRANT

*University of Wisconsin-Madison*

*This article examines the dual meaning of "promise"—hope and vow—in relation to* Brown I *and* II. *It then proceeds to discuss how these two conceptions of promise are carried out in a desegregated junior high school. The article concludes with a discussion of how multicultural education can help meet the dual expectations of* Brown *as promise/vow and promise/hope.*

*Desegregation is not and was never expected to be an easy task. Racial attitudes ingrained in our Nation's childhood and adolescence are not quickly thrown aside. . . . But just as the inconvenience of some cannot be allowed to stand in way of the rights of others, so public opposition, no matter how strident, cannot be permitted to divert this Court from enforcement of . . . constitutional principles.*

—Thurgood Marshall

I begin this article with a discussion of the notion of promise because its interpretation is central to our understanding and expectations of *Brown* v. *Board of Education of Topeka, Kansas.* The word *promise* has many different connotations in our language, some associated with fairly concrete definitions, others with more abstract definitions. Sometimes promise is used to make an explicit statement, or render a vow; other times promise is used to convey an implicit intention, or render hope. For some, *Brown* is a promise/vow to correct the injustices of a dual school system, while for others, *Brown* is a promise/hope to restructure U.S. policy and practices on race and ethnic relations. In *Brown I* and *II* the following promises/vows are stated:

Brown I:

Such an opportunity [education], where the state has undertaken to provide it, is a right which must be available to all on equal terms.

" 'Separate but equal' has no place."[1]

*Brown II:*

> Full implementation of these constitutional principles may require solutions of varied school problems.
>
> In fashioning and effectuating the decrees, the court will be guided by equitable principles.[2]

The promise/hope of *Brown I* is addressed implicitly in several of the statements in the 1954 decision. The Supreme Court said:

> We must consider public education in the light of its full development and its present place in American life throughout the Nation.
>
> Today, education is perhaps the most important function of state and local government.
>
> Today it [education] is a principal instrument in awaking the child to cultural values, in preparing him for later professional training, and in helping him to adjust normally to his environment.[3]

The promise/hope of *Brown* is expressed poignantly in numerous reflections on the decision. Albert Blaustein and Clarence Ferguson note in their book that "this case [*Brown*] has had a greater impact upon American life than any other legal decision in our history."[4] Robert L. Carter, former counsel of the National Association for the Advancement of Colored People (NAACP) and the attorney who worked so closely with Thurgood Marshall in arguing *Brown*, states:

> *Brown* will always stand at the highest pinnacle of American judicial expression because in guaranteeing equality to all persons in our society as a fundamental tenet of our basic law, it espouses the loftiest values of this nation. . . . It is an eloquent statement of our highest ethical values. Because it paints a composite picture of how we want the world to view us and how we like to view ourselves, *Brown* allows us to take pride in ourselves and in the greatness of the nation we live in, and to stand tall and apart from the most of the other countries of the world.[5]

In this article, I plan to examine the dual meanings of promise in connection to *Brown*. Following this examination I will discuss how *Brown* as a promise/vow and *Brown* as a promise/hope was carried out in a desegregated junior high school. Finally, I will discuss multicultural education and how it can help meet the dual expectations of Brown as promise/vow and promise/hope.

## REFLECTIONS ON THE PROMISE OF *BROWN*

"Equal opportunity" is the key component in the *Brown* v. *Board of Education* decision. Equal opportunity to access and participation in American society, according to many constitutional scholars, is located in the Equal Protection Clause of the Fourteenth Amendment. In *Brown*, the Court argued that in our diverse society, segregation was unfair, and answered yes to the question: "Does segregation of children in public schools solely on the basis of race, even through the physical facilities and other 'tangible' factors may be equal, deprive African-American children of equal educational opportunity?" The Court's response asserted that black students had the right to "access," or, in other words, it vowed that black students could and would sit next to white students in school. The Court, however, did not declare that black students had a right to equal results in school. Specifically, the Court stated:

> Segregation . . . has a detrimental effect upon the colored children. The impact is greater when it has the sanction of the law; for the policy of separating the races is usually interpreted as denoting the inferiority of the Negro group. A sense of inferiority affects the motivation of the children to learn. Segregation with the sanction of law, therefore, has a tendency to retard the educational and mental development of Negro children and to deprive them of some of the benefits they would receive in a racially integrated school system.[6]

### PROMISE/VOW OF *BROWN*

*Brown* has been stifled in both categories of meanings of promise. The promise/vow of *Brown* is stifled by avoidance and delay tactics (especially invigorated by the "with all deliberate speed clause") and the "whiteness as property" concept.

#### Avoidance and Delay Tactics

Brown is a promise/vow of access for black students and other students of color, but one that is conditioned by the "with all deliberate speed" clause. On May 31, 1955, when the Supreme Court included the "deliberate speed" clause in *Brown II*, it allowed opponents of racial justice to procrastinate with regard to its implementation.[7] Carter maintains that "*Brown II* represented a break with tradition in constitutional law that constitutionally protected rights were regarded as 'personal and present,' the violation of which required immediate remediation." He adds: "When *Brown II* directed the schools to desegregate with all 'deliberate speed' rather than immediately, it articulated a new and heretofore unknown approach to rectifying violations of constitutional rights—an approach that invited defiance and delay."[8]

In the South, massive organized resistance campaigns leapfrogged across the region. Southern leaders used their political offices, the courts, their newspapers, and White Citizens' Councils to avoid, delay, and evade compliance with *Brown*.[9]

Blaustein and Ferguson report that "there are no constitutional limitations to measurers of 'avoidance.' It is perfectly proper—at least as far as the courts are concerned—for an individual or a state full of individuals to attempt to 'avoid.' "[10] Avoidance tactics used to delay desegregation fell into four categories: (1) interposition and nullification, that is, circumventing *Brown* by arguing states' rights over federal rights (see, for example, *Bush* v. *Orleans Parish School Board*); (2) disqualifying potential litigants, for example, enjoining the NAACP from any activities within the state, prohibiting the employment of any NAACP member by a state agency, and bringing criminal sanctions against an organization that instituted litigation in the state courts; (3) separation by race, but on factors other than race, such as scores on a scholastic achievement or aptitude test; and (4) separation of the operation of the school from state control, for example, establishment of private academies or "free choice" segregated schools for white students. Specific examples of avoidance and delaying tactics include the following.

In South Carolina, a three-judge panel provided an interpretation of *Brown II* that stated that integration was not required, only discrimination was forbidden. The judges said:

> What has been decided, and all that has been decided, is that a state may not deny to any person on account of race the right to attend any school that it maintains. . . . The Constitution, in other words, does not require integration. It merely forbids discrimination. It does not forbid such segregation as occurs as a result of voluntary action. It merely forbids the use of governmental powers to enforce segregation.[11]

In communities throughout the South, segregationist organizations sometimes referred to as White Citizens' Councils instructed white employers to fire black employees; white wholesalers were instructed to cut off credit and supplies to black retailers and customers; and white merchants were instructed to turn away black customers.[12]

Denial of the right of black children to enroll in Central High School in Little Rock, Arkansas, by the governor of the state is a prime example of white officials' using their office to deny compliance with *Brown*.[13] Other methods used to delay compliance with *Brown*, especially during the early years, included declaring that the schools were overcrowded, that there was a lack of funding, and that the curriculum would be disrupted if black students entered in January.[14]

In the decades following *Brown II*, avoidance and delay tactics also took several forms, including white flight, which left the urban areas populated predominately by minorities; negative reactions and resistance to busing of black students to previously white schools and an unwillingness to bus or noncompliance with busing of white students to previously all-black schools; the Department of Health, Education, and Welfare's (HEW) weak enforcement efforts of school integration, especially during the Nixon administration; and the failure of the Supreme Court to support interdistrict integration.[15]

*Whiteness as Property*

The promise/vow of *Brown* was muffled, as Bell has noted, because "whites continued to expect society to recognize an unspoken but no less vested property right in their 'whiteness.' "[16] According to Harris: "Whiteness as property is derived from the deep historical roots of systematic white supremacy that has given rise to definitions of group identity predicated on the racial subordination of the 'other,' and that has reified expectations of continued white privilege."[17]

Although we usually think of "property" as our belongings or possessions, "property also consists of rights in things that are intangible, or whose existence is a matter of legal definition."[18] These include the products of one's labor, potential earnings from a graduate degree, job entitlement, and occupational licenses. It also includes expectations (e.g., being treated a certain way, knowing your race will not work against you in opportunities for jobs and for other societal events) and privileges (e.g., the entitlement and advantages granted to an individual or group). White privilege, according to McIntosh, is like an invisible weightless knapsack of special provisions, maps, passports, codebooks, visas, clothes, tools, and blank checks.[19] Simply put, before *Brown* the law gave holders of whiteness the same privileges and benefits it gave to holders of other types of property. Harris explains that "after legalized segregation was overturned, whiteness as property evolved into a more modern form through the law's ratification of the settled expectations of relative white privilege as a legitimate and natural baseline."[20]

Reflections on the promise/vow of *Brown* lead to the conclusion that, on the surface, *Brown* was a legal mandate to change national educational policy, but at its underbelly, it was a legal mandate guided by folkways and customs based on the notion of whiteness as property. The Supreme Court was willing to declare the dual school system racially unjust, but at the same time, it was hesitant to interrupt the privileges that accompany whiteness. Harris states:

> *Brown* held that the Constitution would not countenance legalized racial separation, but *Brown* did not address the government's respon-

sibility to eradicate inequalities in resource allocation either in public education or other public services, let alone to intervene in inequities in the private domain, all of which are, in significant measure, the result of white domination. . . . What remained consistent was the perpetuation of institutional privilege under a standard of legal equality. In the foreground was the change of formal rules; in the background was the "natural" fact of white privilege that dictated the pace and course of any moderating change. What remained in revised and reconstituted form was whiteness as property.[21]

## PROMISE/HOPE OF *BROWN*

The promise/hope of *Brown*, although its effectiveness and benefits to African-American people have increasingly become an issue of debate (especially within African-American communities), is important to the welfare of black people, other oppressed people of color, white people, and the entire nation.[22] The promise/hope of *Brown* is the dream stuff for nation building and citizen optimism.

### Brown *and Nation Building*

Discussions of the promise/hope of *Brown* mainly focus on what the decision did for African Americans without giving attention to what the decision did for the nation at large. From K–12 textbooks, students most often learn that the *Brown* decision was singularly for and about African Americans. Rarely is there any discussion of the importance of the decision to the entire nation. It is not uncommon to find the discussion located in the section of history textbooks reserved for "minorities." Also, in many instances the discussion of *Brown* is insipid. One history text reads:

> In 1954 the Supreme Court made a landmark ruling in a case called *Brown v. Board of Education of Topeka*. The Court stated that laws requiring separate schools for blacks were unconstitutional. As a result, states could no longer legally segregate children in public schools.

> The school board in Little Rock, Arkansas, made plans to place blacks and whites in the same schools. Arkansas Governor Orval Faubus objected, however. He tried to stop black students from attending Central High School in Little Rock. Many angry white protesters agreed with the governor. Then President Eisenhower sent troops to Little Rock to uphold the law. Under the soldiers' protection, black students began to attend classes at the high school. . . . The Supreme Court's *Brown* ruling was an important victory for blacks.[23]

The school student reading this information is educationally shortchanged regarding an understanding of the importance of *Brown* for all U.S. citizens. Also, when such a discussion is placed in a section on minorities, it becomes marginalized within a discussion of U.S. history.

Discussions of the importance of *Brown* to the nation are available, but most often they are located in legal or scholarly writings.

Carter describes the momentous impact of *Brown* on the nation:

> While *Brown* specifically outlawed segregation in the nation's public schools, what it really stated and [is?] perceived to have done is to have held that the Constitution of the United States guarantees civil equality to all of us in this country. African Americans are not accorded equal citizenship rights because local, state, or federal officials are kind public servants, or because of the liberality or generosity of government luminaries, or because equality for blacks is morally mandated. *Brown* stated unequivocally that equality is a birthright of all Americans.[24]

Harlem Congressman Adam Clayton Powell, Jr.'s earliest written comments on *Brown* were related to the nation's welfare. He wrote that the *Brown* "decision was nothing less than democracy's shining hour and communism's worst defeat."[25] Similarly, Governor Hollings of South Carolina stated, "We of today must realize the lesson of one hundred years ago and move on for the good of South Carolina and our United States.[26]

In *The Fifties*, Halberstam reports that Justice Jackson's reason for supporting *Brown* was that racism by the Nazis had caused a sense of revulsion among American people. Tushnet, however, believes that Jackson's support of *Brown* was political. Regardless of which author is correct, neither reports that Jackson's rationale was to make educational life better for black students. For Tushnet, Justice Jackson did not want to bring the Supreme Court into ill repute. Similarly, Halberstam notes that one of the arguments used to convince Justice Reed, the remaining holdout against *Brown*, to support the decision was the idea that his dissent would damage the Supreme Court as an institution.[27]

In the final chapter of their book *Desegregation and the Law: The Meaning and Effect of the School Segregation Cases*, Blaustein and Ferguson, state that "*Brown* was far more than a 'discrimination-in-education case.' By declaring unconstitutional all state sanctioned racial discrimination, it created the guidepost for determining all issues involving racial classification in all areas."[28]

## Brown: *Uplifting People of Color*

Discussions of *Brown* as promise/hope for African Americans and other oppressed people are well documented. Carter reports that *Brown* gave

African Americans a positive feeling. He states: "As soon as the message *Brown* conveyed was absorbed by African Americans, the submissive supplicant black stereotype was replaced by a militant demanding, assertive black."[29] Greenberg states: "*Brown* decreed an end to school segregation but also transformed how blacks were seen and treated, by law and by society in general, not only in school but in many other areas of life."[30] Kenneth Clark, not too long before he died, addressed the importance of *Brown* to race relations when he said: "When the historic 1954 *Brown* decision pronounced racial segregation illegal, it inspired an optimistic outlook tantamount to euphoria. I felt that was the beginning of major positive change in American race relations."[31]

Similarly, Chambers reports that *Brown*, with all its flaws, set the stage to build a country that would fulfill its promise of equality and justice for people of color.[32] Jones contends that the *Brown* decision planted the seed of hope in the minds and hearts of many other marginalized groups. He states: "This [*Brown*] was without doubt the most momentous decision of the century. The great *Brown* decision has been the locomotive of the train onto which a number of aggrieved groups and individuals have hitched their claims."[33]

## THE PROMISE (VOW AND HOPE) OF *BROWN* IN A DESEGREGATED JUNIOR HIGH SCHOOL

In 1978, two colleagues and I were invited to help the staff and students at a desegregated mainstream junior high school to become more responsive to the race, class, gender, and disability challenges they were facing. This invitation developed into a three-year ethnographic case study that provided an opportunity to learn and understand how the promise (vow and hope) of *Brown* was being carried out. The case study is reported elsewhere, so I will confine my discussion to how the school responded to the three generations of desegregation efforts since *Brown*.[34]

The first generation of desegregation focused on bringing students of all races together under one schoolhouse roof; the second generation of desegregation focused on inequities within school (e.g., access to classroom and programs, suspensions and dropouts among minority students); and the third generation focused on the achievement of equal learning opportunity and outcomes for all students.[35] The school, Five Bridges, was located in a working-class urban community in a midwestern city. The community had been racially integrated since 1976, so the student population at the school was racially mixed. At the time of this study the racial composition of the 580-member student body was 67.5 percent white, 28 percent Hispanic, 2 percent African-American, 2 percent Native American, and 0.5

percent Asian American. Of the forty-six certified teachers at the school, thirty-six were white, three were Hispanic, and two were African-American; twenty-four were male and twenty-two were female. The principal was a white male and the two assistant principals were white, one male and one female. One counselor was a Mexican-American male, and the other counselor was a white female. The educational goals at Five Bridges were multicultural education and increased student academic achievement.

## BROWN—PROMISE/VOW

The faculty and staff at Five Bridges were supportive of the desegregation mandate. When the researchers asked faculty members what they considered the strengths of Five Bridges, two typical responses were:

> Our number one strength, we're not all white, we've got handicapped, Mexican-American, GLD students, and I find this a very nice situation. (White Counselor)

> The community supports the school and the diversity of people that are here. (Assistant Principal)

The school had achieved most of the first-generation desegregation responsibilities, each student had access to all opportunities within the school. Open-seating arrangements existed in most classes, and although students usually separated themselves along gender lines, the seating patterns were racially integrated and students with disabilities integrated themselves within this seating pattern. Racially mixed groups of students usually worked together on curriculum projects and socially; students believed that having friendship groups that were of more than one race was fun.

When students were asked who their close friends were both inside and outside of school, and what their race was, three-fourths of the students named close friends of more than one race. The following comment from an eighth grade student was typical:

> Hal (White): In our gang [a friendship group] we have blacks, Mexicans, and we're gonna have a Korean. None of my friends are prejudiced here.

Many of the procedures associated with second-generation desegregation policies were being addressed: academic expectations were the same for all students; suspensions, expulsions, and discipline referrals were the same across race, gender, and socioeconomic levels. In fact, discipline was not a serious problem, according to both students and teachers, and the disciplinary infractions that did occur were usually handled with after-school detention. These detention classes usually lasted only one-half hour and were not especially populated with any particular race, gender, or socioeconomic group of students.[36]

There were organized sports for both boys and girls and all race, gender, and socioeconomic groups of students were active in the same extracurricular activities (e.g., chess club).

Many of the third-generation desegregation policies were being addressed. Equal learning opportunities and outcomes for all students were available across race, gender, and socioeconomic levels. Teachers treated boys and girls the same in the classroom, and very few teachers were ever heard making sexist statements.

In sum, the students were not only physically desegregated at Five Bridges, they were integrated across race, class, and gender lines, and they believed it was more fun and exciting when different groups of students of color attended school together and socialized together.

## *BROWN*—PROMISE/HOPE

Although the promise/vow of desegregation seemed to have been met, what about the promise/hope of desegregation?

At Five Bridges, although the students were integrated both within and outside of the school, very little was done to capitalize on the racial integration that had taken place within the community. Students were not formally taught about the community's different cultural groups' histories, cultures, and contributions to the United States. The curriculum privileged the white students with its Eurocentric focus and there were few materials that focused attention on women or on sex-role socialization. Discussions about power and knowledge, the nature of prejudice in society, the causes of racism and sexism, were muted. Albeit the students were living in a social system (community and school) that challenged racism and claimed multicultural education as a goal, they were not receiving the knowledge or the social-action skills in school to contest racism outside of their own community.

Teachers treated all students equally without regard to race, gender, or socioeconomic status. Students had access to all courses and activities within the school, but the education offered to students—whites and minorities—was mediocre. It mainly dealt with remediation and basic skills. Teachers primarily used ditto sheets, workbooks, and some easy-reading, high-interest material. Teachers' expectations of the students were low.

> RESEARCHER:  What kinds of things do you think should be taught to the Five Bridges students?

MARJORIE:     (Administrative Intern/Assistant Principal): Everyday type things . . . that might be baby sitting and I know some people don't think that is our function but I think we'd survive better if we just okay this as part of what we are doing. . . . I think we do a fairly good job of the hands-on type things, the metal shop, graphic arts, home economics. . . . I think our seventh-grade life skill program is good.

BETTY:     (Social Studies Teacher): One of the things I am trying to tell them, is the things I am trying to teach you are things you are going to need in the real world. . . . I want them to know practical things. How to write a budget, how to write a check, how to balance your checkbook.

Students, on the other hand, described most school work as boring and not challenging.

RESEARCHER:     Why do you say [social studies] is boring?

ROBIN:     Because I just sat there. We just sit down and listen to him and that gets boring.

RESEARCHER:     Tell me about your English class.

SHIRLEY:     We always do a certain thing through the week. Like the first day we do these little things, we read and then we have to answer questions about it. And the second day, he's got it planned day through day so if you miss Tuesday you know what you did Tuesday because you always do the same thing. Tuesday we have to work out of a workbook. And, Wednesday we finish up the workbook, turn in the assignment and start on our spelling test. Like we write down words and get their meanings and stuff. And it goes on like that. It's boring in his class.

Students were not acquiring the knowledge to compete successfully for money, power, and status in society, or to exercise control of their destiny and future, nor were they being taught to examine traditional gender, race, and class relationships. Although the notion of equal opportunity and open access existed among all students within the school, the notion of achieving equality of results with their peers at other more affluent schools was not an expectation the teachers held for the students or a school goal.

Students were being taught to accept Eurocentric culture as the principal culture and to believe Eurocentric interpretations of reality through the school curricula. Most students did not understand socioeconomic class division or the struggle of poor people to earn better wages. They were also uninformed about the reasons for the race riots in many U.S. cities that had taken place just a little over a decade ago. They knew that family incomes varied, but did not seem aware of the extent of the gap in income and privileges and power between rich, middle-income, and poor people. Some of the boys did have knowledge of the salaries paid to professional athletes, but that knowledge was not accompanied with a realistic understanding of how hard it is to become a professional athlete, or the short career of most professional athletes.

At Five Bridges the promise/vow of *Brown* was being addressed but the promise/hope of *Brown* was not. Perhaps, because the faculty was pleased to work in a desegregated school, they did not understand the promise of *Brown* for each student and the nation. The success of the community to achieve integration, when many other communities across the nation were using avoidance tactics to maintain white privilege, was muted or marginalized during classroom discussion. The idea that Five Bridges could be a showcase for the nation in regard to successful integration within the school was not considered. The school staff lacked an understanding of what the school's goals of implementing multicultural education and increased student academic achievement meant for them.

## EDUCATION THAT IS MULTICULTURAL AND THE PROMISE/VOW/HOPE OF *BROWN*

The promise/vow/hope of *Brown* requires an education that advocates and affirms the belief that equality and equity should be active in all institutions in this country, and will be received by all students. The education best suited for achieving this goal is an eduation that is multicultural and social-reconstructionist. The phrase "education that is multicultural," as I explained in 1978, means that all aspects of schooling should reflect the diverse racial groups in the country; and that schools should be the location where knowledge is analyzed, where the activities of power brokers are critiqued, and skills and knowledge are acquired to enable students to take charge of their life circumstances and develop a positive self-identity.[37] Curriculum, instruction, staffing, testing, and so forth, must be multicultural. Although Sleeter and I have discussed this and other approaches to multicultural education elsewhere,[38] it is important to elaborate on at least two features of this approach here—curriculum and instruction—to explain what I mean.

A curriculum that is multicultural begins with the academic needs and interests of the students. It highlights the history and contribution of all Americans and is infused throughout the entire kindergarten through twelfth-grade program. It also highlights who we are as Americans and how that identity is represented throughout the world. Students are taught about oppression and social equality based on race, class, gender, and disability. Some curriculum concepts are organized around current social issues, including racism, classism, and sexism, and offer discussions about how these and other oppressive dynamics operate in school to produce knowledge and self-identity. Concepts are taught in a manner that includes the experiences and perspectives of several different ethnic groups and uses students' life experiences as a starting point for analyzing oppression. Also, the curriculum includes discussions about the relationship between knowledge and power and how both are acquired. Additionally, the curriculum includes activities that explain the importance of student participation in democratic decision making and the development and use of social-action and coalition-building skills.

Instruction encourages the deconstruction of knowledge and fosters the interrogation of popular events and images (e.g., Columbus Day celebrations). It builds on students' learning skills, thinking, and life experiences and adapts to their skill level. Also, instruction provides students with insights into the role of subject matter (e.g., math and science) within the contexts of society. Additionally, critical-thinking skills are taught; methods for analyzing alternative viewpoints are presented; and students are taught how to develop democratic decision-making and social-action skills.

Education that is multicultural and social-reconstructionist is an education for all students. It requires that schools truly serve all students, especially those who are marginalized. Its objective is to help students acquire the knowledge, skills, power, and positive self-identity to pursue their life goals and remove the barriers that prevent them from achieving the best that life has to offer, including helping others. Education that is multicultural and social-reconstructionist prepares students to grow up to make changes in society so that it better serves the interests and needs of all citizens, especially those who are of color, poor, and female. According to Brameld, a reconstructionist approach to education is visionary. Realistic visions that inspire hope; understanding of personal, cultural, and national identity; and understanding of how to achieve knowledge and power are needed to help students of color take charge of and give meaning to their lives, and fulfill the promise/hope of *Brown*.

Finally, if *Brown* was seen by the Supreme Court as a way not only of interpreting the law but of shaping the sociocultural conscience of the nation, then as we move into the twenty-first century, an education that is multicultural and social-reconstructionist is necessary to make real the belief that the United States is a "Plural Terrain and the Peoples' Domain" inherent in the constitutional ideal of "We the People."

## Notes

1    Brown v. Board of Education, 347 U.S. 483, 74 s. ct. 686 (1954), pp. 493, 495.

2    Brown v. Board of Education, 349 U.S. 294, 75 s. ct. 753 (1955), pp. 299, 300.

3    Brown v. Board of Education (1954), pp. 492–93.

4    A. P. Blaustein and C. C. Ferguson, Jr., *Desegregation and the Law: The Meanings and Effects of the School Segregation Cases* (New Brunswick: Rutgers University Press, 1962), p. ix.

5    R. L. Carter, "Thirty-Five Years Later: New Perspectives on Brown," in *Race in America: The Struggle for Equality*, ed. H. Hill and J. E. Jones, Jr. (Madison: University of Wisconsin Press, 1993), p. 93.

6    Brown v. Board of Education (1954), p. 494.

7    Kenneth B. Clark, "Racial Progress and Retreat: A Personal Memoir," in *Race in America*, ed. Hill and Jones, pp. 3–18.

8    Quoted in C. I. Harris, "Whiteness as Property," *Harvard Law Review* 106(8), pp. 1731, 1714.

9    J. Greenberg, *Crusaders in the Court* (New York: Basic Books, 1994); and N. R. Jones, "Civil Rights after Brown: The Stormy Road We Trod," in *Race in America*, ed. Hill and Jones, pp. 97–111; and M. V. Tushnet, *Making Civil Rights Law: Thurgood Marshall and the Supreme Court, 1956–1961* (New York: Oxford University Press, 1994).

10    Blaustein and Ferguson, *Desegregation and the Law*, p. 241; and Bush v. Orleans School Board, 364 U.S. 500, 81 S. Ct. 260, S L. Ed 2d 245 (1960)

11    H. S. Ashmore, *Civil Rights and Wrongs* (New York: Pantheon Books, 1994), p. 113.

12    Ibid.

13    Blaustein and Ferguson, *Desegregation and the Law*, and Tushnet, *Making Civil Rights Law*.

14    Blaustein and Ferguson, *Desegregation and the Law*.

15    See G. R. Metcalf, *From Little Rock to Boston: The History of School Desegregation* (Westport, Conn.: Greenwood Press, 1983); and Milliken v. Bradley 418, U.S. at 814 (Marshall, T., dissenting)(1974).

16    D. Bell, "Remembrances of Racism Past: Getting Beyond the Civil Rights Decline," *Race in America*, ed. Hill and Jones, p. 78; and Harris, "Whiteness as Property", p. 78.

17    Ibid., p. 1785.

18    Ibid., p. 1725.

19    P. McIntosh, "White Privilege: Unpacking the Invisible Knapsack," *Independent School*, Winter 1990, p. 31.

20    Harris, "Whiteness as Property", p. 1714.

21    Ibid., p. 1757.

22    Bell, "Remembrances of Racism Past"; V. Dempsey and G. W. Noblit, "Cultural Ignorance and School Desegregation: Reconstructing a Silenced Narrative," *Educational Policy* 7 (September 1993): 318–39; and D. O. Leake and C. J. Faltz, "Do We Need to Desegregate all of our Black Schools," *Educational Policy* 7 (September 1993): 370–87.

23    W. J. Jacobs et al., *America's Story* (Atlanta: Houghton Mifflin, 1988), pp. 705–06.

24    Carter, "Thirty-five Years Later," p. 93.

25    W. Haygood, *King of the Cats: The Life and Time of Adam Clayton Powell, Jr.* (New York: Houghton Mifflin, 1993), p. 194.

26    Quoted in Ashmore, *Civil Rights and Wrongs*, p. 252.

27    David Halberstam, *The Fifties* (New York: Fawcett Columbine, 1993), pp. 422–23.

28    Blaustein and Ferguson, *Desegregation and the Law*, p. 273.

29    Carter, "Thirty-five Years Later," p. 93.

30    Greenberg, *Crusaders in the Court*, p. 509.

31    Clark, "Racial Progress and Retreat," p. 17.

32   J. L. Chambers, "Brown v. Board of Education," in *Race in America*, ed. Hill and Jones, pp. 184–96.

33   Jones, "Civil Rights after Brown," p. 99.

34   C. A. Grant and C. E. Sleeter, *After the School Bell Rings* (Philadelphia: Falmer Press, 1986); and idem, "Race, Class and Gender and Abandoned Dreams," *Teachers College Record* 90 (Fall 1988): 19–40.

35   P. Bates, "Desegregation: Can We Get There from Here," *Phi Delta Kappan* 72 (1990): 8–17.

36   Field Notes, 1978–1982.

37   C. A. Grant, "Education That Is Multicultural: Isn't That What We Mean," *Journal of Teacher Education* 29 (1978): 45–49.

38   C. A. Grant and C. E. Sleeter, *Turning on Learning* (New York: Merrill/Macmillan, 1989); and C. E. Sleeter and C. A. Grant, *Making Choices for Multicultural Education: Five Approaches to Race, Class, and Genders*, 2nd ed. (New York: Merrill/Macmillan, 1993).

# Inequalities in Educational Financing

HOWARD A. GLICKSTEIN
*Touro College Jacob D. Fuchsberg Law Center*

*There are sharp inequalities in school financing. The disparity is even more profound given the inverse relationship between per-pupil expenditures and actual educational need. Education, moreover, competes with other major entitlement programs for increasingly scarcer funding resources. Equality in educational financing is a worthy goal but it does not confront the basic cause of educational inequality. Fear of school integration perpetuates the existence of a multiplicity of school districts. This substantially increases the burden to fund education and ultimately costs society dearly.*

In 1968, Demetrio P. Rodriguez sued the State of Texas over the issue of school expenditures in his poor San Antonio school district. He had hoped that, by the time his third-grade son reached sixth grade, his district spending level would equal that of richer ones. By 1993, Mr. Rodriguez's grandchildren attended the school his children did, and conditions there were no better. Often, trailers served as classrooms and the ceilings leaked.[1]

Let me briefly say a few words about the underlying reasons for inequality in school financing and how this inequality is manifested. Then I will discuss some current issues and, finally, I will explain why I think that school finance remedies, and most of the other remedies that are being considered at this conference, are just fiddling with some basic problems this country is not about to confront.

Most of you probably are aware of why our school districts are funded so unequally. Let me remind you of the problem. Local funds, derived almost exclusively from the real property tax, provide nearly one-half the revenue for elementary and secondary education in the nation as a whole. Let us compare what has happened to the source of funds for elementary and secondary education in the last twenty years.

In 1970–1971, local district revenues provided 52 percent of the funds for public education; by 1991, the percentage had fallen to 45.5. In 1970–1971, states provided 44.1 percent of the funding; by 1991, the percentage had risen to 48.3. Federal funding dropped from 6.9 percent in 1970–1971 to 6.2 percent in 1991.[2] There has been some change, but not much.

The amount that can be obtained through a property tax is a function of the tax rate employed and the value of the property taxed. Use of the property tax, therefore, subjects educational financing to the massive disparities in tax base that characterize local governments throughout the United States. Consequently, the richer a district, the less severely it need tax itself to raise funds. In other words, a person in a poor district must pay higher local rates than a person in a rich district for the same or lower per-pupil expenditures.[3] A further glaring inequity resulting from the current system of school finance is that variations in per-pupil expenditures among school districts tend to be inversely related to educational need. City students, with greater-than-average educational deficiencies, consistently have less money spent on their education and have higher pupil/teacher ratios than do their higher-income counterparts in the favored schools of suburbia.[4]

Let me give you some reasonably current examples of inequalities in school financing. An article in the *New York Times* compared two Long Island school districts in Nassau County, Roosevelt and Plainview. The Roosevelt district is 91.1 percent black. It has a school dropout rate of 8.6 percent and a student/teacher ratio of 17:1. The Roosevelt district spends $8,993 per student. The Plainview school district is 94.8 percent white. It has a dropout rate of .3 percent, the student/faculty ratio is 13:1, and it spends $11,271 per pupil. These differences in expenditures have real-life consequences. At Roosevelt, library books from the 1930s describe the Treaty of Versailles as the last word in arms limitation. The football team works out in a cramped room lighted by a bare bulb, on equipment the gym teacher confesses he borrowed from his town's recreation center. At Plainview, a new addition is a dedicated computer network the school was able to buy despite budget tightening. At Plainview–Old Bethpage High School, students enjoy a large, well-lighted weight room with a wide choice of equipment.[5]

Pennsylvania's highest-spending district spends three times the amount of its poorest district—$9,504 per pupil compared with $3,148 per pupil. In Illinois, the disparity is even greater, with a per-pupil expenditure of $14,316 in the wealthiest district and $2,253 in the poorest district.[6]

Let us look at the top five school districts in terms of spending for each pupil in New York State and compare this with the spending in New York City, New York State, and the United States as a whole for the 1990 school year. The top five school districts in terms of spending per pupil are Fire Island—$45,974; Bridgehampton—$31,748; Quogue—$29,458; Pocantico Hills—$28,283; and Amagansett—$27,896. Compare this with New York City, where $6,644 is spent for each pupil. The New York State average is $7,337 and the average spent per pupil in the United States is $5,240.[7]

In Ohio, in 1990, there were school districts that could not afford to install indoor toilets or have running water in the buildings while other districts had $1 million sports fields and Olympic-size swimming pools. In Texas, the property-rich districts were able to "tax low and spend high while the property-poor districts were [forced to] tax high merely to spend low."[8] In 1985–1986, local (property) tax rates ranged from nine cents to $1.55 per hundred-dollar valuation. The hundred poorest districts taxed at an average rate of 74 1/2 cents and spent only $2,978 per student while the hundred wealthiest districts taxed at an average rate of 47 cents and spent at an average of $7,233 per pupil. The property-poor districts found it difficult to improve their tax base because the location of new industry and development, boons to the tax base, depends in large part in tax rates and the quality of local schools.[9]

Does this inequality in funding necessarily mean inequality in quality? In an article I authored in 1973, I concluded that the Serrano case—the California case that was the *Brown* v. *Board of Education* of school finance litigation—might be incorrect in postulating that educational opportunity and money are related.[10] I pointed out that social scientists continue to debate the relative impact of educational spending and environmental influence on school achievement and future success. I indicated that the outcome of this controversy is not yet clear and concluded that "those who expect that additional spending on schools will result in a vastly-increased number of qualified candidates for our colleges and universities may find their hopes unfulfilled."[11] My 1973 conclusion might be as valid today as it was then. Educators still do not agree on the correlation between spending and educational achievement.

A decade after the publication of *A Nation at Risk*, the federal report warning that schools are failing America's children,[12] the performance of U.S. students remains mediocre: American students still underperform those of other industrial countries, despite one of the highest levels of educational spending. Many of the states that spend the most per pupil have the lowest test scores, concludes a recent Heritage Foundation study.[13] An article in *Business Week* magazine pointed out that one problem is that public school bureaucracies absorb money long before it reaches the classroom. Yet, pouring even more funds into an inefficient system will not guarantee better results. The *Business Week* article reports on a five-year experiment completed in June 1993 by the Annie E. Casey Foundation. The foundation committed about $40 million to four cities with a high proportion of disadvantaged groups. With the windfall, the cities—Dayton, Little Rock, Pittsburgh, and Savannah, Georgia—aimed to raise test scores and fix other inner-city problems. Aside from a slight lowering of the dropout rates, which tracked a nationwide decline, the experiment "didn't produce significant changes in the institutions or student outcomes," according to Gary Wehlage, associate director of the Center of Organization and Restructuring of Schools, who studied the program. A key reason: Most of the schools' practices stayed the same. While some schools added after-school programs, for example, they did not change the regular curriculum. Says Wehlage: "Money spent foolishly doesn't make any difference."[14] I will refer later to the need to tie reforms in school practices to school financing.

The courts, however, have been more willing to conclude that there is a relationship between spending per pupil and the quality of education provided. In 1990, for example, the New Jersey Supreme Court concluded: "Today, the disadvantaged are doubly mistreated: First, by the accident of the environment and second, by the disadvantage added by an inadequate education. The State has compounded a wrong and must right it." In that decision, the court also said: "Under the present system, the evidence compels but one conclusion: The poorer the district and the greater its need, the less money available and the worse the education."[15] In 1973, the New Jersey Supreme Court had observed that "it is nonetheless clear that there is a significant connection between the sums expended and the quality of the educational opportunity."[16]

In 1983, the New York Court of Appeals assumed the existence of a "significant correlation between amounts of money expended and the quality and quantity of educational opportunities provided."[17] Nevertheless, the court upheld New York's system of school financing. Perhaps money isn't everything, but it sure does help.

The *New York Times* article reported that students from the Roosevelt school district who visited the Plainview–Old Bethpage High School seemed shocked by the contrast between their own high school and Plainview's. Maybe better physical facilities in Roosevelt would not have a profound impact on the quality of education, but it certainly would have an impact on the way the students perceive themselves as compared with the students in the predominantly white Plainview–Old Bethpage school.[18]

But where is the money to come from to equalize disparities in school financing? Twenty years ago, the likelihood of finding the funds seemed greater than today. Some years ago, education had first call on state and local financing. Today, education is increasingly in competition with Medicaid and law enforcement, particularly corrections, for tight state dollars. Ten years ago, property values, which produce the primary tax source for local education, were rising; today they are stagnant. Today, government's costs for providing services have been passed from the federal to state level and in turn to the local level. Local governments more and more have to cope with state mandates. The states in general have reduced or leveled off their funding for education. We also are faced with an aging population. Only 20 to 25 percent of the voting population have children in school. This means that more senior citizens on fixed or limited incomes have less ability to pay higher taxes and less of a connection with local schools and an interest in supporting them.[19]

The trend in recent years has been to curb government spending to reduce taxes. In November 1992, Colorado voters rejected a 1 percent increase in the state sales tax, which was proposed to fund an anticipated shortfall in elementary and secondary school education revenue. In the same election they approved a constitutional amendment to limit state and local expenditures to the rate of inflation, taking into account population growth. Colorado voters must approve future tax or spending increases above the current year base.[20] Increasingly it appears that finding the funds to remedy inequalities of school financing in these days of fiscal restraint may prove an insurmountable obstacle.

A great deal has been written recently about the need to tie the elimination of fiscal inequities to school reforms. Educators like to talk about "inputs" and "outputs." What many people are trying to learn today is the connection between the various programs the money is spent on and the results in terms of quality of education and student achievement. A 1992 book by Allen R. Odden, the director for the Center for Research in Education Finance at the University of Southern California, calls for the direct funding of local schools, the fostering of school-based management, revamping teacher compensation strategies to reward experience and skills over tenure, creating school performance incentives aimed at achievement goals, providing funding for social services, and paying for expanded teacher recruitment and staff development. Many of those calling for tying school financing to reform insist that we need to have a better system for tracing how school funds are spent. Odden observed, "With this kind of direction, we can begin to answer questions like 'Which is better: higher teacher salaries or lower class size.' "[21] Perhaps Rudolph Giuliani is on to something when he insists that the New York City school system figure out how it is spending its money. I suppose it is reasonable for the mayor to insist that the school chancellor find out how many people are employed in the school system's administration.

Finally, let me say a few words to amplify the comment I made at the beginning to the effect that school finance remedies, and most of the other remedies that are being discussed at this conference, are just fiddling with some basic problems this country is not about to confront.

There are 16,000 school districts in the United States. Texas has 1,040 school districts. Suffolk County, Long Island, has 71 public school districts. The average size of Suffolk's K–12 districts is 3,844 students. A study in

Long Island found that larger districts were more efficient and effective. The study recommended consolidating districts with small enrollments into fewer, larger districts. There has been absolutely no movement to implement this recommendation.[22]

Why do we have so many school districts? The answer generally given is that Americans like local control, particularly for school districts. Perhaps this was a credible answer at one point in our history. Today it is more likely that those who are strong proponents of local control over schools, those who insist that land-use policies be locally determined, are those who are interested in keeping our society separate and divided. It has been quite clear to me that those who most strongly resist school district consolidation on Long Island are those who are fearful of school integration. To be sure, there are bureaucrats, both white and black, who resist consolidation because of concerns about their jobs and power. But I cannot foresee effective remedies for school finance inequalities or school segregation as long as our country retains a multiplicity of school districts. Perhaps full state funding will produce some appearance of equal resources for school districts but you can be sure that in wealthier districts the spending on education will continue to remain higher than in less wealthy districts.

There are many reasons why, forty years after *Brown*, thirty years after the enactment of the Civil Rights Act of 1964, we have become the two nations, separate and unequal, forecast by the Kerner Commission.[23] If there were an interest in reducing some of the separatism, in eliminating some of the inquality in the schools, it does not seem likely that this could be accomplished with 16,000 school districts nationwide. I am extremely dubious that we will ever be able to eliminate inequalities in school financing as long as we continue to pursue the tradition of local control and as long as we provide education through 16,000 school districts. These 16,000 school districts also prevent achieving a promise of *Brown*, at least as I see it. I was in law school when the *Brown* decision was rendered. To me that decision held a hope that our school systems could become a vehicle for achieving respect, unity, and harmony in our country. I saw the decision as a potential force for improving the educational opportunities not only of minority schoolchildren but of all schoolchildren. *Brown* would make it possible to fulfill the early objectives of our public schools. Very early in our history, education was widely regarded as a means of fostering social cohesion. The schools would serve to unify Americans, rather than divide them. Let me conclude with a quote from Samuel Lewis, the first superintendent of common schools in Ohio, who wrote in 1836:

> Take 50 lads in a neighborhood, including rich and poor—send them in childhood to the same school—let them join in the same sports, read and spell in the same classes, until their different circumstances

fix their business for life: Some go to the field, some to the mechanic's shop, some to merchandise: One becomes eminent at the bar, another in the pulpit: Some become wealthy; the majority live on with a mere competency—a few are reduced to beggary! But let the most eloquent orator, that ever mounted a western stump, attempt to prejudice the minds of one part against the other, and so far from succeeding, the poorest of the whole would consider himself insulted.[24]

Samuel Lewis's vision never will be realized through 16,000 school districts.

## Notes

1    Stephanie Anderson Forest, "True or False: More Money Buys Better Schools," *Business Week*, August 2, 1993, p. 62.

2    Ibid.

3    Howard A. Glickstein and William L. Want, "Inequality in School Financing: The Role of the Law," *Stanford Law Review* 25 (February 1973): 337–38.

4    Ibid., pp. 337–38.

5    Diana Jean Schemo, "Persistent Racial Segregation Mars Suburbs' Green Dream," *New York Times*, March 17, 1994, p. A1.

6    National Governors' Association, "Strategic Investment: Tough Choices for America's Future," January 29, 1993, p. 2.

7    Josh Barbanel, "Long Island District Illustrates Paradoxes of School Financing," *New York Times*, February 12, 1992, p. A23.

8    Donald S. Yarab, "Edgewood Independent School District v. Kirby: An Education in Finance Reform," *Case Western Reserve Law Review* 40 (1989–1990): 890, n. 5.

9    Ibid.

10    347 U.S. 483 (1954).

11    Glickstein and Want, "Inequality in School Financing," p. 402.

12    National Commission on Educational Excellence, *A Nation at Risk: The Imperative for Educational Reform* (Washington, D.C. Government Printing Office, 1983).

13    Cited in Forest, "True or False," p. 63.

14    Quoted in ibid, p. 62.

15    Abbott v. Burke, 575 A.2d 359, at 403 (N.J. 1990).

16    Robinson v. Cahill, 62 N.J. 473, 481 (1973).

17    Board of Education v. Nyquist, 439 N.E.2d 359, 363 (1982).

18    Schemo, "Persistent Racial Segregation Mars Suburbs' Green Dream," p. A1.

19    Mary Fulton, "Behind the Funding Crisis Facing U.S. Public Schools," *Christian Science Monitor*, May 20, 1993.

20    National Governors' Association, "Strategic Investment," p. 2.

21    Quoted in Lonnie Harp, "Dollars and Sense: Reformers Seek to Rewrite School Financing to Make It a Powerful Lever for Change," *Education Week*, March 31, 1993, p. 13.

22    Viewpoints, "LI Educational Pie is Cut Unequally," *Newsday*, June 18, 1993, p. 65.

23    The National Advisory Commission on Civil Disorders, Report of the National Advisory Commission on Civil Disorders (1968).

24    Quoted in Glickstein and Want, "Inequality in School Financing," p. 342.

# Race and Choice in Montgomery County, Maryland, Magnet Schools

JEFFREY R. HENIG

*George Washington University*

*Analysis of the pattern of requests to transfer into elementary school magnet programs in Montgomery County, Maryland, suggests that the direction in which choice points may exacerbate, rather than ameliorate, racial segregation. White families were most likely to request transfer into schools with low proportions of minorities (which also were those located in higher-income neighborhoods), and minority families were more likely to opt for schools in low-income neighborhoods (which also tended to be schools with higher proportions of minority students). Significantly, this racial pattern held even when other characteristics of the schools were taken into account. Evidence from parental surveys suggests that, lacking other sharply defined clues about which schools are likely to benefit their children most, both minority and nonminority parents fall back on other criteria, including convenience, informal word-of-mouth, and concerns about their child's social integration. These criteria, while not racially determined, are racially influenced. The Montgomery County, Maryland, experience suggests that unfettered choice has the potential to exacerbate racial separation, even in a relatively liberal and prosperous setting. Choice can be structured so that it promotes racial integration and socioeconomic equality, but doing so requires that public officials take strong stands, and often politically unpopular ones.*

One of the stranger occurrences in the discourse about educational policy has been the subtle but serious redefinition of what magnet schools represent. Originally linked in unambiguous terms to the goal of racial desegregation, magnet schools more recently have been rhetorically linked to the goal of educational excellence. Originally representing the forceful application of government resources and authority to achieve collectively defined goals, magnet schools more lately have been characterized as a testing ground for the principle that market forces—not government policy—are the key to improving our nation's schools.

In my recent book, *Rethinking School Choice: Limits of the Market Metaphor*, I chronicle the political motivations behind this redefinition in greater depth.[1] Early in 1988, President Ronald Reagan went to Suitland High School, a public school in Prince George's County, Maryland, and announced to 2,200 students and guests that its magnet program was "one of the great successes of the education reform movement." In doing so, he was using his considerable powers of rhetoric and symbolism to initiate an interpretive revision of history and a political reclamation of a foundering idea. In spite of his substantial legislative successes in other areas, Reagan had been stymied in his efforts to mobilize support for his vision of school vouchers that could be used in private and parochial schools. Linking the choice agenda to existing public magnet schools helped the administration make the case that school choice was feasible, demonstrably successful, and unlikely to lead to the racial and socioeconomic disparity that his critics seemed to fear.

In this article, I draw on my research on requests to transfer to magnet schools to underscore the danger of misapplying the magnet school experience to bolster calls for more market-oriented school choice plans. The Montgomery County, Maryland, experience suggests, I will argue, that unfettered choice still has the potential to exacerbate racial separation, even in a relatively liberal and prosperous setting. Choice *can* be structured so that it promotes racial integration and socioeconomic equality, but doing so requires that public officials take strong stands, and often politically unpopular ones.[2]

## THE MAGNET SCHOOL OPTION IN MONTGOMERY COUNTY, MARYLAND

The Montgomery County Public Schools (MCPS) is a large district comprising 495 square miles and approximately 103,000 students. The county, which rests on the northern border of the District of Columbia, has a population that is of relatively high socioeconomic status. Although its population is still predominantly white, the minority population in the school system has increased dramatically, both in total numbers and, even more sharply, as a percentage of total enrollment. Between 1970 and 1990, while overall enrollments were decreasing, the number of minority children in MCPS elementary and secondary schools increased just under 290 percent, from 10,034 to 39,543. In 1990, minorities constituted over 38 percent in all enrollments.

In the area of the county that adjoins the District of Columbia, sixteen out of seventeen elementary schools, two intermediate schools, and a high school now boast some kind of magnet program. Within this geographic area, at least, magnet schools are not a specially crafted exception; they are part of a comprehensive magnet network.[3] Children are assigned to a home school based on their local attendance zone; their parents, however, are encouraged to explore the option of transferring their child to another magnet school. Transportation is provided at no charge to students whose transfers have been approved. The county's stated policy holds that transfer requests are to be approved unless they result in racial imbalance, overcrowding, or substantial underutilization in the sending or receiving school. For the 1984 and 1985 school years, 85 percent of all transfer requests were approved either initially or on appeal.[4]

The nineteen schools with magnet programs alone serve a student population of about 10,200—a clientele that is larger than 95 percent of the nation's school districts.[5] Moreover, these magnet schools show much higher levels of racial diversity and special needs than does the county as a whole. Thirteen of the schools have more minority than nonminority students, and in nine of these the composition is over 60 percent minority. In seven of the schools, more than one of every three students is poor enough to be eligible for the school lunch program, and in six schools more than one in ten students is in a program for non–English speaking children.

## RACE AS A FACTOR IN SCHOOL CHOICE

In an analysis, the details of which are provided elsewhere, I related various magnet elementary school characteristics to the racial pattern of requests to transfer into those schools in 1985.[6] There were slightly more than 450 requests by families to transfer into one of the fourteen elementary magnet programs in operation that year. Minority families, which accounted for 57.7 percent of the students in those schools, made 46.5 percent of the transfer requests.

Advocates for more market-based choice systems have argued that there is no necessary tension between individual choice and integration, and they have pointed to the apparent success of some magnet schools in bringing about voluntary integration to buttress their claim.[7] But the pattern of requests in Montgomery County suggests that—unless aggressively regulated by authorities—the direction in which choice points may exacerbate, rather than ameliorate, racial segregation. Both whites and minorities seem to direct their choices toward schools in which their children will be less likely to be racially or socioeconomically isolated. This criterion, however, points them in different directions. Where white families were most likely to request transfer into schools with low proportions of minorities (which also were those located in higher-income neighborhoods), minority families were more likely to opt for schools in low-income neighborhoods (which also tended to be schools with higher proportions of minority students). Significantly, this racial pattern held even when other characteristics of the schools were taken into account.[8]

A survey of over one thousand magnet and nonmagnet school parents, conducted by the county in the spring of 1985, provides some insight into the reason why such a racial pattern exists. The problem is not that Montgomery County residents are strongly or reflexively averse to sending their children to schools with children of different races. To the contrary, in an area in which almost all children attend racially mixed schools, 76.3 percent of white parents and 77.3 percent of black parents indicated they felt the racial composition of their school was "about right."[9]

Rather than being a result of old-fashioned racism, what seems to be happening is this: Lacking other sharply defined clues about which schools are likely to benefit their children most, both minority and nonminority parents fall back on other criteria, including convenience, informal word-of-mouth, and concerns about their child's social integration. These criteria, while not racially *determined*, are racially *influenced*. The concern about social integration, for instance, leads both white and black parents to be unhappy when their children are in the distinct minority. White parents whose children are in schools with over 60 percent minority composition are three times more likely to express dissatisfaction with the racial mix than those in schools with less than 45 percent minority enrollment. Black parents whose children attend schools that have fewer than 25 percent minority enrollment are more than six times as likely to be dissatisfied with the racial mix than those whose children attend schools that are more than 60 percent minority.

## MAKING CHOICE WORK

Given a pattern of requests that might have increased racial segregation, Montgomery County officials have relied primarily on the exercise of government authority to keep choice and integration goals in balance. This is most directly seen in the exercise of the authority to deny transfer requests. By constraining the choice of some parents—by rejecting about 15 percent of the requests for transfer on grounds that they would worsen racial imbalance—officials have been able to keep the magnet program from exacerbating segregation. In addition, county officials have had to face down pressure to dramatically expand the number of magnets, as parents in other areas of the county have demanded to know why their schools should be denied the attention and resources that the magnets seem to garner. The drawing power of magnets, and their utility as tools for managing integration, is likely to be diluted if magnet features are allowed to replicate, willy-nilly, throughout the system.

But the exercise of such authoritative action is politically demanding. School officials are placed in an awkward position when they are forced to deny transfers at the same time they are publicly promoting the availability of choice. The tendency of black parents to shy away from schools in which their children might be racially isolated adds another complication. Because minority transfer requests were more likely to run counter to than support racial-balance objectives, school officials found themselves forced to deny a higher proportion of requests from minorities than from majorities. From 1983 through 1986, officials rejected 20.2 percent of minority requests to transfer into the fourteen magnet schools, while rejecting 13.1 percent of majority requests.[10] And limiting magnet programs to situations in which they will decrease racial integration—which was unproblematic and relatively uncontroversial when undertaken as an alternative to forced busing or when funded by federal programs that made this a requirement—is less easily defended by local officials in the contemporary legal and political climate, which makes judicial intervention less likely.

## SOME IMPLICATIONS

That racial factors appeared to play a strong role, even in the liberal and progressive setting of Montgomery County, should prompt some concern among those who envision a choice dynamic driven solely by parental insistence on educational quality. Such patterns cast doubt on the applicability of the racial neutrality perspective, which holds that freely exercised individual choice will, more or less spontaneously, complement the socially defined goal of greater racial intermixing.

This is not to say that the expansion of choice *cannot* coexist with the continued commitment to important social goals, such as racial integration; rather, it is to acknowledge that bringing about and sustaining such a complementary arrangement is likely to require careful attention to institutional particulars. Moreover, attending to such institutional particulars is not simply a matter of providing model designs to well-intentioned public officials. The difficulties that Montgomery County has encountered suggest that managing choice to promote integration is a problematic exercise, even when undertaken as self-conscious effort by well-informed public officials in a relatively favorable cultural and fiscal milieu. The current fashion of linking school choice to celebrations of the power of markets to succeed where democracy and government are destined to fail, however, misses the boat.[11] Indeed, by systematically delegitimizing the role of collective decision making and authoritative governance, they run the risk of undermining the very institutions on which our hope for the future ultimately must rest.

*Notes*

1  Jeffrey R. Henig, *Rethinking School Choice: Limits of the Market Metaphor* (Princeton, N.J.: Princeton University Press, 1994).

2  This article summarizes data and arguments presented at greater length in "The

Exercise of Choice among Magnet Schools: The Montgomery County Case and Its Implications" (Harvard School Choice and Family Policy Seminar, April 20, 1993). A version of that paper will appear in a forthcoming volume to be edited by Richard Elmore, Bruce Fuller, and Gary Orfield.

3   MCPS established seven elementary-level magnet schools in 1977. The program was expanded to a total of fourteen elementary schools, two intermediate schools, and one high school in 1983; two more elementary schools were added in 1987. For more background on the origin of the program, see Jeffrey R. Henig "Choice, Race and Public Schools: The Adoption and Implementation of a Magnet Program in Montgomery County, Maryland," *Journal of Urban Affairs* 11 (1989): 243–59.

4   John C. Larson and Rita J. Kirshstein, *A Microscope on Magnet Schools, 1983–1985: Implementation and Racial Balance* (Rockville, Md.: Department of Educational Accountability, 1986).

5   Not all of these students are in the magnet programs. While some of the schools offer "whole school" programs, other magnets have distinct identities and entrance requirements. In the 1988–1989 school year, 4.3 percent of all U.S. school districts had enrollments of 10,000 or more  (National Center for Educational Statistics, *Digest of Education Statistics, 1990* [(Washington, D.C.: U.S. Department of Education, 1991], Table 85).

6   Jeffrey R. Henig, "Choice in Public Schools: An Analysis of Transfer Requests among Magnet Schools," *Social Science Quarterly* 71 (1990): 69–82.

7   See, for example, Evans Clinchy, "Let Magnet Schools Guide the Way to Educational Reform—and Diversity," *The American School Board Journal*, May 1985, p. 43; and defenders of choice quoted in William Snider, "The Call for Choice: Competition in the Educational Marketplace," *Education Week*, June 24, 1987, pp. C2–C24.

8   Besides the racial and ethnic characteristics of the existing student population, the analysis considered various indicators of *resources and demands* (including total enrollment, student turnover, overcrowding, the ratio of students to professional staff, the ratio of students to classroom teachers, the ratio of classroom teachers to aides, the percent of teachers with sixteen or more years of experience, and the age of the school structure), differences in *program and grade level* organization (including the nature of the magnet specialization offered, whether the magnet included the entire school or just a portion of its students, and the specific combination of grades offered at the school), and indirect indicators of school *performance* (including standardized test scores and parental satisfaction, as indicated in a survey conducted by the school system's Department of Educational Accountability in the spring of 1985, that included 575 parents of children in the magnet schools).

9   Among the 1,078 parents included in the survey, none attended schools with fewer than 17.3 percent or more than 91.3 percent minority students. The average was 45.6 percent minority, and 63 percent of the respondents had children attending schools with between 25 and 60 percent minority populations.

10   Larson and Kirshtein found that minority requests to transfer among the ten Blair cluster elementary magnets were nearly five times as likely to run counter to racial balance as to be supportive of them (*A Microscope on Magnet Schools*, p. 38). (Although their transfer data do not distinguish among minorities, the survey data suggest the likelihood that this pattern would be even sharper if we could isolate requests by black families.) This left officials with the choice of denying minority requests at a higher rate or allowing minority transfers even when they negatively affected racial balance. The figures suggest that officials did a little of both. While the denial rate for minorities is higher than that for majorities, it is not proportionately as high as might be expected in light of the skewed pattern of requests.

11   For instance, John E. Chubb and Terry M. Moe, *Politics, Markets and American Schools* (Washington, D.C.: Brookings Institution, 1989); and Myron Lieberman, *Public Education: An Autopsy* (Cambridge: Harvard University Press, 1993).

# The False Premises and False Promises of the Movement to Privatize Public Education

**WILLIS D. HAWLEY**
*University of Maryland, College Park*

*The movement to provide parents with financial incentives to send their children to private schools will increase the racial, ethnic, and socioeconomic homogeneity of the nation's schools. The case for privatizing public education is based on several assumptions about the positive effects of reducing the costs of enrolling in private schools. Six of the most commonly cited of these assumptions are examined and found to be false.*

During the last few years, efforts to desegregate America's schools have stalled and demographic changes in urban areas have increased the proportion of children of color who attend schools where few white children enroll. The resegregation of the United States would be accelerated if proposals to provide tuition assistance to parents who want to send their children to private schools were to become public policy.

Given that public investments in private schools would further separate the nation's diverse racial and ethnic groups, what benefits might counter this cost? Advocates of private school choice for parents argue that it will increase the quality of schools for all children. However, this claim is a false promise based largely on false premises. Moreover, the costs of choice are not limited to its effect on the opportunities children of different races and ethnic identities will have to learn with and from one other. Providing public subsidies to parents or to schools in ways that increase private school enrollments is likely to have substantial economic costs, weaken the prospects for reducing social inequality, and undermine support for public education.

The concerns and myths that have fueled the momentum of the private school voucher movement reflect the sense many have that nothing seems to work, that society is out of control, and that our personal and national futures are increasingly uncertain. The search for the shelter of private (or neighborhood) schools, however, is a futile one that weakens our national capacity to solve complex problems, to develop an understanding that we share a common destiny, and to regain our confidence in the wisdom of democratic government.

## THE FALSE PREMISES OF PRIVATE SCHOOL CHOICE

There are at least six commonly heard justifications for private school choice that are either wrong or so unlikely that they should be dismissed. Without these justifications, the case for giving public money to parents to spend on private school tuition becomes one of narrow self-interest or political ideology.

*False Premise 1*

*The quality of public schools has declined in the last several years.* There is no responsible analysis of educational trends over the last fifteen years that supports this commonly held belief. It is true that there has been little overall improvement in student achievement. It is also true that virtually every social condition that affects student learning has worsened. One might say that public schools have maintained speed while the hill has become more steep.

*False Premise 2*

*Private schools are more effective in facilitating student achievement than public schools.* The consensus view among those who have reviewed the available research is that students in private schools are likely to score only slightly higher (two-tenths of a standard deviation) on tests of academic performance than public school students from the same socioeconomic background.[1] Even this small effect is suspect because private schools can select the students they enroll (and most say they do) and can dismiss students who misbehave or have learning problems with which the school cannot or will not deal. Moreover, since evidence of the small private school effect is confined almost completely to students in Catholic schools, the difference is probably the result not of differences in quality but of the exceptional motivation of the predominantly non-Catholic parents of students in urban Catholic schools and the fact that many Catholic schools are not coeducational.

If private schools do not enhance student learning any more than do public schools, why would having more students, whose parents would be less willing to make sacrifices for a private education than the current cohort of private school parents, lead to improved education?

*False Premise 3*

*Providing parents with options in the private sector will cause schools to compete for students and this will lead to improvements in the overall quality of instruction and the rigor of the curriculum in both public and private schools.* If this assumption were correct, private school students would outperform public school students from similar backgrounds and private schools would compete for students by developing new and powerful strategies for enhancing student learning. But, of the hundreds of articles on the issue of choice, virtually none have identified innovation as a characteristic that differentiates private and public schools.

It is very difficult for parents—or researchers—to know how much difference (added value) one school makes in student learning compared with another. This reality, coupled with the desire of parents to have their children attend schools with people like themselves (or people they want to be like) and to avoid unfamiliar school settings, means that parental choice seldom turns on evidence of school quality. Student characteristics, location, physical facilities, religious preference, and ideology are the bases of parental choice. Not only does competition on these criteria not lead to educational excellence; it probably detracts from concern for academic differences among schools.

The political advocates of tuition vouchers argue that market forces will increase competition in ways that increase the general welfare. However, the theory of welfare economics holds that effective competitive markets should have several characteristics: relatively simple and reliable ways to assess product quality, equality (or symmetry) of information among consumers, low needs for regulation related to safety or equity, independence of purchasing acts, and no third-party payments.[2]

*False Premise 4*

*If more parents were economically empowered to choose private schools, this would encourage private entrepreneurs to enter the marketplace and this would drive out weak schools and drive up the quality of both private and public schools.* However, not only do the conditions for quality-producing competition not exist, but good private schools do not seek to maximize profits—they maximize services. Maybe there are entrepreneurs waiting in the wings, but much publicized claims by business adventurers like Chris Whittle have been abandoned once careful analyses are completed. There were fewer children attending private schools in 1993 than in 1984 even though the total number of students increased.[3] Over the last few years, virtually all new private schools have been religious schools and many of these paid teachers abysmal salaries (resulting in high teacher turnover). Thus, the choices most new entrants to private schools are likely to have will either be Catholic schools or small Christian schools, many of which are *not* characterized by academic rigor.

*False Premise 5*

*Providing parents with tuition vouchers will give all children the same opportunity to attend private schools.* There are many reasons why this outcome is highly unlikely. First, some schools—particularly those thought to be the best—will remain selective and this selectivity will limit choice. Second, schools that already have waiting lists (if the market works at all, these are the best) will increase their price rather than their enrollment, putting them further out of the financial reach of most families than they are now. Third, rural Americans are unlikely to have more choice because a critical mass of consumers, especially consumers who can pay the price of quality schools, seldom exists in rural areas. Fourth, parents will compete for access to the limited supply of high-quality schools. Even if some private schools do not require selective tests as a condition for admission, parents will differ greatly in their access to information, transportation for their children, time to analyze options and act on their decisions, and knowledge about what to expect of schools. All of these differences among parents are related to income and this means that poorer families will have the options that are left over after the more wealthy have made their choices.

*False Premise 6*

*The potential effectiveness of providing public funds for private school tuition is illustrated by the expansion and success of public school choice plans.* In other words, if public school choice is good, private school choice is simply more of a good thing, if not better.

In a remarkable number of cases, the advocates for private school choice use the successful implementation of public school choice plans—such as specific magnet schools or District 4 in New York City—as evidence of the validity of their position without acknowledging that public choice plans in the United States are fundamentally different from the tuition voucher strategies they really favor. Indeed, opponents of tuition vouchers for private schools have often said that they would support private school choice if only it included the safeguards of public choice plans—a condition lost on a confused public and conveniently ignored by private school choice advocates who point to support for public school choice in national opinion surveys as evidence of the rightness and inevitability of their cause.

There are many variations of public choice plans but, when they are well designed, they have the following attributes that set them apart from private school choice proposals:

1.  Parental choice is controlled or limited to ensure that racial and ethnic diversity is maintained whenever possible, that resource allocation among schools is more or less equitable (but not, necessarily, equal), that the needs of students with learning disabilities are addressed, and that there are commonalities among the schools with respect to core curricula.

2. The choices parents have are determined primarily by the politically defined needs of the community and the judgments of professional educators rather than by consumer interests. Among the consequences of this is that certain parental preferences, such as religious instruction, get no consideration and specific education innovations often become the rationale for implementing new options.

3. As any businessperson knows, most innovations cost more in the short run than the processes they have been using. Thus, innovations often need extra investments and time to build a following. School *systems* can make such investments and tolerate, even encourage, low enrollment in schools of choice that "break the mold."

4. Public plans often invest heavily in information for parents. Most private choice advocates propose information systems too but there is a big difference: Public information systems seek to *shape* parental choice and direct the flow of students toward underused or more innovative options and often focus extra efforts on low-income parents. Parent information programs for public school choice are, in short, part of a systemic strategic plan that seeks to shape consumer choices for the public good.

5. Public school options usually incorporate systemwide or statewide curriculum plans that seek to ensure not only equity but continuity across schools and across grades so that students who move from school to school, whether by choice or by necessity, can build on what they have learned in the school they previously attended. This is no small concern in an increasingly mobile society and it is particularly important for low-income children.

6. Schools of choice within public systems have a greater chance to influence change in other schools because the motivation of schools to replicate successful ways to attract students is complemented by a school system capacity to both publicize innovations (do private companies advertise the key reasons for their comparative advantages?) and to move resources, especially leaders, to settings at which the changes are to be diffused and newly implemented.

7. Schools of choice within the public sector have a distinct advantage in building relationships with other community institutions, such as business and social service agencies. To be sure, many private schools link to other institutions, such as churches or a patron business, but the capacity of individual private schools to build such bridges on their own, especially for schools serving low-income children, is limited.

## SOME PROBABLE COSTS OF TUITION VOUCHERS FOR PRIVATE SCHOOLS

### COSTS TO TAXPAYERS

Surprisingly, the economic cost of tuition vouchers has received relatively little attention. If tuition vouchers were to be provided for those now attending private schools and an equal number of students now attending public schools, the additional public cost of education in the United States would be more than $25 billion. To this conclusion, the advocates of choice have two responses: (1) Private school education does not cost as much as public education and (2) vouchers would be limited to those with low incomes. The second response is disingenuous. The leading advocates for private school choice argue that everyone should eventually get a voucher. Beginning with the less well-off is but a strategy for getting started and, as the advocates of this strategy surely recognize, it would be politically difficult to avoid the extension of vouchers to everyone.

With respect to the cost of private education, it is important to recognize that most nonreligious private schools spend as much as or more than public schools and seldom provide the range of services offered by public schools. Religious schools tend to be less expensive than public schools for three major reasons: The sources for the learning they provide are limited; they pay much lower salaries to teachers and administrators; and they use instructional facilities whose cost is not counted in their expenditures. Would these reasons for the lower cost of the average private school stay constant if private school enrollments increased? More important, how could we justify providing vouchers that only paid the cost of religious schools? Thus, directing choice toward religious preference? And, will the quality of schools increase if salaries of teachers and administrators decline?

### DECREASED SUPPORT FOR PUBLIC EDUCATION

Private school vouchers would undermine public education in at least three ways. First, funding for public education would probably decline. The money to pay for vouchers for students now in private schools would have to come from somewhere. The most likely source is public expenditures for education. Moreover, the most effective advocates of public spending for education are not parents but education professionals. The private school choice movement seeks to weaken the political voice of professional educators. Second, the idea of paying parents public money to purchase services essentially defines education as a private rather than a public good. The logic of sustaining tax expenditures for a private school is likely to be lost on nonparents. The proportion of households without children has grown steadily and is now more than double the proportion of households with children. Third, once we have isolated most low-income children in "their own schools" it will be difficult to sustain the significantly higher-than-average expenditures such children need to receive a quality education. This, in turn, means that all children in public schools that serve low-income students will have a lower quality education than they now have.

## THE FURTHER FRAGMENTATION OF AMERICA

Without substantial constraints on parental choice, the consequences of the widespread use of tuition vouchers that can be used in private schools will be to sort the nation's children, and thus the country, according to religious beliefs, social class, race, ethnicity, and political ideology. This is the experience of most other nations where school choice is substantially supported by government.

It seems worth remembering that the idea of tuition vouchers first received serious attention in America from advocates for empowering the underclass. But that effort was abandoned by its initial proponents when they realized that the protections needed to avoid inequality and fragmentation would so constrain private school choice that vouchers would not create markets that produce quality education.

## UNDERSTANDING THE INTEREST IN CHOICE AS THE SEARCH FOR PERSONAL CONTROL

If the potential benefits of tuition vouchers for private school choice are so problematic and the potential costs are so high, how could the issue have gained so much attention? Part of the answer to this question is that parental choice enjoys the support of an articulate elite, most of whom send or have sent their children to private schools. Part of the answer also is that the advocates have used their control of the presidency, the Republican party, and some business groups to wage a skillful and persistent campaign for choice as a basic right. But more important, the increasing support for private school choice seems based on three widespread concerns that have profound implications for the nation's willingness and capacity to be a society in which differences—real or perceived—are accommodated and resolved in accord with democratic values.

First, many Americans appear to be alienated from government and politics. They do not trust public officials and government cannot seem to get things done about anything remotely complicated. Not surprisingly, the single most influential argument for maximizing school choice asserts that democratic politics is *the* reason to support vouchers. Second, the world—

life in general—seems to have become increasingly less predictable. The streets are less safe, relationships between the sexes are more strained, and the prospects of economic well-being are much less certain. What happened to the time when obeying the law, working hard, and minding your own business resulted in the good life for you and a better one for your children? Third, there are more people in America who seem to speak another language and have values, habits, and skin color that are different from our own.

Having one of these concerns would be threatening enough. When all three bother us, it is not surprising that we want to find a way to get control over the events and situations that seem to put us and our children at risk. What more reasonable and sure way to regain some certainty in one's life than to be able to choose where one's children go to school and who their classmates and friends are and to "know" that the values and beliefs taught in that school are those to which you subscribe?

## THE SEGREGATION OF EDUCATION AND NATIONAL VULNERABILITY

The idea that school choice can provide us control over our private lives, that it can shelter our children from the chaos and complexities of modern society, is an illusion. Indeed, *the* critical issue society must face is how to arm children intellectually and morally so that they can solve complex problems that require collaboration with persons different from themselves and cope calmly with uncertainty. The furor over the quality of our schools was fueled a decade ago by the realization that we needed to reach standards of academic performance throughout the entire country that we had never reached before. It would be ironic if the consequence of this furor is to retreat from complexity and opportunities to learn from our diversity and to privatize educational policy so that the possibility of pursuing the development of the nation's human resources is left to goodwill and the workings of a market that is fundamentally flawed. If we decide to pursue the false promise of privatizing education, the nation will be increasingly divided and, therefore, at risk economically, socially, and politically.

### Notes

1   H. M. Levin, "The Theory of Choice Applied to Education" in *The Theory of Choice and Control in American Education, Vol. 1*, ed. W. H. Clune and J. F. Witte (New York: Falmer Press 1990).

2   C. V. Schultz, *The Public Use of Private Interest* (Washington, D.C.: Brookings Institution, 1977).

3   U. S. Department of Education, *National Center for Education, 1994* (Washington, D.C.: Author, 1994).

# After Forty Years: The Other Half of the Puzzle

JOHN A. MURPHY
*Charlotte-Mecklenburg Schools*

*Although many school districts are finally integrated, integration alone has not had the anticipated effect on minority academic performance promised by* Brown *over forty years ago. Years of adjusting school attendance areas and busing have not had the desired effect on minority achievement. I discuss the positive effects that raising minority student expectations coupled with aggressive educational strategies have had on minority academic performance in Charlotte-Mecklenburg Schools. I also suggest the necessity of shifting the burden of societal integration from schools alone to the community at large.*

*Brown* v. *Board of Education of Topeka, Kansas,* was a major turning point in American education. It clearly signaled that our nation would no longer tolerate second-rate education for minority students. School systems wrestled with ways of moving students from one school building to another—moving them to achieve the "ideal" ratio—while, at the same time, *assuming* that the performance of minority youngsters would improve. Well—the assumptions were wrong. In many cases, we achieved the correct mix of students by race but *never* saw the hoped-for improvements in achievement.

After a few years of being on this "treadmill" (or perhaps more appropriately, on this "freeway"), most of us have come to realize that integrating only by the numbers does not work. The number and percentage game is fair neither to students nor to our greater society. By now, I think that most of us realize that (1) integrating schools by numbers without raising our expectations for the performance of minority youngsters will not change the nature of educational outcomes for most; (2) teaching higher-level classes to one group, while others are taught in competency-level classes, is unforgivable; and (3) expecting one group of students to achieve less because of problems that they have *outside* of school is an excuse for inaction *inside* of the school.

Given this perspective, there are two points that I would like to make: first, that the achievement of black students can be dramatically improved in a variety of settings if we are willing to change the ways in which we do business, and second, that we need to initiate a new call for our business and community institutions to become actively involved in the issue of school integration.

## THE FIRST POINT: IMPROVING THE EDUCATIONAL OUTCOMES FOR BLACK STUDENTS

I have had personal experience with this issue in Charlotte-Mecklenburg, the site of the important and ground-breaking *Swann* decision.[1] This decision required full school system integration and, to its credit, the Charlotte-Mecklenburg community took it to heart. Specifically, the school system instituted procedures that resulted in numerical compliance with the court decree; it created a system that showed the rest of the nation that integrated schools could be created without destroying the social or economic fabric of the community; and it created a school system of which the community can be justifiably proud.

But—the question has to be asked—was the integration of school buildings the "end" in and of itself, or was there some other key purpose to be served? Of course, although integration by itself is a highly valued condition, it must be accompanied by high expectations and effective education for all students. Its ultimate purpose should be to create situations in which children of different races and ethnicities attend school together and learn to the same extent and at the same rate. Anything less than this as the ultimate goal is totally unacceptable.

When I arrived in Charlotte-Mecklenburg in 1991, the very first thing that I did was to analyze the state of education for all of the system's children. In those earliest days, I was not interested in knowing how much money was spent, or what the conditions of the textbooks were, or what future plans there were for new schools. My sole focus was to figure out "who was learning what" and to determine if there were any disparities in that learning. (I want to remind you that by 1991, *Swann* had been institutionalized and an elaborate system to integrate the schools was in place including paired schools, schools with satellites of students who were bused from far away, a few magnet schools, and schools with ever-changing boundaries to respond to demographic shifts.)

The results of this review were both shocking and eye-opening. The average performance of black students in Charlotte-Mecklenburg was dismal. It was equally dismal for the students in the few schools that were still predominantly black and for those that were, by any standard, integrated. The fact of the matter was that attitudes and practices that were characteristic of black segregated schools in our past remained in most of our schools and classrooms, no matter what the degree of integration. The course of action was clear—in the context of integrated schools, we had to find a way to improve the quality of education for all of our students.

Before I tell you what we did to address this problem, I want you to understand the nature of the results that we achieved in only three years—results that prove, once and for all, that given sufficient flexibility, the right attitudes, and effective practices, we can achieve the dual goal of integration and effective education for all. As you consider these gains, consider that they (1) represented a reversal of past trends, (2) were achieved in only two to three years, and (3) still leave us with "a way to go" before complete equity of educational outcomes is achieved.

I am now going to briefly review our data concerning the academic achievement of black students in each of five areas. Please understand that I am doing this in summary form and therefore may have a tendency to underestimate the significance of the changes.

## AREA 1: SCHOLASTIC APTITUDE TEST (SAT) SCORES

From 1991 to 1993, SAT scores for black students rose 32 points (from 711 to an all-time high of 743). Note that this was accomplished *without a reduction* in the number of black test takers. In fact, 22 percent of all of our test takers are black, compared with only 11 percent nationwide.

In 1992, Charlotte-Mecklenburg black students outscored black students nationwide for the first time (742 in CMS and 737 nationally).

The gap between black and white scores decreased from 202 in 1991 to 193 in 1993 even though white scores increased during this time period.

## AREA 2: ADVANCED PLACEMENT (AP) COURSES AND PERFORMANCE

Enrollments in AP courses by black students increased from 84 in the 1990–1991 school year to 376 in the 1993–1994 school year, a 348 percent increase (during the same period, white enrollments increased 198 percent).

The number of black students taking AP exams increased from 28 in 1991 to 86 in 1993, a 207 percent increase.

The number of AP exams "passed" by black students (score of 3 or higher) increased from 14 in 1991 to 42 in 1993, a 200 percent increase.

AREA 3: PARTICIPATION IN HIGHER-LEVEL CLASSES

In 1992, 9 percent of courses taken by black high school students were higher-level, compared with 25 percent in 1994, a 168 percent increase (during the same period, white enrollments increased 100 percent).

In 1992, 25 percent of black secondary school students were enrolled in foreign language courses, compared with 37 percent in 1994, a 50 percent increase (during the same period, white enrollments increased 26 percent).

In 1992, 38 percent of black seventh-graders were enrolled in pre-Algebra, compared with 56 percent in 1994, a 48 percent increase (during the same period, white enrollments increased 6 percent). In terms of academic performance, these students are performing quite well.

In just one year (from 1992 to 1993) the percentage of black students who stated an intent to go on to higher education increased from 75 percent to 78 percent.

AREA 4: INDICATORS OF DISCIPLINE AND BEHAVIOR

Retentions are down (from 12 percent of black students recommended for grade retention in 1991 to 11 percent in 1993).

Suspensions are down (from 38 percent of black students in 1991 to 24 percent in 1993).

Fewer students are dropping out (from 12 percent of black students in 1991 to 11 percent in 1993).

AREA 5: INDICATORS OF EARLY READINESS

In 1993, 57 percent of all black first-graders were ready for second grade in reading, up from 51 percent in 1992.

In 1993, 51 percent of black second-graders were ready for third grade in reading, up from 42 percent in 1992.

Given these early but significant indicators of improvement, the question now is how this was accomplished.

First, we addressed the needs of all students in every facet of our operations.

We developed performance standards that define what every student should know and be able to do at every grade and in every subject.

The same standards apply to all children. There are *no* exceptions except in the case of severe handicaps.

We established a public accountability system that did not allow us to hide behind our failures. Included in this information are school-by-school report cards that include disaggregated data, by race.

Second, we gave extra attention to students with traditionally lower achievement.

We created a schoolwide bonus program in which teachers and others receive a financial bonus if the entire school meets a set of academic goals that are established at the beginning of the school year. It is important to note that for each school we establish separate goals for black and white students, and meeting the academic goals for black students requires that they learn "at a faster rate" than other students. This is the only way that the "gap" will ever be closed.

We eliminated lower-level and "fluff" courses from the curriculum and replaced them with more demanding courses.

We developed a set of criterion-referenced tests (CRTs) that are administered several times a year and provide teachers with early warning signs that students are having difficulties. Building principals and others have been trained to assists teachers in adjusting their instruction based on the results of these tests.

We eliminated the use of IQ tests—tests that had been used to identify and assign black students to long-term, low-level ability groups.

We allowed and encouraged schools to use staff and time flexibly in ways that increase the direct instructional time for students who are farther behind.

Third, we provided specific programmatic support for each of the outcome measures.

For the SAT:

We administered the Preliminary Scholastic Aptitude Test (PSAT) to all ninth- and tenth-graders at system/state expense and used the results to assist students in selecting appropriate coursework.

We provided in-service training to teachers, administrators, and counselors on preparing for the PSAT/SAT and analyzing and using the results.

We involved parents and students in learning from, and acting on, PSAT results.

For the Advanced Placement tests:

We provided additional training to over 100 teachers in AP course content and instructional strategies.

We added AP courses at every high school.

We provided financial support to students, when needed, for taking AP exams.

We moved the AP examination sites from one central location to each high school, eliminating transportation problems.

We collaborated with the College Board on adding Pacesetter Math/English to course offerings at pilot sites.

For the Higher-level courses:

We eliminated lower-level "fluff" courses.

We added the International Baccalaureate (IB) program to three high schools, three middle schools, and two elementary schools.

We added foreign language offerings.

We added staff development on teaching higher-level thinking skills.

We provided additional pre-algebra summer staff-development programs for teachers with a practical lab site for students for those with the lowest entry-level achievement.

For First- and Second-grade Readiness:

We implemented an assessment process that identifies critical skills areas.

We initiated literacy projects in those schools with the lowest reading performance—including a literacy specialist for each school and intensive in-service work.

We expanded school media center offerings.

We increased staff development for all teachers and made it school-based.

We distributed brochures entitled *CMS Performance Standards* to parents at each grade level as a means of familiarizing them with what their children should be taught and should learn.

Fourth, we involved the entire community in understanding and addressing the needs of our black students.

I meet regularly with black and other clergy in the community to share concerns and ideas for action.

We have involved all facets of our community in the development and monitoring of *The Charlotte Legacy*, our five-year plan of action for achieving excellence in our schools, and will continue to do so.

Our school board has passed a resolution strongly commiting us to integration.

Although we have a long way to go to achieve our ultimate goal of absolute equality of outcomes by race and ethnicity, we are convinced that we know how to get there. You will note that the strategies described above are designed to elevate the entire system with a special focus on those who are not yet competitive. Focusing merely on the equality of outcomes will just not work. Truly eliminating the gap between white and black students requires that the quality of education be elevated for all. It requires that school staffs understand that children who enter their classrooms "behind" in their studies require special services—not remedial services, but accelerated services. This, in turn, requires basic changes in the ways in which our schools and classrooms are run and organized. Embedding these and similar strategies in schools that are also integrated will represent the best case for all. Once again, one without the other is not nearly as powerful, or even acceptable, as the two combined.

I would like to address this point a bit further. Recently, a study was released that claimed that experiences with the Milliken II Programs reveal that they were not successful.[2] Without getting into what I believe was more of an editorial position than a solid piece of research, there is positive evidence that extremely significant outcomes have been achieved in Milliken II Schools. Before going to Charlotte, I was superintendent in Prince George's County, Maryland. In Prince George's we had a very aggressive and successful Milliken program. We used a variety of strategies—several similar to the ones noted above—and the results were striking. For example, between 1984 and 1989 standardized test scores increased for nearly every school in the system. Countywide averages increased from the fifty-ninth to the seventy-fifth percentile; the gap between black and white third-graders closed from 26 to 16 points. The Milliken average, once in the mid-forties, rose to within four percentile points of the systemwide average for all students. The Milliken fifth-grade student scores also increased significantly.

The issue is clearly not which particular integration strategy works (schools that are naturally integrated or integrated via assigned busing, magnetization, or some other strategy, or in court-approved nonintegrated settings such as the Milliken model). We know that the best solution will ultimately include several of these approaches. However, no matter what the strategy, it must be characterized by special efforts to elevate the quality of education for *all* students.

## THE SECOND POINT: INVOLVING OTHERS IN THE INTEGRATION ISSUE

We must all recognize the fact that what has been seen as school system policies must be redefined as problems that require communitywide solutions. School districts can continue to move students around with buses, but school systems cannot create policies and practices that determine where they live. As noted by Douglas Massey and Nancy Denton at the University of Chicago, "segregated schools, like high rates of unemployment and minority crime, are the result of white, black, and brown neighborhoods." They continue, "Residential segregation is the institutional apparatus that supports other racially discriminatory processes and binds them into a coherent, uniquely effective system of racial subordination."[3]

School systems can only react to these neighborhood patterns. It will take the full force and commitment of all parties in a community to change those patterns. In the meantime, it would be helpful if our university colleagues and other social commentators could spend more of their energies on finding ways to make this happen, rather than on studying the relative impacts of alternative student assignment strategies on achievement, strategies that in and of themselves are isolated from the academic achievement.

## SUMMARY

Until now, the burden of integrating schools has been placed on the courts and on local school systems. In truth, all remedies have the characteristics of compensatory mechanisms—compensating for a lack of integrated housing in our communities. And, as demographics continue to shift, schools will be expected to compensate more and more by adjusting school boundaries and attendance rules. It is absolutely appropriate for school systems to play this role in the short run. But in the long run all citizens and institutions must assume much more responsibility for creating the kinds of communities in which compensating for a lack of integration will no longer be necessary.

### Notes

1   Swann v. Charlotte-Mecklenburg Board of Education, 4902 U.S. I 1971.
2   Milliken v. Bradley (II), 433 U.S. 267 1977.
3   Douglas Massey and Nancy Denton, interview 1994.

# The Promise of Accountability and Standards in the Achievement of Equal Educational Opportunity

EDMUND W. GORDON

*City College of New York and College Entrance Examination Board*

*The recent history of development in accountability in a variety of educational settings is discussed. Focus is on the national standards for educational achievement and the complexity of the problems in setting those standards. Among these complexities are issues that flow from the facts of diversity in the populations served by these institutions, and pluralism in the standards students must meet. In response to the considerable confusion around much of the policy planning as concerns these issues, emphasis is given to definitional clarity relative to constructs like diversity, pluralism, and equity. Attention is called to the ways in which chauvinism and communicentric bias may compromise the development and implementation of equitable systems of educational assessment that may also be universally applied.*

The modern history of accountability in education dates back to the early 1980s with the Chief State School Officers' efforts to come to agreement on a few key indicators of the quality of educational productivity in the public school sector. The focus was on reading, math, writing, and attendance. This modern history was preceded by modest efforts at the turn of the century and slightly before mid-century by some of the discipline-based associations and accrediting groups to specify minimal offerings in elementary and secondary schools. These earlier efforts at standardizing the curriculum also included efforts by the College Entrance Examination Board and the College Testing Service to standardize the process of and standards for admission to college. These efforts had important implications for educational standard setting, but explicit attention given to standards for educational achievement in the United States is a late-twentieth-century development.

In a related effort, the then U.S. Office of Education in the mid-sixties developed the National Assessment of Educational Progress (NAEP) under the leadership of then Commissioner Francis Keppel. Ralph Tyler was asked to provide leadership in the development of an assessment system that could enable the nation to determine what American students know and know how to do. Although this was a major assessment effort, the determination of criteria or standards for such a system was required. NAEP has emerged as the nation's principal source of information concerning the extent to which elementary and secondary schools are producing educational achievements related to patterns of such achievement in other nations.

In 1990, the chancellor of the New York City public schools issued what were, perhaps, the nation's first minimum standards for elementary and secondary schools. These standards, recommended by a blue ribbon commission, were directed at levels of productivity for the schools of the city. The standards specified attendance rates, number of school disturbances, percentages of students passing specific achievement tests, and percentage of students passing the New York State Regents' Examinations. In addition to these outcomes, the standards also provided that schools were to be held to progress standards applied to students in the bottom achievement percentiles. For those students whose achievement was lowest, schools were to be required to demonstrate specified annual gains, even if the standards for achievement were not met. Individual schools were to be held accountable for meeting these standards. The report of the commission was prophetic in that it called for greater attention to be given to symmetry between student outcomes and staff/school inputs (opportunity to learn), to the specification of the quality of course content, and to the improvement of the instruments and procedures of assessment. This work in New York City was driven by a concern for student, school, and staff accountability.

The developments in New York City were followed by the movement within the council of governors of the nation's states to build a national agenda for school reform, with assessment and accountability at its center. Major initiatives were begun in the states of Arkansas, California, Kentucky, Maryland, South Carolina, and Vermont. Declaring himself the "Education President," George Bush seized the education issue with his Education 2000, the enunciation of five goals for the nation's schools, and for a brief while focused on a national educational achievement test as the centerpiece of his initiative. National standards and a national education test were expected to drive upward the quality of educational achievement in this country. It never became clear whether the expectation was that the standards would model and challenge schools to greater productivity, or that low results from a national test would threaten embarrassment sufficient to push schools to higher levels of achievement. What was clear was that the "Education President's" agenda for education did not include more money, only greater accountability.

Thus much of the modern accountability movement has been about the specification of expectations and standards for improvement in the educational achievement of students. Little national attention has been given to specifications for or the actual improvement of the capabilities of schools and their staffs. Almost as an anticipation that these efforts would not work, the so-called choice movement emerged. The advocates of choice appear to have concluded that the public sector simply cannot serve adequately the education requirements of the society. Their solution is to privatize schooling. If their pessimism were justified, privatization is one possible solution. However, we know that excellent education can be provided through the public sector. We also know some of the problems that privatization produces for the human services. Health care comes to mind. Here we have a national capacity for quality health care that is, perhaps, unmatched in the world. Yet our delivery of such care, filtered through an essentially private system, is hardly competitive with that of some Third World nations. In such a climate, it is interesting and somewhat discouraging that the movement toward standards should be focused so sharply on the productivity of students and not on the quality of the system by which academic achievement is enabled.

In the current educational reform movement, attention has been focused on the establishment of higher standards for educational achievement, and improved instruments and procedures for educational assessment. The New York State Council on Curriculum and Assessment is an atypical example of this movement. The council has been charged with responsibility for making recommendations directed at strengthening the curriculum of elementary and secondary schools in the state, and improving the system by which educational achievement is assessed. General concern has been expressed for ensuring that our new and higher standards are universal, that is, that they apply to all of our students and that they be equitable, in the sense that the imposition of these standards not treat unfairly any of our students, and especially those students with whom our schools have traditionally been less than successful.

Movement in support of higher standards and effort directed at improved assessment have proceeded at a faster rate and with greater clarity than has concern for the provision of sufficient opportunities to learn, and the enablement of equity in educational assessment procedures. Yet any realistic examination of the demographic trends in the nation reveals that the goals of educational reform cannot be achieved without real progress in the achievement of a higher degree of equity in the educational productivity of our state and nation. It is thus for practical as well as moral reasons that our curriculum and assessment review and reform must take seriously a commitment to equity.

The current debate concerning the appropriateness of a set of national standards for educational achievement in the United States has been cou-

pled with a renewed debate concerning the utility of standardized testing
(a) in the monitoring of educational progress and (b) as a basis for cre-
dentialing for a wide variety of purposes. Unfortunately, for those of us
who prefer to deal with simple problems, this one is complex beyond measure. Yet the work of the national standards–setting efforts cannot proceed
far without the serious engagement of these complex issues.

One source for this complexity is the ubiquitous distortions that flow
from classism, nationalism, racism, sexism, and other forms of chauvinism
in our society. These distortions have been traditionally thought to be
unrelated to the processes of education and educational assessment. This
is because the tendency has been to focus on the impact of racism or sexism on the persons who are the targeted victims of such communicentric
biases rather than on the social processes and institutions that reflect those
biases. But all of us and all segments of our society are victims or possible
victims. The distortions and otherwise negative fallouts have an impact on
practically all that we seek to do. Nowhere is this more obvious than in our
efforts to educate diverse populations effectively and to assess educational
needs and outcomes in people whose life conditions, experiences, and values differ from those that have achieved hegemony in the society.

It is to the credit of many of the recent efforts at reform in education
and the education measurement community that several of us have
agreed to try to engage seriously the possible implications of diversity in
human characteristics for more adequate and hopefully more equitable
systems of education and assessment. Implicitly, we seem to have agreed
to try to make teaching, learning, and assessment procedures more
authentic with respect to what we know about learning and human competence, as well as with respect to the educationally relevant characteristics of the various populations whose members must be educated and
assessed. The concern with pedagogy has concentrated on the establishment of higher standards for all students and the diversification of
approaches to the achievement of these standards. The concern with
authentic measures has focused on the development of assessment probes
that require performance—that is, that the respondent do things to
demonstrate competence and understanding as in solving problems or
explaining relationships. However, this shift to higher achievement standards and from more static measures of ability to performance measures
of developed competence may not be sufficiently responsive to the diversity in populations served by our schools. Our concern for authentic and
effective reform also requires that we recognize that the members of these
various populations live their lives in multiple contexts, and that authenticity may vary not only with population characteristics but also with these
varied contexts. Thus, in modern societies authenticity requires that com-

petence be achieved and measured by multiple criteria met by the same person functioning in multiple contexts. This is readily seen in relation to languages, where those of us who are monolingual are increasingly disadvantaged in a multilingual world, or in relation to cultures where we often fail to understand people who see and react to the world in ways that differ from the culture each of us happens to know.

This sensitivity to diversity and pluralism has not been reflected in our concern with universal standards of achievement. Increasingly we hear the assertion that all children can learn at high levels of achievement, but we hear little of the call for a guarantee of adequate and appropriate opportunities to learn. Rather, such claims are actively resisted in some circles. There are some who are sympathetic to high standards and rigorous assessment, but insist that it is immoral to begin by measuring outcomes before we have seriously engaged the equitable and sufficient distribution of inputs, that is, opportunities and resources essential to the development of intellect and competence.

The development of such opportunities and the making available of such resources may require a higher level of understanding of the dimensions of the problems with which we are faced. Toward that end, some clarification of the relevant constructs may be helpful.

*Diversity in human characteristics* refers to differences in position or status and differences in function. *Status* defines one's position in a social hierarchy and that status or position often determines one's access to sociopolitical power and material resources. Status influences access to opportunities and rewards. It influences how other people treat you, what others expect of you, and too often what one expects of oneself. Traditionally, differential status has been assigned based on social class and caste, ethnicity and race, gender and sex, language and national origin, and a host of other less prominent social dividers. Diversity in *functional* characteristics refers to the how of behavior, the manner in which behavior is manifested, the way people act. These functional characteristics may be colloquially associated with certain status groups, but the manner of behavior is not invariably associated with status. We include among functional characteristics such traits as culture, cognitive style, temperament, interest, identity, and motivation.

*Pluralism* refers to the social demand for the demonstration of multiple, concurrent competencies in situationally relevant contexts. We recognize pluralistic demands most readily with respect to cultures and languages. Those who are bilingually and multilingually competent have clear advantages over us poor monolingual folk in our rapidly shrinking world. Too many of us are fighting, chauvinistically, against it, but what thinking person fails to recognize the importance of multicultural competence and multiperspectivist thought? Pluralism implies the recognition of diverse routes to the mastery of both universal and population-specific standards.

*Equity* speaks and refers to fairness and social justice. It is to be distinguished from equality, which references sameness and the absence of discrimination. Rawls eloquently reminds us that one of the fundamental tenets of social justice is unequal distribution that favors the weaker members of the society.[1] In societies of unequal members, equal distribution is not equitable. Equity requires that the distribution of resources be sufficient to the condition that is being treated. If I need penicillin and you need tetracycline, and the hospital gives us both penicillin, you may be treated equally, but it certainly cannot be claimed that you have been treated equitably. Or if I need three doses and you need one of the same medicine, and we are both given one dose, I would be treated equally, but I would also have been deprived of what is sufficient to my need and thus treated inequitably.

It is becoming more and more obvious that these sources of variance in human populations influence:

1.  the motivation to engage academic learning and to master its content;

2.  opportunities to learn and be reinforced by academic competence and literacy;

3.  the conditions in and under which knowledge and skills are learned, and attitudes and dispositions are developed; and

4.  the nature of the processes by which academic attitudes, dispositions, knowledges, and competencies are assessed.

Thus it can be argued that one of the most complex problems with which we are faced as we generate educational standards and improve educational assessment in the interest of greater accountability in education is this problem of the concurrent honoring of diversity, pluralism, and equity. The challenge is to arrive at, and enable students to meet, standards that are *high, plural, universal,* and *equitable,* and to hold all of us—students, staff, and systems alike—accountable for doing so.

*Support for the preparation of this article was provided by the College Entrance Examination Board through an arrangement between the board and the Institute for Research on the African Diaspora in the Americas and the Caribbean at the City College of New York. The opinions expressed, however, are those of the author and are not to be understood as the official position of either institution.*

## Note

1    John Rawls, *A Theory of Justice* (London: Oxford University Press, 1973).

# Fulfilling the Promise of *Brown*

JUDITH A. WINSTON
*U.S. Department of Education*

*This article summarizes the U.S. Department of Education's efforts to promote deseg-regation in order to implement the mandate of* Brown v. Board of Education of Topeka, Kansas, *and the Civil Rights Act of 1964. The article describes the depart-ment's use of traditional tools in enforcing civil rights laws, including the provision of technical assistance and policy guidance to states and educational institutions on topics such as minority scholarships and racial harassment. The article also provides an overview of the new strategies the department is pursuing to promote high-quality education and equal educational opportunity and diversity in all schools.*

Commemorating the landmark *Brown* v. *Board of Education of Topeka, Kansas,* decision is particularly important to me, because I have spent my professional career in public service as an advocate for, and defender of, racial equality and equal opportunities for all.[1]

I want to share with you some thoughts about the U.S. Department of Edu-cation's activities over the years to promote equal educational opportunity and equity through desegregation and other vehicles, and to discuss what we have learned about the evolving face of desegregation and where we need to go to make equal educational opportunity and equity a reality for all.

## HIGHLIGHTS OF THE DEPARTMENT OF EDUCATION'S ACTIVITIES TO PROMOTE DESEGREGATION OF PUBLIC SCHOOLS

The enactment of the Civil Rights Act of 1964 provided the federal govern-ment with the statutory authority to protect the civil rights of students through technical assistance, administrative enforcement procedures, and federal or state court litigation.[2] It also provided protection against dis-crimination based on race, color, or national origin by tying federal fund-ing to antidiscrimination policies and practices. Additionally, it authorized the then commissioner of education at the old Department of Health, Edu-cation, and Welfare (HEW) to provide both technical and financial assis-tance to deal with problems incident to desegregation of public schools. Since that time, the department has been awarding millions of dollars every year to state and local governments and desegregation assistance centers through the Title IV desegregation assistance program established by the Civil Rights Act.[3] However, I do not mean to imply that this funding has been even nearly adequate to address the need.

The department's Office for Civil Rights (OCR) has also engaged in enforcement of Title VI of the Civil Rights Act, through the investigation of complaints of discrimination in, and compliance reviews of, programs or activities in educational institutions.[4] Enforcement has engaged the department in litigation, the promulgation of regulations and guidelines, and the provision of technical assistance to recipients of federal financial assistance. Indeed, it was guidance from OCR with respect to educational opportunities for limited-English-speaking children that formed the basis for the ruling by the Supreme Court in *Lau* v. *Nichols*—an example of how the department's activities have had a profound effect on the law.[5]

Congress increased support for desegregation in the early seventies in response to the urgent need to provide federal assistance to desegregating school districts. From 1972 through 1981, the department supported school desegregation efforts through the Emergency School Aid Act (ESAA). ESAA was designed to (1) meet the special needs incident to the elimination of minority-group segregation among students and faculty in elementary and secondary schools, (2) encourage the voluntary elimination, reduction, or prevention of minority-group isolation, and (3) aid school children in overcoming the educational disadvantages of minority group isolation.[6]

ESAA was expanded in 1976 to include support for planning and implementing magnet schools. However, the ESAA program was repealed in 1981, and support for desegregation was folded into the Chapter 2 block grant program.[7] This dramatically *decreased* the federal financial assistance available for school districts engaged in desegregation activities. In response to the repeal of ESAA, Congress enacted the Magnet Schools Assistance Program in 1984.[8] The Magnet Schools program provides financial support for magnet schools that are part of an approved desegregation plan, either a plan ordered by a court or agency or a plan voluntarily adopted by a local school board. A magnet school offers a special curriculum that is capable of attracting students of different racial backgrounds. Since its enactment, the department has provided over $700 million to school districts across the country under this program.

## WHAT WE HAVE LEARNED IN ATTEMPTING TO PROMOTE DESEGREGATION

We in the department recognize that the primary strategies developed to address desegregation have evolved over time—from almost a single-minded focus on the physical movement of students to a more comprehensive approach that includes the enhancement of educational opportunities for students in desegregated schools *and* for those who remain in racially isolated settings. Throughout this evolution, the department has used the tools available to it—enforcement of Title VI and the administration of targeted funding programs such as the Title IV Emergency School Aid Act, and Magnet Schools programs—to effect positive changes. However, over the years the capacity and willingness of the department, as well as its authority to act, have been limited by political expediency, public resistance, and legislative and judicial initiatives—or, more accurately speaking, deterrents.

Even when operating effectively, the tools available to the department are not sufficient to address the ever-increasing challenges to quality public education in desegregated settings, most notably the increase of children living in poverty, changing demographics (much of it related to white flight), particularly in urban communities, and changing housing patterns. We all know too well the disparities that exist in our educational system for rich and poor children, children of color and white children, children in urban communities and children in the suburbs. There is no simple solution to eliminating these disparities. Many of the factors that perpetuate them are outside the control of any one government agency and cannot be addressed solely through strategies directed at, or undertaken by, the public schools, state education agencies, or the federal government. To move effectively toward comprehensive solutions, we must recommit to the effective use of traditional strategies and tools, and to the creative and thoughtful development of new comprehensive strategies that involve coordination and partnerships among various federal agencies, state and local governments, and the private sector.

As a first step in understanding how the department intends to proceed, I would like to describe how we intend to utilize what I have called the traditional tools available to the department to achieve equal educational opportunity.

## STEP ONE: USE OF TRADITIONAL TOOLS

The department is committed to carrying out, more vigorously, its traditional role in enforcing civil rights laws. The enforcement role will be supplemented through the provision of technical assistance to states, local governments, and other recipients of department funds in their efforts to promote desegregation, equal access, and full participation in high-quality educational programs.

Recently, in the area of civil rights enforcement, the department has published several notices providing guidance to educational institutions on issues ranging from minority scholarships to racial harassment. In January

1994, OCR published a notice outlining how it will apply the Supreme Court's 1992 decision in *U.S.* v. *Fordice* to the public higher education systems in the southern and border states.[9] In *Fordice*, the Court held that states may not simply adopt race-neutral policies as a remedy for correcting a previously segregated higher education system. Rather, states have an affirmative duty to eliminate all vestiges of the *de jure* segregated system. The notice emphasized that (1) the standard announced in *Fordice* comported with the department's policy under its "Revised Criteria Specifying the Ingredients of Acceptable Plans to Desegregate State Systems of Higher Education" requiring that the vestiges of prior segregation be eliminated systemwide[10] and (2) the department would not allow states to place a disproportionate burden on black students or traditionally black institutions during the desegregation process. The notice also reiterated that the Supreme Court based its decision in *Fordice* on the precedent established in *Brown* and its progeny.[11]

In February 1994, OCR published final policy guidance on minority scholarships.[12] The notice specifies how colleges can use minority-targeted financial assistance to remedy the effects of discrimination and to promote campus diversity. The guidance furthers the integration and diversity principles of *Brown* by recognizing that diversity objectives provide a compelling rationale supporting race and national origin–targeted financial aid. Recently, the department, in conjunction with the Department of Justice, filed an appellate *amicus* brief in *Podberesky* v. *Kirwan*, a case involving a challenge to a scholarship program targeted to African-American students.[13] We argued to the court of appeals that the district court judge had been correct in ruling that the University of Maryland could use scholarships designated only for black students as a tool to dismantle the vestiges of Maryland's formerly *de jure* segregated system.[14] Finally, in March 1994, OCR published investigative guidance regarding racial incidents and harassment at educational institutions.[15] The guidance outlines the procedures and analyses that OCR will use when investigating possible violations of Title VI based on incidents of racial harassment. It was published to apprise schools and students of the legal standards governing their rights and responsibilities. OCR will be working to ensure that schools are not allowed to become racially hostile environments so that the integration and diversity principles of *Brown* can be fulfilled.

During the next three years OCR plans to devote substantial time and resources to conducting compliance reviews in addition to investigating complaints. These compliance reviews will address issues that continue to be very important concerning the desegregation of elementary and secondary schools and higher education institutions, access to programs for limited-English-proficient students, and gender equity in athletics. OCR also plans to target "second-generation" issues in its compliance reviews concerning overrepresentation of minorities in lower-track classes and special education programs, underrepresentation of minorities and women and girls in math and science and high-achievement programs, testing and assessment practices, and racial and sexual harassment.

Thus, through its civil rights enforcement activities and its administration of targeted funding programs, the department will continue its historical—though often interrupted and sometimes less than vigorous—efforts:

1.  to achieve desegregation at all education levels;
2.  to eliminate within-school segregation, that is, placement of minority children in lower tracks, including special education, and the exclusion of minorities from higher achievement level courses;
3.  to ensure that diversity goals of *Brown* are met after integration, by encouraging affirmative recruitment efforts and seeking to eliminate racially hostile environments;
4.  to expand the guarantees of equal protection of the laws specified in *Brown* to limited-English-proficient students and to women and girls; and
5.  to provide funding, technical assistance, and training in the areas of race, sex, and national-origin discrimination.

## STEP TWO: NEW STRATEGIES TO PROVIDE A HIGH-QUALITY EDUCATION FOR ALL STUDENTS

The second prong of our efforts to realize the promise of *Brown* focuses on new education initiatives emerging from Congress and within the Clinton Education Department under the leadership of Secretary Richard Riley. Before I elaborate on this second prong, a few words about the *Brown* decision are in order. When we think about the *Brown* decision, we sometimes forget that there were two decisions: *Brown I*, where the Court in 1954 pronounced that constitutional imperatives could not be met by a separate but equal formulation, and *Brown II*, where the Court in 1955 focused on guidelines for the lower courts to use in fashioning remedies with "all deliberate speed."[16] *Brown I* speaks of the importance of education in our society as the "foundation of good citizenship" and as "a principal instrument in awakening the child to cultural values, in preparing him for later professional training, and in helping him to adjust normally to his environment."[17] The Court in the *Brown* decisions recognized that a state that has undertaken to provide education must provide it as a right to all children on equal terms. We read these principles from the *Brown* decisions as a clarion call for a high-quality education for *all* children, one that includes as a fundamental prerequisite to quality an appreciation of the diversity that makes up our American culture. In the context of today's America, that means that we must ensure that all of our nation's children, from the many races and ethnic groups that make up America, have a realistic opportunity to achieve high standards *wherever* they are.

In the past, the principles of *Brown I* were submerged into the strategic goals of *Brown II* remedies. Our ability to pursue the promise of *Brown I* was seen to depend solely on the extent to which the physical movement of students was possible, that is, busing and student reassignment strategies. Thus, in 1972, when President Nixon's pursuit of a southern strategy had the effect of reducing the number of federal resources available to black plaintiffs pursuing the implementation of court-ordered desegregation, *equality of educational opportunity* was said to be essentially stymied. However, what was stymied was our ability to place more students in desegregated educational settings—albeit an important and significant factor in the achievement of equal educational opportunity.

The remedial strategies of *Brown II* were all but abandoned during the Nixon era. Federal education officials were prohibited from providing technical assistance in drafting desegregation plans. Title IV–funded desegregation centers had to demonstrate that the state or public school system board of education invited their participation in local desegregation efforts—invitations that were not readily forthcoming.

In 1969, the Justice Department, with the support of the Department of HEW, for the first time since *Brown I* opposed counsel for black plaintiffs before the Supreme Court in *Alexander* v. *Holmes*, a school desegregation case in which the plaintiffs sought to require thirty-three Mississippi school districts to adopt desegregation plans.[18]

During the mid to late 1970s, renewed impetus was given to the pursuit of desegregation strategies when the Emergency School Aid Act made funds available to support some desegregation activities. In addition, in the latter part of the 1970s, litigation efforts to achieve equal educational opportunity were centered on defining when segregated northern and western school systems were obligated to desegregate and the circumstances under which voluntary desegregation could be pursued in the face of resistance. Plans that could achieve incremental desegregation of schools without extensive transportation were favored and pursued, although white flight from many of our urban areas made it difficult. Indeed, Congress passed the Eagleton-Biden Amendment, which prevented OCR from requiring busing as a remedy, and the Esch Amendment, which effectively prevented the Department of Justice from seeking—and courts from ordering—busing as a remedy under Title VI by limiting that remedy to constitutional violations.[19] Again, equal educational opportunity as a guiding principle of *Brown I* was submerged within a physical movement remedial strategy.

During the 1980s, many people began to recognize that, because racial balance and student movement had become the singular focus of the *Brown* strategy, there was little or no attention being paid to equalizing educational opportunity beyond the bus ride. There was also growing discontent among black families and intense hostility among both black and white parents and students to transportation decrees, especially where the opportunity for significant desegregation in the face of growing white flight was remote—and black students were disproportionately burdened. Additionally, the 1980s was another period of retrenchment during which the enforcement of the civil rights laws by the executive branch was lackluster.

Accordingly, the tools available to pursue the remedial mandate of *Brown II* were much more limited as we approached the 1990s and the promise and principles of *Brown I* were essentially relegated to a holding pattern as the concept of equal educational opportunity was made synonymous with the reassignment of students. Do not misunderstand my meaning here. We must continue to use the tools available to us at the federal level to desegregate schools and provide high-quality education in a racially and culturally diverse setting. But the concept of equal educational opportunity must be pursued in *all* of the schools where children are today. We cannot afford a "one-burner" philosophy, ignoring the opportunity to provide quality education to the extent possible until diversity is achieved.

We cannot postpone the opportunity to educate *all* children to high standards while we are strengthening our resolve and seeking additional resources to coordinate the multilayered efforts that will transform schools into the culturally and racially diverse schools envisioned and promised by *Brown*. As the federal government's primary voice on education, the department has the obligation to develop the vision for what a quality education should be and a strategy for realizing that vision across the entire spectrum of American schools. We then must identify those aspects of the strategy that can be addressed most effectively by the federal government, recognizing that we alone cannot reform education.

The Goals 2000: Educate America Act, which President Clinton signed into law on March 31, 1994, and the department's other efforts to promote school reform have begun. The focus of Goals 2000 is voluntary systemic and comprehensive reform. It makes strong demands for students to meet high standards, to learn challenging subject matter, and to be tested to find out whether they have learned what children ought to know to succeed in our global economy. It is designed to establish, for the first time, a national vision of educational excellence, which would be realized and put into practice by partnerships with local communities. In essence, Goals 2000 endorses the National Education Goals and not only establishes the National Education Goals Panel but also creates a means to set voluntary national standards and assessments that allow us to compare what our students are learning and doing with what students learn and do in other developed nations. The assessments and assessment systems adopted to measure the degree to which the standards are met must be reliable and valid measures of their intended purpose. They will have to be fair in assessing knowledge of skill levels of all students regardless of the race, gender, ethnicity, and language proficiency and must provide for the participation of all students with diverse learning needs.

Furthermore, federal funds must be leveraged to encourage states and local communities to design strategies that: (a) improve curriculum and instruction; (b) create assessments that tell us whether students are successfully meeting the standards; (c) prepare teachers and principals to deliver challenging content; (d) increase parental and family support; (e) restructure schools; and (f) provide real opportunities for students to move from school to work and/or to college.

The systemic reform envisioned under Goals 2000 will encourage actions by school districts, institutions of higher education, and other recipients of federal funds to address the needs of all students and teachers, including those with special needs. Accordingly, as companion legislation to the Goals 2000 Act, the administration has introduced and the House has passed, as part of the reauthorization of the elementary and secondary education programs, an amendment to one of the department's administrative statutes, the General Education Provisions Act, or GEPA, designed to promote and require equity for students, teachers, and other program beneficiaries. Under the proposed GEPA provision, an application for departmental funds must include a description of the steps that will be taken to overcome barriers to participation in the program, including barriers that are based on race, color, national origin, sex, age, or disability. Our intent is to focus early on the barriers to equitable participation so that we will all work together to avoid or reduce costly civil rights compliance proceedings that may arise after federal funds have been spent. We think that the present and future costs of these barriers to society and to economic progress in the United States far outweigh the efforts that applicants would have to make to comply with this new provision. Our hope is that, in this way, we increase the likelihood that the National Education Goals will be achieved by all students and that all students will be provided every opportunity to achieve high standards.

## CONCLUSION

In *Brown I* Chief Justice Warren said, "It is doubtful that any child may reasonably be expected to succeed in life if he [or she] is denied the opportunity for an education."[20] These words are no less true today than when they were written forty years ago. I would add that an education, in the fullest sense of *Brown*, includes an appreciation of people from a variety of backgrounds and viewpoints.

Today we face what seem to be insurmountable odds in striving to provide a high-quality public education for our children. In addition to the disparity of resources among school systems, we also have children who come to school hungry, and children and teachers fearful of random violence in schools. It is, therefore, especially important for us to heed the message of *Brown*: that a quality education "is a right which must be made available to all [children] on equal terms."[21] We have learned that just moving children to different schools is an important but not a sufficient strategy if the education they receive at the end of the bus ride will not prepare them for a competitive world, or to be good citizens, or to have an appreciation for people unlike themselves. The children left behind in racial isolation also need an education to prepare them for these challenges and opportunities. Recognizing the evolving face of our schools, we must implement a range of strategies to promote high-quality education and diversity that are tailored to the needs of our children in all of the education settings where we find them.

## Notes

1   Brown v. Board of Education of Topeka (Brown I), 347 U.S. 483 (1954).

2   42 U.S.C. 2000a *et seq* (1964).

3   42 U.S.C. 2000c (1964).

4   42 U.S.C. 2000d (1964).

5   Lau v. Nichols, 414 U.S. 563 (1974) (holding that failure to provide English-language instruction to non-English speaking students denies them a "meaningful opportunity to participate" in public education). The Supreme Court cited HEW regulation 35 Fed. Reg. 11595 (May 25, 1970) in support of this decision.

6   20 U.S.C. 3192 (1972).

7   20 U.S.C. 3831 (1981).

8   20 U.S.C. 3021-3032 (1984).

9   "Notice of Application of Supreme Court Decision," 59 *Fed. Reg.* 4271 (January 31, 1994); and U.S. v. Fordice, 112 S.Ct. 2727 (1992).

10   "Revised Criteria Specifying the Ingredients of Acceptable Plans to Desegregate State Systems of Higher Education," 43 *Fed. Reg.* 6658 (February 12, 1978).

11   States with expired desegregation plans that OCR is now reviewing are Texas, Maryland, Florida, Virginia, Kentucky, and Pennsylvania.

12   "Nondiscrimination in Federally Assisted Programs," 36 *Fed. Reg.* 8756 (February 23, 1994).

13   Podberesky v. Kirwan, 38 F.3d 147 (4th Cir. 1994), vacating 838 F. Supp. 1075 (D. Md. 1993) (holding that race-based merit scholarship program that considered only African-American students could not withstand strict scrutiny under equal protection analysis), *reh'g en banc denied*, 1994 U.S. App. LEXIS 37083, at *1 (4th Cir. Dec. 10, 1994).

14   See Podberesky v. Kirwan, 838 F. Supp. 1075 (D. Md. 1993) (holding that University of Maryland's race-based merit scholarship program was necessary to remedy past discrimi-

nation against African-Americans and that program served "compelling governmental interest" and was "narrowly tailored" to withstand strict scrutiny analysis).

15  "Racial Incidents and Harassment against Students: Investigative Guidance," 59 *Fed. Reg.* 11448 (March 10, 1994).

16  Brown v. Board of Education of Topeka (Brown II), 349 U.S. 294 (1955).

17  Brown I, 347 U.S. at 493.

18  Alexander v. Holmes, 396 U.S. 19 (1969).

19  Eagleton-Bidon Amendment, P.L. 95–205, 91 Stat. 1460 (December 9, 1977); Esch Amendment, 20 U.S.C. 1702, 1714 (1975).

20  Brown I, 347 U.S. at 493.

21  Id.

# Educational Equity Issues in an Information Age

DENNIS SAYERS
*New York University*

*Equity in access to educational resources faces new challenges in our age of rapid technological change, threatening to produce a society of information "haves" and "have-nots" through schools where disparity in access to educational technology is already glaring. These challenges occur at a time when efforts toward the privatization of the "information superhighway" and of public schools themselves have dominated the discourses on public policy. An alternative direction is proposed for equity of access to* global learning networks *as a catalyst for genuine educational reform that preserves the legacies of* Brown *v.* Board of Education of Topeka, Kansas, *and* Lau *v.* Nichols.

Forty years ago, *Brown* v. *Board of Education of Topeka, Kansas,* affirmed the principle of equity of access to educational resources. Twenty years later the *Lau* v. *Nichols* decision laid the groundwork for equity of access to educational resources and instruction appropriate to language-minority students' learning needs.[1] I will argue that threats to these decisions are arising on a new and, for many, unfamiliar terrain, an arena where important decisions likely to affect all educators, parents, students, and concerned citizenry—and especially those concerned with minority and language-minority education—are now being made daily. Worse, these irreversible decisions are largely going unquestioned. They involve access to computer networking and telecommunications.

For readers of the print mass media in every industrialized country, the rumblings surrounding the construction of the "information superhighway" have been fairly constant over the last few years. Generally, the popular press either (a) heralds the advent of the Internet or (b) discusses maneuvers by the communications industry to control access to—and take tolls on—activity conducted over international computer networks. Key examples include the special number of the *Nation* ominously entitled "The 'Information Highway'—Who will control it?" and the *Wall Street Journal* special section, "Wired," a twenty-eight page insert, with ordering information for accompanying disks, and including articles with such headings as "Chasing the Gold."[2]

It is clear that we are witnessing the same scramble for gatekeeping rights over a powerful communications technology that is similar in scope and import to the introduction of telegraphy, the telephone, radio, motion pictures, or television; indeed, since this technology promises to dwarf and subsume all these previous communications technologies, the stakes are quite high and the bidders numerous. Most disturbing of all, the present administration in Washington is auctioning off segments of the information bandwidth to the highest corporate bidders, selling for a "quick fix" of billions of dollars what is essentially an irreplaceable commodity that will garner trillions of dollars in profits for corporations in perpetuity.[2] Meanwhile, discussion of safeguarding the free access of educators to what amounts to a national natural resource is notably absent, and hastens the day when schools, like society at large, will be delineated as "information haves" and "have-nots."

In her review of recent research on computer equity issues, Delia Neuman discusses not only computers but also "teleconferencing, interactive television, electronic mail, and expanded telecommunications networks," and warns that

> despite the promise of emerging technology, it is important to remember that technology and equity are not inevitable partners. . . . The literature on computer equity reveals that many students—not only minority, disadvantaged, and inner-city but also female, handicapped, and rural—have been hampered by inequitable access to computers and by widespread patterns of inequitable distribution and use of computers within and across schools.[3]

How technology is used and who gets to use it are realities that tend to conform to the broader pedagogical orientations that prevail within schools. Put another way, schools as they are presently constituted show a remarkable ability to conduct business as usual—with or without computers, and whether networked or not.

The gaps between the technological haves and have-nots are glaring. While an increasing number of computers are being placed in schools, early surveys reported wealthy districts with a 54:1 student-computer ratio while poor ones had a ratio of 73:1, and more recent surveys show this pattern persisting.[4] Female students and those from low-income and ethnic and linguistic minorities tend not to have the same access to computers as do their male, middle-income, nonminority counterparts.[5] Generally, the more exciting programs are reserved for students in the upper tracks; when lower-track and minority students do get access, they are much more likely to be assigned to drill-and-practice rather than to problem-solving activities.[6] In recent years, high-level administrators of school districts with many "at-risk" students—that is, with large numbers of culturally diverse students from immigrant and racial and ethnic minority backgrounds— have been targeted for the marketing of "computer-managed instructional systems" that dispense programmed lessons throughout each specially wired school. Here "learning" consists of pressing the keys "a," "b," "c," or "d" in response to cartoon graphics and robotlike voices.[7]

I want to make clear that my position advocating equity of access to computers and networking resources is not one that champions the curative powers of technology as the remedy for all that ails today's schools. The unalloyed boosterism of many uncritical advocates of educational technology is all too commonplace. Virtually all popular writing on the place of computers and telecommuncations in education, including magazines and journals that target educators as their principal readership, are full of untested assumptions, void of research backing or any theoretical discussion based on modern learning theories, touting the unquestioned virtues of classroom computers as machines that can be programmed to teach students, thus "freeing up" educators to do more important work than mere teaching.

Rather, I wish to signal the danger to the legacy of *Brown* and *Lau* posed by a second group of educational technology advocates who collectively advance what I view as disturbing proposals that attack the very basis of public-funded education. These proposals fall into two categories: (a) those that link high-tech classrooms with the conservative campaign to promote "school choice" through student vouchers, that is, vouchers with a cash value that can be "spent" by parents in the public or private school of their choice, thus eroding public funding for many already desperately underfunded schools; and (b) privatization schemes in which profit-taking corporations are invited to take over the running of schools or, more recently, entire school districts.

Chris Whittle, chairman of Whittle Communications, illustrates both of these tendencies. As Jonathan Kozol details in a *Nation* article entitled "Whittle and the Privateers," Whittle has racked up an impressive string of achievements that all point in the direction of privatizing and commercializing education.[8] Described by the *New York Times* as "the impresario of captive-audience marketing," Whittle has found a huge public-school audience for his commercial television programming effort, Channel One. More than 8 million students—fully a third of all junior and senior high students in the United States, in 12,000 schools located in 47 states—are required to watch twelve minutes of commercial television while attending compulsory public-funded education, a captive audience, indeed![9] While educators everywhere are debating the benefits of a longer school day and increasing the days in the school calendar, schools that sign up with Channel One are dedicating what amounts to an entire school day each year to requiring students to watch commercials.

Whittle has created this massive captive audience by making schools an offer—with important strings attached—that many cannot resist. In return for the installation of a satellite dish on the school's roof wired to a "free" television monitor installed together with two VCRs in each classroom, a school must agree to require 90 percent of its students to watch the shows first thing in the morning 90 percent of the time. Whittle can afford to make such a generous offer, considering that Channel One brings in $630,000 a day in advertising fees. In fact, his is not such a generous offer as it may appear at first blush: All equipment is leased, and can be confiscated if used for any but Channel One programming.[10] But many schools, strapped for human and material resources, have a hard time just saying no.

What kind of schools sign up with Whittle Communications? A study conducted by Michael Morgan of the University of Massachusetts–Amherst has found that urban schools with middle-to-high concentrations of minority and culturally diverse students were more likely to require their students to watch the Whittle Educational Network programming.

> Channel One is most often found in schools with the largest proportions of low income, underprivileged students, and in schools that have the least amount of money to spend on conventional educational resources. Ironically, these schools have more high-tech equipment, in no small part due to Whittle Communications' own contributions, but they invest substantially less in teachers, texts, or other instructional materials. The relationship between spending on texts or other instructional resources and accepting Channel One is especially striking: Channel One is apparently used instead of traditional materials when resources are scarcest. Schools that can afford to spend more on their students are much less likely to utilize Channel One.[11]

These often are the same school systems, as noted previously, whose superintendents are targeted for direct sales of expensive computer-managed instructional systems, another technological quick fix.

Just as troubling as Channel One is the Edison Project, Whittle's next venture into technology-mediated education. The Edison Project first proposed a chain of 1,000 technology-intensive private schools, but financing woes at Whittle Communication have forced a shift in focus to securing contracts to run public schools instead. Each private school, Kozol wrote, was to have

> charge[d] tuition of $5,500—roughly the same as the national average spent per pupil in the public schools. In order to cut costs, Whittle proposes saving on teacher salaries by using volunteers, classroom

aides and computerized instruction, and he proposes using the students themselves to do some of the work of school custodians.[12]

Even though Whittle abandoned his plans in 1993 to build a chain of private schools as too-rapid expansion led to loss of confidence from his financial backers, it is important to understand how his original proposal contained the seeds of a "taxpayers' revolt" against public education. Kozol warned in 1992:

> Once a handful of Whittle's schools exist—and, with the corporate funds he has available, the first schools he opens are likely to be dazzling creations—they may well be exploited as a further selling point for vouchers. Parents, he says, who already "pay tax dollars" for the public schools, "are going to have to make a decision about whether they want to pay twice." Whittle undoubtedly hopes that the parents of the children he enrolls—and the favorable press he orchestrates—will generate a national demand for the diversion of tax money into private education.[13]

However, after $60 million invested in research and development, the Edison Project has yet to open the first of its initially projected one thousand private schools. Trying to make do with less, Whittle turned to the public-school sector in an effort to lower the costs of educating each pupil in the Edison Project from $5,500 by using taxpayer-financed schools as its "plant," while still requiring public schools to ante up $3,000 per pupil for the Edison Project's technology-intensive curriculum. Yet not a single contract has been negotiated with a public school system.[14] However, Whittle's competitor in the public-school privatization market, John Golle of Educational Alternatives, Inc. (EAI), has succeeded where Whittle has faltered. Since 1991, Golle's company, again relying heavily on educational technology to keep payroll costs down, has managed single public schools for a profit in a dozen communities around the country, and in 1992 landed a contract with the Baltimore Public Schools to run nine schools. Golle hit the privatization jackpot in another eastern city, convincing the school board of Hartford, Connecticut, to turn over all of its thirty-two schools to EAI's control, beginning with the 1994–1995 school year.[15]

Whittle, Golle, and others have many conservative allies in this technology-intensive effort to undermine public-funded education. The board of directors of the Edison Project is headed by Benno Schmidt, former president of Yale University, and includes Chester Finn, former Bush and Reagan appointee to numerous posts, and John Chubb, a principal proponent of school vouchers. Diane Ravitch, former assistant secretary of education in the Bush administration, has written an article in the *Economist* devoted entirely to the implications of the "information superhighway" for the future of education. In the high technology of the future, with 500 cable channels available and vast networked computer resources, she asks:

> Will it matter if state systems [of public-funded schools] are replaced by something else? . . . In future, the state "system" is likely to be different. Instead of a programme of publicly funded schools administered uniformly by a bureaucracy, it is likely to become a mechanism for allocating public money to improve and promote education, which will take place in variety of institutions and settings. . . . Some schools will be adjacent to the workplace, so that parents and children can go to work and go home together. Others may be administered by religious organizations or universities. Some will have private boards of trustees, much as colleges and other quasi-public agencies. All may be part of the reconfigured state system, in which the state establishes performance standards (on such matters as health, safety and quality) and provides basic financial support.[16]

Ravitch's vision of privatized yet publicly subsidized schools is based on the economies of scale achieved by reducing the numbers and constricting the role of teachers in face-to-face interaction with students through extensive use of educational technology, viewed as machines for delivering programmed—that is, prepackaged—instruction.

## BRAVE NEW SCHOOLS: ANOTHER VISION

Jim Cummins and I have attempted to outline an alternative direction for genuine educational reform that, we assert, responds to the global realities of an interdependent world in the twenty-first century.[17] In *Brave New Schools*, we are proposing, as a fundamental catalyst for widespread educational renewal, the adoption on the broadest possible scale of *global learning networks*, that is, long-distance intercultural team-teaching partnerships that seek to take advantage of accessible and culturally appropriate educational and communications technology. We argue that such partnerships can promote academic development across a broad spectrum of content and skill areas including literacy skills development, critical thinking, and creative problem solving in domains such as science and social studies, citizenship and global education, and second-language learning.[18]

When we talk of long-distance intercultural teaching partnerships or global learning networks, we are acutely aware that differences in language and cultural experience can themselves create enormous "distances," and not only across continents and oceans or between regions and countries; there are also enormous cultural distances to be bridged within a particular country (and often within a single community) between racial, ethnic, and other immigrant or national minority groups. The diverse cultural enclaves that comprise a single urban center like Chicago, Los Angeles, Miami, Montreal, New York, or Toronto may live under the same sky but look out on very different horizons. In contrast to neoconservative academics who view the increase in cultural diversity as a threat to social cohesion and an occasion for hand-wringing over the loss of a "golden age," we propose to embrace the conjunction of diversity and technological innovation as an opportunity for unprecedented educational development that can benefit all students.

International trends towards greater population mobility and increased global interdependence, both economically and politically, highlight the need to develop more effective ways of promoting intercultural cooperation and understanding in our education systems. In order to foster interdependence and cooperation we need global education programs that will prepare students to function in multilingual/multicultural contexts both nationally and internationally. The best preparation for effective international cooperation in the future is clearly direct experience of cooperative learning activities—ideally involving students from other cultures—in the present.

If educators at every level—elementary, secondary, and tertiary—do not seek common cause in the effort to demand equal access to communications and computing resources, we will in fact have squandered whatever potential computer networking may hold for creating, nourishing, and sustaining the genuine learning communities so desperately needed if we are to confront the social, cultural, economic, and ecological challenges of the coming years—that is, the sort of learning communities that have deep local roots in the community as well as an extensive global reach. Instead, the information "haves" will retain or strengthen their ability to shape technological innovations to their own advantage, and the "have-nots," when not completely excluded from access to technology, will be more often manipulated by computers and computer networking than in control of these powerful technologies. The legacy of *Brown* v. *Board of Education* and *Lau* v. *Nichols* will have been irreparably vitiated.

## Notes

1   Lau v. Nichols, 414 U.S. 563.

2   See especially Herbert Schiller, "The 'Information Superhighway:' Public Way or Private Road?," *Nation* 257 (July 12, 1993): 64–66; and in the same issue, Leo Bogart, "Present Laws Are Outmoded: "Shaping a New Media Policy," pp. 57–60; and Kevin Cooke and Dan Lehrer, "The Internet: The Whole World Is Talking," pp. 60–64; and John J. Keller, "Net Assets: There's Nothing Virtual about the Money Being Made by Those Providing On-line Services," *Wall Street Journal,* November 15, 1993, p. R20.

3   Delia Neuman, "Technology and Equity," *ERIC/IR Digest* EDO-IR-91-8. (1991): (ERIC Number ED339400).

4   John Hood et al., "Microcomputers in Schools, 1984–85: A Comprehensive Survey and Analysis," (May 1985) (ERIC number ED 265 822); and Henry J. Becker, *How Computers Are Used in United States Schools: Basic Data from the 1989 I.E.A. Computers in Education Survey* (Baltimore, MD: Johns Hopkins University, Center for Social Organization of Schools, 1990), p. 20.

5   Elisabeth Gerver, "Computers and Gender," in *Computer in the Human Context: Information Technology, Productivity and People,* ed. Tom Forester (Cambridge: Massachusetts Institute of Technology Press, 1990), pp. 481–501.

6   Henry J. Becker, "Using Computers for Instruction," *BYTE* 12 (February 1987): 149–62 (ERIC number EJ 349 598).

7   Dennis Sayers, " 'Computer Literacy' vs. Computer Networking: Equity Issues for Bilingual Education," *NABE News* 17 (March 15, 1994): 14, 20, 36, 45.

8   Jonathan Kozol, "Whittle and the Privateers," *Nation* 255 (September 21, 1992): 272, 274, 276–78.

9   Kozol, "Whittle and the Privateers," p. 272; and *New York Times,* July 30, 1993, pp. D1, 4.

10   Michael Apple, *Official Knowledge: Democratic Education in a Conservative Age* (New York: Routledge & Kegan Paul, 1993).

11   Michael Morgan, *Channel One in the Public Schools: Widening the Gaps* (Washington, DC: Unplug, 1993).

12   Kozol, "Whittle and the Privateers," p. 274.

13   Ibid., p. 276.

14   *New York Times,* January 19, 1994, pp. D1, 15.

15   *Education Week,* August 3, 1994, pp. 1, 19.

16   Diane Ravitch, "When School Comes to You: The Coming Transformation of Education and Its Underside," *The Economist* 328 (1993): 43–44, 49.

17   Jim Cummins and Dennis Sayers, "Education 2001: Learning Networks and Educational Reform," *Computers and the Schools* (special issues on Language Minority Students and Computers, ed. Christian Faltis and Robert DeVillar) 7, nos. 1 and 2: 1–29.

18   Jim Cummins and Dennis Sayers, *Brave New Schools: Challenging Cultural Illiteracy through Global Learning Networks* (New York: St. Martin's Press, forthcoming).

# *Brown* and *Lau:* Seeking the Common Ground

ROSA CASTRO FEINBERG

*Florida International University*

*This article includes a brief description of commonalities between* Brown *and* Lau *compliance efforts and outcomes, an analysis of those outcomes, and some recommendations for advocacy and policy strategies for the next decade that take into account that analysis. The recommendations include techniques that may help reduce residential segregation, desegregation on the basis of socioeconomic status, reduction of tracking, funding initiatives, support of family-friendly policies, and greater involvement in the political process on the part of academics and civil rights advocates.*

## COMMONALITIES IN IMPLEMENTATION

Both race and national-origin school desegregation efforts are based on court decisions, and on the legislation and regulations developed to implement those court decisions. The primary enablers include Title VI of the Civil Right Act of 1964, the May 1970 HEW Memorandum, and the Equal Educational Opportunities Act of 1974.[1] Title VI prohibits discrimination or exclusion from benefits on the ground of race, color, or national origin. The 1970 Memorandum prohibits denial of access to participation in school programs because of language; segregation by tracking, ability grouping, and assignment to special education; and exclusion of parents from school information. The Equal Educational Opportunities Act prohibits state action that denies equal educational opportunity to any individual. These provisions were developed to support the requirements of *Brown* v. *Board of Education of Topeka, Kansas*, and its progeny, and of *Lau* v. *Nichols* and related cases.[2]

Initial race desegregation efforts focused on physical features of school life such as movement of students and school facilities, and subsequently moved to consideration of curriculum and educational reform. National-origin desegregation reversed the process.

## COMMONALITIES IN OUTCOMES

According to Liebman's analysis presented in the *Virginia Law Review*, the results of school desegregation have been positive.[3] The life chances of blacks have been improved, substantial positive effects on achievement have been noted, and white flight may have decreased rather than increased as a result of desegregation plans.

According to Orfield, director of the Harvard Project on School Desegregation, school segregation is increasing. The proportion of black students in 50 percent or more minority schools has reached the level that existed before 1971, and Latino students are far more likely than African-American students to be in predominantly minority schools. Furthermore, "segregation by race was very likely to mean segregation by poverty. . . . If poverty is systematically linked to educational inequality, as it consistently is in educational research, the very powerful link between racial and poverty segregation is a central element in perpetuating the educational inequality of minority students".[4] According to Lee, writing for the American Council on Education, college participation and retention rates of minority and poor students reflect this same pattern of inequality.[5]

## ANALYSIS OF OUTCOMES

Present strategies promote school desegregation, which has had its intended beneficial results, but segregation is increasing nonetheless. The present set of strategies is necessary, and should be augmented (as Orfield suggests[6]) through revitalized enforcement, technical assistance, and research efforts, but a review of outcomes leads to the conclusion that present strategies are not sufficient.

Recent action taken by a large southern school system in a gateway city illustrates the limitations of the current status for both racial and national-origin minority students. A contingency plan for the anticipated arrival of large numbers of refugees, most likely from Haiti and or Cuba, was approved by the school board on June 22, 1994.[7] The plan called for leasing commercial space in which to establish Orientation Centers for the newcomers. The rationale for the plan cited the need to focus resources in order to meet the special educational and linguistic needs of the new students, who would then be better served in the separate location than in the regular schools of the overcrowded system. In actuality, however, nothing in the plan offered benefits or services beyond that which the system is already providing to language-minority students in the regular schools, by virtue of a statewide consent decree (which requires services to limited-English-proficient students, including specially trained teachers, English-language instruction, understandable instruction in the content areas, and individual education plans that take into consideration previous academic achievement)[8] and of the provisions of a Memorandum of Understanding entered into with the Regional Office for Civil Rights in 1976.

It was estimated that up to 20,000 national-origin and racial-minority students might be placed in ethnically isolated and identifiable alternate school facilities, segregated from the rest of the school system and its children, for up to a year, with no discernible educational justification. Only one board member voted against this plan, calling for either voluntary participation and an expanded level of services beyond that available in the home schools to be directed to the newcomers in alternative facilities, or the sharing of leased commercial space with all students, new and old. Two day's later, the *Miami Herald*, the area's major newspaper, gave its editorial approval to the plan by deeming it fair because it is temporary, and because it avoids disruption of existing schools and programs. In a district with a court-ordered desegregation plan, thirty years of experienced success in incorporating refugees via placement in home school settings, a majority-minority population, and enviable status as a pioneer in bilingual education, such a plan was approved with barely a murmur of protest.

Our common problems as advocates for racial and national-origin minority students are revealed as we consider the situation of politically and economically helpless refugee (primarily African-origin, Haitian and Cuban) students slated for exile to alternative facilities. We are all in the same boat, and it sometimes seems to be sinking.

## ADVOCACY AND STRATEGY POLICIES FOR THE NEXT DECADE

It appears that we have to add to our present set of strategies in order to reach our goals. Pamela Barnhouse Walters reminds us that education is a politically determined good, and that political regimes serve the interests of some groups better than others.[9] The best served are not generally the groups at the bottom of the economic hierarchy. As Herbert Kohl puts it in his discussion of educational restructuring, approaches differ "according to the values and educational preferences of people with the power to make changes."[10] The proposed supplementary strategy, therefore, is for us, the members of the civil rights, academic, and advocate communities, to become the people with the power to make changes, to become the school board members, commissioners, and state representatives who make the rules, establish the policies, and appropriate the funds needed to enable schools to be successful in educating minority students. Proposed elements in the platform of such candidates are described in the following sections.

### RESIDENTIAL DESEGREGATION

Elected officials who choose to could, for example, cause school systems to collaborate with other agencies to help bring about greater residential desegregation. A system of graduated impact fees, for example, could be developed to encourage the creation of planned desegregated housing developments. Reductions in property taxes could be planned to encourage home ownership by families with children in multiethnic neighborhoods.

Grandparent/caretaker areas could be established, again with tax incentives for multiethnic communities. Foster home placements could favor multiethnic placements. Adoption agencies could insist that prospective parents live in integrated communities. The fees and taxes paid when homes are sold could be altered to favor residential diversity in race, ethnicity, and class. Government agencies and civic-minded private sector employers could favor applicants for employment who live in desegregated settings within the county. Utility providers could provide a discount for all residents of mixed neighborhoods. University tuition could reflect the same type of discount. Chamber of Commerce members (particularly those who do business with government agencies) could be persuaded to offer discounts on their services along the same lines. Federal income tax incentives could serve the same purpose. The benefit of such measures to school desegregation is obvious. An additional benefit would be the equalization of residence neighborhood opportunities. "Since neighborhoods appear to impart considerable advantages and disadvantages to children growing up in them, we need to view neighborhoods as a potent source of unequal opportunity."[11]

## DESEGREGATION BY SOCIOECONOMIC STATUS

Similarly, elected officials could legislatively raise to priority status plans to develop pupil-assignment plans on the basis of socioeconomic class (such a plan is in operation in LaCrosse, Wisconsin), as advocated by Julius Menacker. After analysis of 1988–1989 student test data from the Chicago public schools, he concluded that "student income level, irrespective of race/ethnic distribution, is the critical variable to be addressed in student assignment policy in urban school systems that are increasingly characterized by minority-group populations."[12] Income inequality among children is greater now than at any time since the 1950s, and the potential for accelerated differentiation is greater now than at any time in recent history.[13]

The effects of current and or persistent poverty are correlated not only with low educational achievement, but also with mental health problems, poor nutrition, exposure to hazardous environments, and exposure to violent crime or criminal victimization.[14] In addition, severe poverty is positively associated with lethal violence (homicide and suicide) rates.[15]

## UNTRACKING

Similarly, elected officials, particularly school board members, could establish policies that reduce or change the structure of tracking procedures, a form of within-school segregation. The perpetuation of social inequality through school tracking mechanisms has been amply described.[16] It seems clear that participation in the higher tracks leads to higher achievement status. Additional analysis of longitudinal data from Israeli students shows that tracking can also affect measured levels of verbal intelligence.[17]

Hugh Mehan describes the San Diego Public Schools Advancement Via Individual Determination (AVID) Program, developed by the district in response to a court-ordered desegregation plan that brought minority students from predominantly minority schools to Clarement High School, a predominantly white school. AVID's goal is to prepare students for college. To reach this goal, selected students from the minority schools are placed into regular college-prep classes and provided support and counseling services. Minority and low-income students who participated in the program for three years enrolled in four-year colleges at rates that compared favorably with district and national enrollment rates. The success of this untracking program has led to its replication by sixty-four other schools in San Diego County and by eighty-four schools in other school areas. Policymakers would do well to import such an innovation into their own districts.[18]

### FUNDING

Policy goals and funding guidelines could be established that recognize the high cost involved in developing programs designed to help *all* students meet the standards set by the widespread adoption by state education agencies of competency standards and Education 2000–related education goals. This could be accomplished legislatively, as Clune suggests, or through litigation, as suggested by Liebman.[19] In either case, the result would be recognition of legal rights of the poor.

### FAMILY-FRIENDLY POLICIES

Linguistically and culturally appropriate early childhood programs could be expanded, in conjunction with outreach efforts to enroll parents in adult and vocational education programs. In the case of mothers with no high school diploma, outreach efforts should be linked to access to a job with a future.

Students could be provided opportunities to earn money on a daily or weekly basis as part of school fund-raising activities (50 percent to the student, 50 percent to the school) and entrepreneurial training activities.

Such a program is part of the Dade County Public School Alternative Education TROY Center, operated in cooperation with the Juvenile Justice System. At this recently opened center, students operate and profit from a lunch wagon that serves the office workers in a building next to the school site. This project offers promise of success with high-risk students with delinquency records.

Parental involvement policies could be adopted that accord due priority to efforts to tap the strength of the family in support of the education process. Full-service schools, support of interagency collaboration, community and adult school programs in appropriate languages, and collaborative efforts to improve the economic condition of children and youth would add support to parental involvement goals.

As Burke observed, "though the stage may be the schools, the drama is essentially political."[20] None of these proposals are likely to be implemented in widespread fashion without considerable and continual demand by elected officials with "the power to make changes." That this has *not* happened means that enough of us, the readers of this article and participants in this conference, have not ourselves acquired positions as elected officials. When we do, we must resist the temptation to be sufficiently moderate to hope for reelection. Light your candle your first term, then help your colleague get elected to take your place. After all, change/reform is the goal, not career redirection for midlife educators. I wish you, and the children you serve, God speed and good luck in these endeavors.

## Notes

1    Title VI, Civil Rights Act of 1964 (1964) 20 U.S.C. sec.2000d; J. S. Pottinger, Memorandum to School Districts with More Than Five Percent National Origin-Minority Group Children regarding Identification of Discrimination and Denial of Services on the Basis of National Origin, 35 *Federal Register* 11595, May 1970; and Equal Education Opportunities Act of 1974 (1974) 20 U.S.C.

2    Brown v. Board of Education, 1954, 347 U.S. 483, 74 S.Ct. 686, 98 L.Ed. 873; Brown v. Board of Education, 1955, 349 U.S. 294, 75 S.Ct. 753, 99 L.Ed 1083; Green et al. v. County School Board of New Kent County, Virginia, et al. 1968, 381 US 430, 20 L.Ed. 2nd 716, 88 S.Ct. 1689 [no. 695]; Swann et al. v. Charlotte-Mecklenburg Board of Education et al., 1970, 402 U.S. 1, 26, 91 S.Ct. 1257, 1281, 28 L.Ed.2d, 554; Freeman et al., v. Pitts et al., 1992. 112 S.Ct. 11430; Lau v. Nichols (1974) 414 U.S. 563; Castaneda v. Pickard (1981) 648 F.2d 989 (5th Cir.); Gomez v. Illinois State Board of Education (1987) 811 F.2nd 1030 (7th Cir.); Idaho Migrant Council v. Board of Education (1981) 647 F.2nd 69 (9th Cir.); Keyes v. School District No. 1 (1983) 576 F. Supp. 1503 (D. Colorado); Jose P. v. Ambach (1979) EHLR 3 551: 245 (E.D.N.Y.); and Plyler v. Doe (1982) 457 U.S. 202; See Rosa Castro Feinberg, "Bilingual Education in the United States: A Summary of *Lau* Compliance Requirements," *Journal of Language, Culture and Curriculum* 3 (1990) for more information on Lau-related court mandates; and James L. Liebman, "Implementing *Brown* in the Nineties: Political Reconstruction, Liberal Recollection, and Litigatively Enforced Legislative Reform," *Virginia Law Review* 76 (April 1990): for race desegregation cases.

3    Liebman, "Implementing Brown," p. 336.

4   Gary Orfield, *The Growth of Segregation in American Schools: Changing Patterns of Separation and Poverty since 1968: A Report of the Harvard Project on School Desegregation to the National School Boards Association* (Alexandria, Va.: NSBA/CUBE, 1993), pp. 1–22; quotation on p. 22.

5   V. Lee, *Access to Higher Education: The Experience of Blacks, Hispanics and Low Socio-economic Status Whites* (Washington, D.C.: American Council on Education, 1985).

6   Orfield, *The Growth of Segregation in American Schools*, pp. 24–30.

7   Office of Superintendent of Schools, Refugee Emergency Contingency Plan, Dade County Public School [sic], Revised June 1994.

8   LULAC et al. v. Florida Dept. of Education et al., 90-1913 Civ. Scott (S. D. Fla., Miami Div. Aug. 14, 1990).

9   Pamela Barnhouse Walters, David R. James, and Holly J. McCammon, "Accounting for Racial Inequality in Southern Education: A Reply to Ramirez," *Sociology of Education* 63, (April 1990): 146–48.

10   Herbert Kohl, "Education in a Fix," *Vocational Education Journal*, October 1992, p. 70.

11   Jeanne Brooks-Gunn et al., "Do Neighborhoods Influence Child and Adolescent Development?" *American Journal of Sociology* 99 (September 1993): 385.

12   Julius Menacker, "Equal Educational Opportunity: Is It an Issue of Race or Socioeconomic Status?" *Urban Education* 25 (October 1990): 323.

13   D. T. Lichter and D. J. Eggebeen, "Rich Kids, Poor Kids: Changing Inequality among American Children," *Social Forces*, March 1993, pp. 761–80. See also M. E. Thomas, "Race, Class and Personal Income: An Empirical Test of the Declining Significance of Race Thesis, 1968–88," *Social Problems* 40 (August 1993): 328–42.

14   See Jane D. McLeon and Michael J. Shanahan, "Poverty, Parenting, and Children's Mental Health," *American Sociological Review* 58 (June 1993): 361.

15   Lin Huff-Corzine, Jay Corzine, and David C. Moore, "Deadly Connections: Culture, Poverty, and the Direction of Lethal Violence," *Social Forces* 69 (March 1991): 715.

16   See generally Jeannie Oakes, *Keeping Track: How Schools Structure Inequality* (New Haven: Yale University Press, 1985); and Adam Gamoran and Mark Berends, "The Effects of Stratification in Secondary Schools; Synthesis of Survey and Ethnographic Research," *Review of Educational Research* 57 (1987) 415–35.

17   Yossi Shavit and David L. Featherman, "Schooling, Tracking and Teenage Intelligence," *Sociology of Education* 61 (January 1988): 49.

18   Hugh Mehan, Lea Hubbard, and Irene Villanueva, "Forming Academic Identities: Accommodation without Assimilation among Involuntary Minorities," *Anthropology & Education Quarterly* 25 (1994): 97–98.

19   W. H. Clune, "The Shift from Equity to Adequacy in School Finance," *The World and I* 8 (1993): 389–405; and Liebman, "Implementing Brown."

20   F. G. Burke, "Bilingualism/Biculturalism in American Education: An Adventure in Wonderland," *The Annals of the American Academy of Political and Social Science* 454 (1981): 177.

# Of Promises and Visions:
# *Brown* as a Gift to American Democracy

JOSHUA P. BOGIN

*New York University*

*Two of the highlights of the "Brown Plus Forty" Conference were the general session panel discussions. "The Promise of Brown" and "Visions for the Future." A senior project associate at New York University's Equity Assistance Center and a former senior trial attorney with the U.S. Department of Justice's Civil Rights Division, I moderated one of these panels, and offer both a synthesis of the panelists' " expressed views and my own thoughts on the legacy of the Supreme Court's 1954 opinion, a legacy I see as one of opportunity—not just equal educational opportunity, but opportunity for redemption—for a nation riven from birth by the internal hypocrisy of institutionalized racial discrimination, freed in a way by Brown to try finally to realize our democratic ideals.*

## INTRODUCTION

In the winter of 1959, some of us in the New Rochelle public schools had our big day on what was then known as "Educational TV." Several of the district's elementary schools had been asked to send groups of students to perform, live, from the Channel 11 studio. My third-grade class at Trinity School had a "percussion band," which consisted of about fifteen white kids playing on an assortment of bells, triangles, sticks, and wood blocks to the accompaniment of Tchaikovsky's *Nutcracker Suite*. I was the drummer and cymbals crasher in that rag-tag little band, and while I am sure that several other New Rochelle schools were represented both on the bus taking us down to the New York studio and on the show itself, the only other group I can now remember was the sixth-grade choir from the Lincoln School. Like the sixth-graders at Trinity, they seemed big and loud and scary, but they were different. They were all black. Incidentally, I can distinctly remember that while we white third-graders sat in the front of the bus that took us into New York City, the Lincoln School kids all sat in the back.

At about the same time, my mother became quite active in what came to be known in New Rochelle as "the Lincoln School case," which won some notoriety as the case in which for the first time a federal judge using *Brown*

v. *Board of Education of Topeka, Kansas,* as precedent, ordered a northern school district to racially integrate its schools. I can remember thinking, when the one or two black kids who suddenly started appearing in each of our classes would be introduced, that these were the kids to whom I was supposed to be particularly nice. Still, I knew they were different, I felt the difference, and I was acutely aware that, unlike the basic shyness I experienced with all new friendships, with these kids I simply felt that I did not know how. For a white kid in New Rochelle, my contacts with blacks were relatively extensive. Yet, extensive as those contacts were, I can remember vividly the self-awareness of difference and awkwardness, and I know just how easy it was for all of us—of whatever racial or ethnic stripe—to come away with unformed, fear-driven, enormously magnified visions of people perceived through narrow lenses as different and scary.

*Brown* has been in my thoughts for a long, long time, and as I have recently pondered this great marker in the American experience, I have found that personal reflection, viewed now with the refreshing perspective that history and time permit, offers us some of the most important insights not only as to where we have been, but also as to where we might want to be traveling. In this piece I will attempt to recapitulate the flow of the Brown Plus Forty conference's two general-session panel presentations, "The Promise of *Brown,*" and "Visions for the Future," and to offer my sense of the collective import of our panelists' views, in the light of history, experience, commentary, and personal reflection.[1] I will offer a view of *Brown* as a benchmark of American democracy, as a second—perhaps last—chance for us as a people to live up to and to live out the promises that gave birth to our nation's democratic consciousness.

## *BROWN* AS PROMISE

The Brown Plus Forty conference set out to explore the underpinnings of the Supreme Court opinion, the idea of *Brown* as a promise, and the imperatives for future policy and action aimed at fulfilling any such promise. If *Brown* was a promise, we wanted to know, what was its nature, to what extent has it been fulfilled, and to the extent that work remains to be done to deliver on it, where should we be heading? It is hard to imagine that anyone in this day and age would attempt to deny that the Supreme Court's pronouncement on May 17, 1954, outlawing all state laws mandating racial segregation in public schools constituted some important promise. But, as we found in our "Promise of *Brown*" session, every one of us who has given the subject some thought seems to have a profoundly personalized sense of what it was that was being guaranteed.[2] No seemingly logical groupings can be used to classify these views. Civil rights advocates, for example, still struggle in their efforts to find consensus among themselves concerning the premise for the Court's opinion, with some arguing strenuously that the notion of "stigma" articulated by the Court lent the Court's own imprimatur to the very notions of racial inferiority on which it took dead aim through *Brown.*[3] It was difficult, at our conference, to discern any groupings of participants—whether by professional, racial/ethnic, age, political, or geographical background—whose view of *Brown*'s promise was internally congruent.

One could ponder this lack of consensus and reach the conclusion that *Brown* is all things to all people and therefore ultimately without long-term consequence or meaning.[4] On the other hand, we can—and in my judgment should—view this multiplicity of interpretations not as a lack of consensus, but rather as important information that helps to teach us more about our progress as a society over the past forty years, and about how we might want to take aim on the future.[5] To limit our analysis of the sometimes divergent views offered in our panel discussions to a discourse on which was the "right" take on *Brown*—and therefore to whether the Supreme Court's decision represented *a* promise—simply distracts us from the possibilities offered by the intricacies of our collective individual experiences of the past forty years.

The two panels about which I write were instructive in this regard. It seemed clear to me, for example, as I moderated a panel with three of the most important civil rights lawyers of our time, that while our audience (comprised mostly of educators) was fascinated by the observations of each of our panelists, they felt most connected to the practical concerns expressed by the panel's one nonlawyer (and only woman), Patricia Carey. Carey, herself a black student in a northern elementary school when *Brown* was decided, spoke from the crucible of her own personal experience, recounting what it felt like to be one of two blacks in class and having to listen to her white teacher lead all her white classmates in a regularly performed rendition of "Old Black Joe." That she had the internal wherewithal to substitute the word "white" each time the word "black" came up in the song, and that she had the additional support at home that helped her to transcend the insults that came with growing up black in a white public school system, tells us much about the long-term significance of family expectations and support; her impressions of what integration felt like at a young age are equally instructive. While she paid tribute to the value of integration, she forcefully cautioned us to focus on educational achievement rather than on integration as "an end." Her concern, like that of Kevin Brown and Judge Robert Carter, now fastens itself on making public schools "effective for all children," and on eliminating what she called "the growing sense of hopelessness in public education."[6]

Perhaps Carey's analysis resonated so fully with the participants because it was offered free of (and at times in the face of) the intricate debate that was presented by the panel's distinguished lawyers concerning the Court's underlying premises, and, in effect, the purposes of the *Brown* litigation itself. For example, Brown tangled with Carter, Greenberg, and Landsberg over the Court's approach in *Brown*, contending that by focusing on segregation's long-term deleterious effects *on blacks*, the Court simply reinforced the very notions of racial superiority and inferiority it was being called on to redress. If, as Brown suggests the Court was stating, segregation caused *blacks* to suffer long-term injuries to their hearts and minds, then whites, he argues (particularly those in newly desegregated settings), would simply be inclined to view blacks as wounded and inferior in academic and other life skills. By viewing "separate but equal" through the lens of victimized blacks, Brown argues, the Court avoided the greater issue of our nation's essential system of cultural values, particularly as those values deal (or do not deal) with the issue of race. Carter, Landsberg, and Greenberg rose to the Court's defense, reminding us that the time was 1954, and the Court was being asked by black plaintiffs to outlaw an entrenched, state-sponsored system of education that was at its core designed to minimize the educational opportunities available to black schoolchildren.

This colloquy is representative of a debate that began long before Thurgood Marshall and the Legal Defense Fund (LDF) of the National Association for the Advancement of Colored People (NAACP) initiated the litigation that led to the Supreme Court's landmark ruling. It has its roots in the essential argument between separatists and integrationists, many of whose primary concern has always at heart been the same—as Carey put it, a "sharing of the wealth."[7] The history of post–Civil War race relations is checkered with the ongoing vigor of this debate, shouldered by generations of black leaders in the face of their abandonment by whites, after the Compromise of 1877,[8] to the purgatory of Jim Crow, and by *Plessy* v. *Ferguson* to a second-class status approved by a wink of the U.S. Supreme Court.[9] Whether the debate was waged between Booker T. Washington and W. E. B. Du Bois, Du Bois and Marcus Garvey, Martin Luther King, Jr., and Malcolm X, or Bayard Rustin and Stokely Carmichael, the question has always revolved around the issue of means rather than ends.[10] All of these leaders, irrespective of their particular approach, "struggled for freedom and . . . were caught up in the same web."[11] The question throughout the history of American race relations—explored and tested by separatists and integrationists alike—has remained fundamentally the same: What must be done to free America from what Kenneth Clark has characterized as our "moral schizophrenia," and to guarantee that black Americans shall be incorporated as so many other minority groups have been into the fabric of American life?[12]

Historical context creates needed parameters for any discussion concerning *Brown*'s meaning, its promise, and our responsibilities as we look to the future. Brian Landsberg, speaking on the federal government's role in school desegregation litigation, reminded us that the Justice Department's *amicus* brief in *Brown* was written and filed by the Truman administration, in the aftermath of World War II and in the infant glow of the United Nations. Embarrassed perhaps by the evident hypocrisy of an international stature as a symbol of freedom growing under the long shadow cast by a legally enforced caste system of citizenship at home, the government's brief in *Brown* was built on the premise that "racial discriminations imposed by law inevitably tend to undermine the foundations of a society dedicated to freedom, justice and equality."[13] Jack Greenberg, asked to offer his sense of *Brown*'s promise, was quick to explain that the school desegregation cases were but one important part of a systematic attack against segregation and overt racial discrimination in all walks of American life.[14]

Hugh Price, speaking on the "Visions" panel, echoed Greenberg's observation. *Brown*, he tells us, must be viewed in a larger context, as one part of the civil rights movement as a whole. To the new executive director of the National Urban League, the decision was about "the elimination of segregation, legal segregation, the elimination of the Jim Crow laws, *the lowering of barriers to the American Dream and the leveling of the playing field* so that there could be a natural sorting according to various forms of ability—be it intellectual, financial, or physical—without consideration of color."[15] The debate seems to be joined when *Brown* is viewed as the linchpin of the entire movement, that is, that equal educational opportunities (read, through *Brown*, as integration) must precede blacks' entrance onto the major league playing field, the stage of American democracy.[16]

Carter sees this problem, and carefully navigates his way through it. He agrees in principle with Price, contending that *Brown* was viewed by LDF as necessary to announce the death of legally enforced discrimination, so that blacks could be freed to turn their attentions to their broader entitlements as Americans. Here Carter strikes gold, observing that *Brown*, by stating that official discrimination would no longer be a bulwark of American society, "revolutionized how black people looked at the country."[17]

This, really, is the essence of Thurgood Marshall's legacy, not only to black Americans, but to all of us.[18] Thelma Esteves, a Latina school principal in a highly diverse (both racially and economically) middle school, described her school's performance of *West Side Story*, in which the cast read like a list of delegates to the U.N. General Assembly, and in which the technical crew included as many girls as boys, and several "handicapped children." As a school principal, she sees every day the broad societal benefits we have all reaped from legislation such as the Americans with Disabilities Act, the Education for All Handicapped Children Act, Title IX, and *Lau* v. *Nichols*, and views all of that enabling legislation and precedent—for women, people with disabilities, and students with limited English proficiency—as being rooted in a revolutionary spirit embodied by *Brown*.[19] In effect, she sees *Brown* as a landmark call to arms for all disenfranchised Americans.[20]

A call to arms, of course, is not a promise of what lies ahead. Perhaps the Supreme Court did issue a promise, one that said, simply: "The highest Court in the land will no longer cast a blind eye to the second-rate treatment you suffer *in the name of law.* We shall no longer countenance this travesty of justice, and we will not stand in your way." That said, what was promised for the future? Regardless of how people have come to interpret its words, the Court did not define equal educational opportunity in *Brown*. Nor has it addressed—in *Brown* or any of the other now famous school desegregation opinions issued over the next twenty-five years—whether racially disparate educational outcomes demonstrate or even are evidence of unequal educational opportunity.[21] Carter, in his keynote address to the conference, bemoans the continuing saga of disproportionate minority underachievement in America's public schools. And while he does not fault *Brown*, or even the legal reasoning behind the Court's decision, he is willing to abandon some of the assumptions that have followed in *Brown*'s wake, particularly the assumption that integration itself, for a host of possible reasons, should increase black academic achievement. Not so Robert Crain, a noted expert on the effects of school desegregation, who stated on the "Visions" panel that indeed desegregation has produced quite substantial gains among black public schoolchildren—that between 1970 and 1980, the achievement gap between black and white students, as measured by standardized tests, was reduced by "one-third."[22] Equally insistent on the continued validity of the thesis linking black underachievement to segregation is Kenneth Clark, whose research and testimony on the injurious impact of segregation on black (and white) schoolchildren was a key component of LDF's case at trial and on appeal. "In forty years of work in this field," he told us during one of the planning sessions for the NYU conference, "I have seen nothing to change my conclusions."[23]

Here is where Kevin Brown enters the fray. Whatever the playing field looked like in 1954, he maintains, the landscape has changed, so that in 1994, urban centers are so highly minority concentrated as to defy any practical attempts at desegregation. If accepted universally, Clark's analysis would imply, Brown believes, that inner-city blacks could never improve their academic status, creating an even more insidious stigma, with its imprint ostensibly forever inscribed on this and future generations of urban black schoolchildren.

We have, of course, now come full circle, back to the question of separation or integration, a question that may not lend itself to singular correct answers, no matter how much the two ideas seem to compel mutual exclusion. Derrick Bell, like W. E. B. Du Bois half a century ago, maintains that the struggle requires a variety of strategies.[24] Like Carter, he now regards some of his own early views on school desegregation as naive, a mistaken belief that segregation itself was the evil to be eradicated.[25] He takes issue with school desegregation advocates, such as Jack Greenberg, who argue that no measure of desegregation's impact could be attempted until 1970, when finally, after fifteen years of ceaseless litigation, the Supreme Court abandoned its failed "deliberate-speed" approach for a more immediately measurable "maximum practicable desegregation" standard.[26] Bell believes that Greenberg and his colleagues spent so much time and energy addressing in court the staunch resistance to desegregation that they were diverted from realizing "that you can have continued deprivation and discrimination in a perfectly racially balanced school."[27] Patricia Carey gave it a slightly different tilt: *Brown*, she observed, didn't guarantee "quality of instruction or human sensitivity."[28]

We can see here a continuum of disagreement about the promise of *Brown*, about what has happened to the promise, and about where we should focus present and future energies. Greenberg believes that *Brown* was the first shot in a long war whose next significant battles were won with the Court's termination of the deliberate-speed doctrine. Since that time, he reiterates, we have witnessed "considerable successess," particularly in the South, with blacks who went to integrated schools attending four-year colleges in significantly greater numbers, ending up in better jobs "and making more money than people who haven't."[29] Carter, though he acknowledges some of the successes reaped through desegregation, is acutely troubled by the failure of desegregation to touch the lives of urban blacks, whose continuing failure to enter the American mainstream in large numbers he views as the critical issue facing American society. Bell, for his part, simply views *Brown* as a failure, not because it could not lead to full desegregation of American schools, but because it does not address the issue of unequal power. One of the many suggested theories about *Brown*'s conceptual underpinnings is in fact rooted in concepts of political power: Educational benefits (whether through additional resources or programmatic accountability), the theory goes, necessarily follow political and economic power. Since white parents can be expected to exert dominant political influence on behalf of their own children's education, blacks will reap otherwise unavailable educational opportunities simply by being in the same schools.[30]

But Bell contends that so long as whites will not give up control, a control that pervades attitudes, treatment, and cultural assumptions, perfect

racial balance will bring no gain for blacks.[31] On the other hand, he sees
*Brown* as a useful part of an overall strategy to secure blacks' rightful share
of the levers of power. He would be content, it would seem, if "separate
but equal" could in fact mean equal, and so he is prepared to use whatever tools are at his disposal—including both integration and separation—to gather the equal share to which blacks are entitled. "This neither
represents paradox nor defeat," he maintains, "if we recognize that the
challenge is to keep moving, testing, prodding, always eschewing dogma
or ideology."[32]

## A LOOK FORWARD

From every vantage point the view of *Brown* is different. Was it fundamentally a case about black achievement? Was it fundamentally about entry
into the society, "the leveling," as Price put it, "of the playing field?" Was it
fundamentally about looking into the future and understanding that an
America divided in any meaningful way by race or religion or ethnicity or
caste would cease to be the model that we in the post–World War II era
are determined to show off to the rest of humankind? Was there some
kind of recognition, even back in 1954 among all the white male judges
who ruled on the desegregation cases, that ultimately America would
internally destruct if we as a people could not begin to live as one among
people different from ourselves? Thelma Esteves, in looking to the future,
cited Shakespeare, saying "we have scorched the snake, not killed it."[33] But
what exactly is the snake?

The snake, I would suggest, is a hydra, not a monster with a head and a
body and a tail, but a multiformed, amorphous, ever-changing manifesta-
tion of a fierce virus. The virus attacked the roots of our culture as our
nation took its first prenatal breaths, in the early treatment of America's
native people, and with the arrival and sale of the first American slaves.
All Americans, and particularly blacks, continue to reap the foul harvest
of what William Styron has referred to as the "renewed bondage" that
awaited newly freed slaves after Reconstruction, a bondage "from which
white Americans have always averted their eyes." Styron, like Derrick Bell,
sees American slavery as "a world that may be dead but has not really been
laid to rest."[34]

Theodore Shaw spoke of *Brown* as a watershed in American history. For
American blacks, he said, there was life before *Brown*, and there is life
after *Brown*. But Shaw is well aware that it is *Brown* the symbol that is a
watershed, for *Brown* as a statement of substantive law and even of policy
was—though hugely significant—but a first step in a new effort to lay
American slavery finally to rest. And while Shaw promised further legal

assaults on "work undone," such as racially segregative tracking and ability grouping that may negate the benefits of desegregation, he, like the rest of us who may debate the true foundations of *Brown*, knows that we are now at a point where many of the problems of American education are deeply rooted in the vicious cycles of poverty and a rapidly and radically changing economic landscape, both within the United States and internationally.[35] The solutions, as both Hugh Price and Patricia Carey so forcefully noted in their respective panels, require a breadth of vision that may embrace but must transcend school desegregation, separate schools for black males, or even the restructuring of state school aid formulas.

One of the most poignant moments of our three-day conference came when Price paid tribute to his friend, Shirley Comer, from whose funeral he had just come. Price extolled her work, and that of her husband, James Comer,[36] and referred to an inner tension between the benefits of integration, on the one hand, and the importance of close bonding between family and school, on the other. He takes issue to some extent with Bell, noting that racial barriers have been significantly lowered since *Brown*, but agrees with Carter and Bell that much was not foreseen by black leadership back in 1954. Unlike Bell, however, who attributes his own "naiveté" to an underestimation of the depths of individual and institutional white racism, Price names the unforeseen critical piece as "profound changes in the world economy that would realign work and wealth throughout the world, that would redefine the value attached to various skill levels and that would create enormous schisms among classes in our society."[37] Indeed, both Price and Carey cautioned us not to forget that class schisms exist within the minority community as well and affect the character (if not the racial makeup) of urban public schools. And while Judge Carter assails the community of educators for its failure to bring about more significant achievement among black urban kids, Virginia Mayo Hardy, herself a black educator, emphasizes the need to bring a wide range of community services to the school level, noting that experience has taught her that the task is too great, in present urban America, for educators alone. In order for schools to be "once again . . . the center of a community," she states, basic services such as health clinics, juvenile justice programs, social services, and so forth, must become a part of the school itself. Like Thelma Esteves, she urged the audience to focus on the teacher-student level, where "the real changing of lives" occurs.[38] Each of the "Visions" panelists, like Carey the day before, spoke eloquently of the importance of making educational improvement in our urban areas a priority commitment. Price, like Keven Brown, noted that this commitment is essential, not only for vindicating the educational opportunities of minority schoolchildren, but for sustained economic viability of the American society as we know it.

## CLOSING THOUGHTS

Brian Landsberg compared *Brown* to the Ten Commandments, noting that both are "aspirational in nature."[39] To view *Brown* any other way would be to do a great disservice to the lawyers who tenaciously built the complex and powerful structure on which it had to stand, and would trivialize defining moments in the evolution of our nation's self-concept. It is simply impossible to find in *Brown* proposed solutions to all of the problems visited on our nation's black population by centuries of institutionalized slavery and other forms of overt and insidious discrimination. Like a hydra, this country's history of race discrimination, and the sediment such discrimination leaves behind, is "a multifarious evil not to be overcome by a single effort."[40] The justices of the Supreme Court certainly could not have anticipated all of the twists and turns that would affect American race relations (and American society in general) even in the first ten years that followed the issuance of its landmark opinion, let alone in the past forty years. Moreover, already by 1954, race relations, and the imperative of curtailing discrimination, were matters that looked quite different to people depending on where in the country they lived. While Martin Luther King was the voice for millions of southern blacks who continued to live under the heel of an overt dual system that deprived them of rights as basic and essential to self-determination as the right to vote,[41] many northern black leaders were giving voice to an anger born of years of dashed expectations, of what Kenneth Clark once referred to as "the broken promises of the white community."[42] Integration was a meaningful priority for those living in the South, and for those northerners living in multiracial communities; for many others, economic interests naturally took precedence.

To many, *Brown* has become a symbol of every hope and aspiration of every black American—as Price suggested, a "lowering of barriers to the American Dream." I think, in this respect, that Kevin Brown need not concern himself with whether *Brown* perpetuates notions of racial inferiority, thereby blocking the way to potentially creative ideas such as schools for black males. I do not happen to like the idea of schools that continue to separate people based on race or any other particular criteria, but I am not sure that *Brown* stands in their way. *Brown* was written about a specific situation—it happened to be the norm, and that norm was a system of segregation institutionalized by whites to promote and perpetuate their continued domination over blacks in American society. In decrying the injuries caused by this system, the Court rightfully noted the message of stigma sent to all Americans, that is, that blacks in this country, notwithstanding the official emancipatory language of the thirteenth, fourteenth, and fifteenth amendments, were still second-class citizens.

*Brown*, in my judgment, can be viewed as a straightforward case about liberation. "If you institutionalize a dual system of citizenship," the Court seemed to be saying, "one group will tend to feel superior and to usurp its power in ways that cause lasting injuries to the second-class group, while those with inferior status will experience the impact of their injuries and will tend to feel less worthy, and that is not what our country purports to stand for." Nothing, I submit, was implied concerning innate characteristics of any member of our society, or of any child in an American school. If whites control the schools and say blacks must be separated, then blacks and whites will be aware of the message, and all—but especially those condemned to second-class status—will be injured.[43] The promise was that, after the terrible post-Reconstruction betrayal, America would be given perhaps one last chance to fashion for the first time a democratic society that might live up to its purported ideals of freedom and equality, thereby freeing us not only from a "moral schizophrenia," but from internecine conflict that invariably will limit our long-term ability to compete in the international marketplace.

Finding the way, however, is not simple. Far from it. Not only does change take time, but the remedies are elusive in concept and practice. Notions of "equality" will vary not only among individuals and groups, but over time. It is a difficult, somewhat ambiguous concept, and, as one commentator has noted, its "very ambiguity gives the concept much of its power to motivate, incite and disappoint."[44] Progress will continue to come in bits and pieces, forged no doubt from many different conceptual constructs, both across and within different racial groups. We must constantly struggle to explore the relationship between egalitarianism and excellence, to arrive at approaches that exalt both without taking away from either. That consensus concerning some specific approaches may be difficult to forge should not undermine the important basic agreement over a commitment to equal opportunity and equal justice. The evolving political power and influence of the nation's now multifaced minority communities—a factor that was almost nonexistent at the time of *Brown*—as well as the processes that lead to the formulation of positions within that political sphere can now be expected to exert a forceful influence in this continued evolution.

## CONCLUSION

Let us return to my early years. Great debates raged about how to desegregate New Rochelle's elementary schools. Eventually, the dilapidated Lincoln School was closed, its students bused to schools in surrounding neighborhoods. Was integration a positive experience for the Lincoln School kids who came to Trinity? I have my doubts. They were certainly strangers in what must have been for them a very stange land.[45] What about that bus that took us to New York, though? Were those kids feeling their power in the back of the bus, like the "cool" sixth-graders always seemed to be doing? Or were they feeling their second-class status as symbolized by the back of a bus? Would everyone have profited more if white students had been bused to a newly built Lincoln School? Perhaps, unless, as Bell would have us believe, white power would ultimately have been felt to diminish the self-image of blacks even in their own neighborhood. And what about the barriers of difference that I (and, I would guess, all my classmates, white and black, throughout my [elementary and secondary, undergraduate, law and graduate] school life) experienced as uncertainty, strangeness, on occasion discomfort? Even in our facially integrated institutions, we struggle to find vehicles to break down these barriers. Why do we seem to have such difficulty actually *integrating* the very concept of integration into our day-to-day activities? Do we not place a high enough value on integration itself? Do integrationists (and I count myself among this group), as Brown and Shaw suggest, mouth words of integration without examining the unspoken assumptions we carry that might include an intolerance of alternative cultural "thes[es] of belief?"[46] Must the broader social benefits that would surely come with a more comfortably integrated society stay on hold until we address more successfully the issue of black academic achievement? If so, are we still at a point where racial separation is perceived ultimately by blacks as a symbol of their second-class status in an unjust society? These are questions that require continued vigilance of thought, and to which solutions will not come easy.

I tend to agree with Hugh Price, who values integration but is wary of what he called its "internal contradictions." Indeed, I think that all of the members of the "Promise" and "Visions" panels shared that sense, the knowing that integration, as well as sensitivity to and respect for people with different cultural mores, is the best (and, perhaps, only) hope we have to make our nation a worthy model for the world's admiration, but that in the short run we must explore every creative solution to address the immediate needs of the living children for whom educational success effectively can mean the difference between life and death. In this way, our panelists, as a collective of uniquely dedicated and visionary individual thinkers and practitioners, give life to *Brown*, as a spirit that drives us as we work in our various fields, trying to help find the way to a just society. This is the essence of a flourishing democracy, where, like so many goals to which we as a society aspire, "racial justice remains elusive," but where the continued struggle to define the goal, and then to touch the brass ring, defines the inherent goodness (and frustration) of our system.[47] Martin Luther King, Jr., observed that while "social change cannot come overnight," his commitment was to a movement that "causes one to work as if it were a possibility the next morning."[48]

*Brown* was a gift, long overdue, of spirit and opportunity, a gift of achievable good health to a society ravaged since birth by self-inflicted disease. As 1954 recedes ever more rapidly into the distance of the past, we must focus not so much on the words of the Supreme Court's opinion as on our collective individual experiences in living with its spirit, and on our own collected individual wisdom, crafted to make sense of the world we now are living in, so that future generations, as they try to make their America a healthier one still, will try—as we now attempt to do with our forebears—to make use of *our* vision, and of *our* promise.

## Notes

1    The opening general-session panel on April 14, 1994, "The Promise of *Brown*," featured the following speakers: Kevin T. Brown, Associate Professor of Law, Indiana University School of Law; Patricia M. Carey, Assistant Chancellor, New York University and Associate Dean for Student Services and Public Affairs, NYU's School of Education; Hon. Robert L. Carter, U.S. Senior District Judge for the Southern District of New York, former General Counsel to the NAACP, and one of the original trial and appellate lawyers on the *Brown* case; Jack Greenberg, Professor of Law, Columbia University School of Law, former Director-Counsel of the NAACP Legal Defense and Educational Fund, Inc., and a member of the *Brown* litigating team; and Brian K. Landsberg, Professor of Law, McGeorge School of Law, and former Chief of the Education and Appellate Sections of the Civil Rights Division of the U.S. Department of Justice. I was the moderator of this general-session panel.

The last general-session panel, on April 15, 1994, entitled "Visions for the Future," was moderated by Lovely H. Billups, Director of Field Services in the Educational Issues Department, American Federation of Teachers. Panelists included Robert L. Crain, Professor of Sociology and Education, Teachers College, Columbia University; Thelma Rodriguez Esteves, Principal, Isaac E. Young Middle School, New Rochelle, N.Y.; Virginia Mayo Hardy, Deputy Superintendent of Schools, Community School District 19, New York N.Y.; Hugh B. Price, Executive Director, National Urban League, and at the time of the conference, Vice President, the Rockefeller Foundation; and Theodore M. Shaw, Associate Director-Counsel, NAACP Legal Defense and Educational Fund, Inc., and Assistant Professor of Law, University of Michigan Law School. All references to the speakers in the article refer to this note.

2    One commentator has observed that the ostensible meanings of *Brown* "have multiplied like fruit flies" (David L. Kirp, *Just Schools: The Idea of Racial Equality in American Education* [Berkeley: University of California Press, 1982], p. 14). Brian Landsberg, speaking at the conference, concurred, finding, it seemed, value in this multiplicity of interpretations; he characterized *Brown* as "a 'big tent' kind of opinion that provided shelter for lots of different views as to what racial justice might mean" (Conference Proceedings, "*Brown* Plus Forty," April 14, 1994).

3    For a comprehensive discussion of the various theories offered by scholars to explain the Court's school desegregation jurisprudence, see generally James S. Liebman, "Desegregating Politics: 'All-Out' School Desegregation Explained," *Columbia Law Review* 90 (October 1990): 1463–664. Regarding the argument, see Kevin Brown, Conference Proceedings, "Brown Plus Forty," April 14, 1994. Cf. "Equal Educational Opportunity and Race: School Desegregation in the '90s," *Quality Education for All in the 21st Century: Can We Get*

*There From Here?* (Des Moines, Iowa: Drake University, Constitutional Law Resource Center, 1994), pp. 53–54 (comments of Theodore Shaw); and Lori S. Robinson, "Court Cases Are Still Key," *Emerge* 5 (May 1994): 26 (comments of Theodore M. Shaw concerning what "*Brown* stood for at its core").

4    Or one can argue, like Kevin Brown, that the premise of *Brown* rested on a continued notion of black helplessness and inferiority, and thus does long-term damage to present-day blacks' ability to help themselves through autonomous public institutions such as public schools for black males. See text below.

5    See R. G. Collingwood, *The Idea of History*, rev. ed. (New York: Oxford University Press, 1994), pp. 268–74.

6    Patricia Carey, Conference Proceedings, "Brown Plus Forty," April 14, 1994.

7    My use here of the term "separatists" is meant to refer only to those who view separation as a tool for advancing the standing of blacks in American society, and not to those intent on perpetuating a racial hierarchy with whites at the top and blacks somewhere below. See ibid.

8    See generally, C. Vann Woodward, *The Strange Career of Jim Crow*, 3rd. ed. (New York: Oxford University Press, 1974), pp. 67–74. Woodward's chronicle of blacks in the late nineteenth century as the losers in the reconciliation among northern and southern whites is echoed by Derrick Bell in "The Space Traders," a parable that finds the American government accepting an alien offer to completely eradicate the national debt and all forms of pollution, while at the same time providing a safe and everlasting supply of fossil fuels, in exchange for deporting all of the nation's blacks (*Faces at the Bottom of the Well: The Permanence of Racism* [New York: Basic Books, 1992], pp. 158–94).

9    163 U.S. 537 (1896).

10    See, e.g., W. E. B. Du Bois, *Against Racism: Unpublished Essays, Papers, Addresses, 1887–1961,* ed. Herbert Aptheker (Amherst: University of Massachusetts Press, 1985); Robert A. Hill, ed., *The Marcus Garvey and Universal Negro Improvement Association Papers, Volume V* (Berkeley: University of California Press, 1983), pp. 395–96. See generally, Lerone Bennett, Jr., *Before the Mayflower: A History of the Negro in America 1619–1964,* rev. ed. (New York: Penguin Books, 1966).

11    Aldon D. Morris, *The Origins of the Civil Rights Movement: Black Communities Organizing for Change* (New York: The Free Press, 1984), p. 88 (Comments of Rev. Fred Shuttlesworth).

12    Kenneth B. Clark, "Overview III," in Studs Terkel, *Race: How Blacks & Whites Think & Feel about the American Obsession* (New York: The New Press, 1992), p. 334.

13    When asked by the editor of the *Chicago Defender* to comment on Germany's defeat by the Allies, W. E. B. Du Bois telegrammed this message: "We have conquered Germany but not their ideas. We still believe in white supremacy, keeping Negroes in their place and lying about democracy" (Herbert Aptheker, ed., *The Correspondence of W. E. B. Du Bois [Vol. III]* [Amherst: University of Massachusetts Press, 1978]), p. 39; Brief of United States as Amicus Curiae, *Brown v. Board of Education*, p. 3.

14    "Blacks in 1953 couldn't go to professional or graduate schools in the south. Delaware didn't admit black college applicants. Interstate busses and trains were all segregated; public accommodations from DC south were segregated" (Jack Greenberg, Conference Proceedings, "Brown Plus Forty," April 14, 1994). It would be another ten years after *Brown* before Congress would pass the omnibus Civil Rights Act of 1964, eleven before passage of the historic Voting Rights Act of 1965, and fourteen years before passage (in the wake of Dr. Martin Luther King, Jr.'s assassination) of the Fair Housing Act of 1968. In discussing the school cases' place in LDF's overall litigation strategy, Greenberg noted that when he joined LDF, it had a staff that included but six lawyers.

15    Hugh B. Price, Conference Proceedings, "Brown Plus Forty," April 15, 1994 (emphasis added).

16    See, for example, Ed Wiley III, "Black America's Quest for Education," *Emerge* 5 (May 1994): 32–33.

17    Hon. Robert Carter, Conference Proceedings, "Brown Plus Forty," April 14, 1994. Jack Greenberg, agreeing with Judge Carter, stated that LDF strategy planning documents reveal a determination to "stir the spirit of revolt among black people" (ibid.).

18    The late Justice Marshall was the first Director-Counsel of the NAACP Legal Defense and Educational Fund, Inc., and coordinated the complex web of litigation that culminated in *Brown*. For a comprehensive discussion of Marshall's role, and of the litigation's history, see Richard Kluger, *Simple Justice: The History of Brown v. Board of Education and Black America's Struggle for Equality* (New York: Vintage Books, 1975).

19    Americans with Disabilities Act of 1990, P.L. 101-336, 42 U.S.C. § 12101; P.L. 94-142, 20 U.S.C. § 1400 *et seq.* (since 1990 entitled "Individuals and Disabilities Education Act [IDEA]"); Title IX of the Education Amendments of 1972, P.L. 92-318, 20 U.S.C. § 1681 *et seq.*; 414 U.Sl 563, 94 S.Ct. 786 (1974).

20    Thelma Esteves, Conference Proceedings, "Brown Plus Forty," April 15, 1994. Indeed, it has been averred that *Brown* was not only the embodiment of revolutionary spirit, but that it in fact triggered "a social revolution of mammoth proportions" (Mark G. Yudof et al., *Educational Policy and the Law*, 3rd ed. [St. Paul: West, 1992], p. 469). Dr. Martin Luther King, Jr., was later to characterize the movement as a "revolution for human rights" (*Why We Can't Wait* [New York: Harper & Row, 1964], p. 168).

21    To the contrary, the Court has carefully limited the permissible use of remedial school desegregation decrees to those cases where trial judges have made findings of systemic discriminatory intent. See, e.g., *Columbus Board of Education* v. *Penick*, 443 U.S. 449, 99 S.Ct. 2941 (1979). But cf. *United States* v. *Yonkers Board of Education*, 833 F. Supp. 214, 222 (S.D.N.Y. 1993), in which U.S. District Court Judge Leonard B. Sand finds that continuing disparate outcomes on standardized measures in Yonkers, N.Y., are "the consequence of conditions which are themselves more properly regarded as vestiges" of previous unlawful segregation. See also note 27, below.

22    Robert Crain, Conference Proceedings, "Brown Plus Forty," April 15, 1994.

23    Kenneth Clark, "Brown Plus Forty" Planning Session, New York, N.Y., June 7, 1993.

24    That segregation and integration might both end up as important vehicles in promoting black educational achievement was anticipated by Du Bois years before *Brown*. When asked his views on school desegregation, Du Bois stated: "What I want is education for Negro children. I believe that in the long run this can be best accomplished by unsegregated schools but lack of segregation in itself is no guarantee of education and fine education has often been furnished by segregated schools" (Letter to *Chicago Defender*, October 6, 1945, quoted by Meyer Weinberg, "Du Bois and Desegregation," in *Just Schools* ([Special Report of *Southern Exposure*, vol. 7, p. 119]). See also Aptheker, ed., *The Correspondence of W. E. B. Du Bois*, pp. 120–22 (letter to Charles E. Toney, November 14, 1946) ("segregation or no segregation, American Negro youth must be educated"). For Bell, See "Public Education for Black Children: A Future Role for Dramatic Crisis," *Quality Education for All in the 21st Century: Can We Get There From Here?*, p. 82. Bell, a former school desegregation advocate and presently a professor of law at New York University School of Law, has written extensively concerning the current state of American race relations. See, e.g., his *Faces at the Bottom of the Well.*

25    Ironically, this sense of personal naiveté concerning integration is shared both by Bell, who now decries integration as secondary in importance to control, and by Kenneth Clark, who continues to maintain that integration is essential to the survival of our democracy. Clark says that he was naive in thinking that *Brown* would be a turning point not only for blacks for for whites as well, that it would provide America with a release from its "moral schizophrenia." "I thought," he recounts, "that within ten years or so, America would be free of it" ("Overview III," in Terkel, *Race*, p. 334). Dr. King himself, ten years after *Brown*,

gave voice to a similar faith: "The revolution for human rights," he declaimed, "is opening up unhealthy areas in American life and permitting a new and wholesome healing to take place" *(Why We Can't Wait,* p. 168).

26   The deliberate-speed standard is in *Brown* v. *Board of Education,* 349 U.S. 294, 300-01 *(Brown II)*; it was abandoned in *Alexander v. Holmes County Board of Education,* 396 U.S. 19 (1969) (desegregation remedies must be implemented "forthwith"). The maximum practicable desegregation standard is embraced in *Swann* v. *Charlotte-Mecklenburg Board of Education,* 402 U.S. 1 (1971), and its companion cases.

27   Greenberg, in a way, concedes Bell's point, to the extent that he acknowledges that school desegregation lawyers believed that they could not concern themselves—in the litigation context—with the legally more complex educational quality issues until legally mandated segregation was eradicated. Ironically, in *Freeman* v. *Pitts,* __ U.S. __, 112 S.Ct. 1430 (1992), a decision viewed with trepidation by many civil rights advocates because it appears to facilitate removal of many school desegregation decrees from court supervision, the Court for the first time highlights "quality of education" as a relevant area of inquiry for determining whether the vestiges of unlawful segregation have been eliminated. As in the recent district court opinion in *United States* v. *Yonkers Board of Education* (see note 21, above), this issue has been visited by the Eighth Circuit Court of Appeals in the Kansas City, Mo., desegregation case. In that case, the court upheld a district court's order that the State of Missouri direct substantial expenditures of state monies to the Kansas City school district, to remedy disparities in black and white achievement levels characterized as vestiges of the prior unlawful segregated system (Jenkins v. Missouri, 11 F.3d 755, 764-69 [8th Cir. 1993]), *cert. granted,* no. 93-1823, September 23, 1994). The Supreme Court, which has not to date addressed the issue, granted certiorari and heard arguments in *Jenkins* this term.

28   Patricia Carey, Conference Proceedings, "Brown Plus Forty," April 14, 1994.

29   Jack Greenberg, Conference Proceedings, "Brown Plus Forty," April 14, 1994. See also Robinson, "Court Cases Are Still Key," p. 26 (comments of Theodore M. Shaw); and Liebman, "Desegregating Politics," pp. 1624–25.

30   Liebman describes this in somewhat different, "redistributive" terms, whereby integration would ensure for blacks a place in society's dominant educational institutions ("Desegregating Politics," p. 1624).

31   The insidious impact of white-controlled and dominated cultural assumptions in the public schools was noted on our panels, not only by Kevin Brown and Theodore Shaw, who drew attention to the issue specifically, but implicitly by Judge Carter, who acknowledged that *Brown* was crafted with a view to gaining entry for blacks into white society: "All of us assumed that the dominant culture would be the white culture" (Carter, Conference Proceedings). Indeed, Marcus Garvey lashed out at W. E. B. Du Bois over this issue in 1919, accusing Du Bois of seeking to incorporate American and African blacks into a white "capitalist" world (Hill, ed., *The Marcus Garvey and Universal Negro Improvement Association Papers,* pp. 395–96). That we have now moved to a point where a variety of minority groups are subjecting the dominant cultural assumptions of our society to close scrutiny, and where cultural issues are being raised as a component of equal educational opportunity, highlights the distance we have come—from simply gaining entry to insistence on an equitable playing field—since 1954.

32   Bell, "Public Education for Black Children," p. 82.

33   Thelma Esteves, Conference Proceedings, "Brown Plus Forty," April 15, 1994, quoting from William Shakespeare, *The Tragedy of Macbeth,* Act III, Scene ii (New York: Signet Classics, 1963), p. 80.

34   William Styron, "Slavery's Pain, Disney's Gain," *The New York Times,* August 4, 1994, p. A23.

35    That poverty and race overlap to a great extent in America's cities is, to be sure, neither coincidental nor irrelevant to this discussion. On the other hand, the problems that severe poverty brings with it into schools and classrooms often must be addressed with comprehensive remedial approaches that require far greater reconstructive vision than the simple desegregation of student bodies and/or faculties. See generally, James P. Comer, *School Power: Implications of an Intervention Project* (New York: Free Press, 1980); and Lisbeth B. Schorr, *Within Our Reach: Breaking the Cycle of Disadvantage* (New York: Doubleday, 1988), especially pp. 179–255. As Dr. King observed thirty years ago, "What will it profit the Negro to be able to send his children to an integrated school if the family income is insufficient to buy them clothes?" (*Why We Can't Wait*, p. 148).

36    See, e.g., Comer, *School Power.*

37    Hugh B. Price, Conference Proceedings, "Brown Plus Forty," April 15, 1994.

38    Virginia Mayo Hardy, Conference Proceedings, "Brown Plus Forty," April 15, 1994. James Comer concurs, stating that "schools are being asked to solve social problems they did not create," such as malnutrition, housing decay, unemployment, and various forms of invidious, systemic discrimination (*School Power*, p. 16).

39    Brian Landsberg, Conference Proceedings, "Brown Plus Forty," April 14, 1954.

40    Webster's New Collegiate Dictionary (Springfield, Mass.: G. & C. Merriam Co., 1977), p. 559.

41    Dr. King, of course, was a spokesperson for blacks (and many whites) from throughout the country. His rise to legendary status, however, clearly sprang from his efforts to break down formal barriers to equal opportunity in the South. See generally, Martin L. King, *Stride Toward Freedom* (New York: Harper & Row, 1958) (Perennial Library ed., 1964); and idem, *Why We Can't Wait.*

42    Kenneth B. Clark, "Introduction," in Mario Fantini et al., *Community Control and the Urban School* (New York: Praeger, 1970), p. x.

43    Du Bois actually anticipated the Court's reasoning in *Brown* when he wrote, ten years prior to the decision, "No separation of schools by race or class must be permitted *which involves any limitation of educational opportunity for anyone*" (*Against Racism*, ed. (Aptheker; from his proposed "Program of Organization for Realizing Democracy in the United States by Securing to Americans of Negro Descent the Full Rights of Citizens," March 19, 1944), p. 225 (emphasis added).

44    Kirp, *Just Schools*, p. 9.

45    In a study marking *Brown*'s twenty-fifth anniversary, a southern black educator and parent noted that "a big part of the problem [with integration] is that our children don't know who they are in desegregated schools" (Charles Hardy, "Making the Extra Effort . . . Again," in *Just Schools*, p. 96).

46    Kevin Brown and Theodore Shaw, Conference Proceedings, "Brown Plus Forty," April 14 and 15, 1994.

47    "Not Just Another Monday," Editorial, *The New York Times*, October 4, 1994, p. A20.

48    King, *Stride Toward Freedom*, pp. 197–98.

# *Brown* at Forty:
# Six Visions

BURT NEUBORNE
*New York University*

*This article, originally delivered as an address to a conference of public school edu-cators, argues that the Supreme Court's decision in* Brown *was an act of prophecy calling the nation to a new level of moral consciousness. I argue that current efforts to denigrate* Brown *as a failure overlook the opinion's effect as a social catalyst for the movement toward equality. Nevertheless, I concede that the promise of* Brown *has not yet been fulfilled. I urge a rededication to the principles of moral decency on which the opinion is based and a recognition that* Brown *was the beginning of our journey, not its culmination. I offer six visions of* Brown *in an effort to grasp its contemporary meaning:* Brown *as triumph, aspiration, catalyst, failure, challenge, and promise.*

I am grateful to have this opportunity to share my thoughts about the *Brown* v. *Board of Education of Topeka, Kansas,* decision and about some of the most important issues that face us today. My life is bound up with the decision in *Brown*. I was a young man of thirteen visiting Charleston, South Carolina, when the decision came down. I remember the day starkly. I remember an extraordinary sense of shock that settled on the people in that community as they were forced (and forced is the right word) to come to grips with an equality that they did not dream they would have to deal with in their lifetimes. Equality was upon them in a way that would change their world forever.

When I read today's academic critiques of *Brown* suggesting that the case really did not achieve much in American life, that it is overvalued as a precedent, that it is an icon we have idealized but do not look closely at, I wish those critics could have been in Charleston that day as the idea of equality, spoken in the firmest tones possible by the highest court of the land, was assimilated into the thinking of a caste of people who never dreamed that they would have to confront black people as equals. In many ways, my road to the American Civil Liberties Union (ACLU) and to the New York University Law School began that day in Charleston when I saw the power of law as an instrument of social justice.

These are challenging days for the *Brown* decision. There is an academic assault on *Brown*. Some are asking difficult and troubling questions about precisely how much impact *Brown* really has had on American life. They ask: "Were the welcome changes that came to the United States in the years after *Brown* really propelled  by the decision or was *Brown* simply a symptom of an underlying social trend dating from World War II and from changes in the economics and the structure of society?" "Would these trends have caused widespread racial change and even greater opportunities for racial justice in the absence of *Brown*?" These critiques, especially Gerald Rosenberg's work several years ago, call into question not just *Brown*, but the very use of law as an effort to achieve social justice.[1] The challenge is to prove that law really does change things and that law is capable of being utilized as an engine for social justice—and not (as it has been in virtually every society) as an engine of oppression, an engine by which the powerful recycle their power, using law as a club to keep the weak in place.

The dream we have had during my life as a public-interest lawyer is that we could make law something different. Instead of a club that had been used in virtually every other society as a way of freezing the status quo, we hoped that we could use law to break the status quo: to pave the way for change and to use the moral power of the Supreme Court as a way of calling the nation to be better than it had been.

But Rosenberg's work asks some very troubling questions about law and social change. It asks, have you really been successful? How much have you actually done? Are we really better off now than we were before *Brown*? The sobering reality is that many people of color are also asking troubling and difficult questions about whether *Brown* really has made a difference, a positive difference in their lives. For the first time in debates and discussions, especially with my students, I am hearing the following questions in the classrooms: "Are we really better off now forty years after *Brown*? Are we really better off than we were before *Brown*? Would people of color have been better off if *Brown* had never been decided? Would they have been better off if they had been left to develop their own institutions and their own lives without the golden challenge of being pushed into the mainstream by a Supreme Court that announced an aspiration but no means to enforce it? Should we abandon the aspirations of universality that underlies *Brown* and retreat back to a world without the challenge of attempting to live together?"

I never heard those questions until recent years. Most of my life has been spent committed to the proposition that *Brown* was the most important moral moment in the American law in this century—that it began to undo the stain of *Dred Scott*,[2] that it began to try to redeem a promise of equality that is in the Constitution, but is often buried there and never becomes a reality; and that the use of law to achieve social justice was the highest calling that an American lawyer could aspire to. I must tell you that when I hear these questions, when I read books like Rosenberg's book, which is a challenging and troublesome book by a serious academic,[3] when I hear questions from the best of my students, from students who care, from students whose anger would once have been channeled into the civil rights movement, when I hear them ask if it was worth the candle, I realize that we who have lived with *Brown* as an article of faith have a great deal of explaining to do: that the challenge of *Brown* is not only making it a reality, but keeping the flame alive in an era in which there are many who would give up the struggle.

I think the first thing that I have to do as an academic, an educator, and a civil rights lawyer is to acknowledge the power of the critique. Lawyers have often oversold law as the way to deal with social justice. When I began as a civil rights lawyer in the 1960s, there was a naiveté. It was a naiveté that I wish we could recapture. The world seemed simpler then; the assumption was that if we could only remove the legal chains that bound people into apartheid, then equality would inevitably and inexorably follow. We assumed that what was stopping equality in this nation was not deep wellsprings of racism and deep economic inequality, but an artificial impediment caused by law, and if we could just get rid of the impediment, equality would then follow. I once believed that. Much of my younger life was spent in courts all over the country desperately trying to break those chains of inequality, and I am proud of every moment of it. I think it was worth it and would urge people to continue to do it. But I must confess to you that I now realize that the task is much more complicated than any of us understood in the 1960s.

We thought we were at the end of a great moral journey. We now realize that we were merely at the beginning of a much more difficult moral journey. We now know that the removal of the chains of law that locked people into inequality make it possible for us to move toward moral greatness as a people, but it does not guarantee that we are going to get there. Just getting rid of the legal chains does not get rid of the social chains and the psychological chains and the behavioral chains that centuries of oppression have imposed on us all. And so one thing that people who care about *Brown*, people who care about law as an instrument of social justice, must do is that we must acknowledge that lawyers cannot solve the problem alone.

What lawyers can do, and what we must do, is unlock the society so that it can begin to work out its own problems in two ways. You unlock the society first by removing legal impediments to decency. When law impedes decency by preventing people from acting in decent ways, there is no way that a society can achieve moral greatness. So one of the first requirements, one of the first obligations of American lawyers, is to continue to search out legal impediments to decency and to get rid of them. Once that occurs, there is a complicated process of healing that involves educators, psychologists, doctors—that involves the entire spectrum of the society in a cooperative effort to undo the harm that years of oppression impose on a society. In short, we have to acknowledge that changing the law does not change the society. It just begins the process of change.

Second, I think we have to acknowledge that for many people of color in this society today, life is so bleak, so friendless, so without opportunity, that it is rational for them to reject the notion of integration, to reject the notion of living with a white society that has simply refused to carry out the promise of *Brown*—a society that continues to starve education and desperately needed services in the inner cities. We cannot pretend that the rage that fuels these young people is an aberrational event that we can cure by just having them read a few more books. The rage that fuels these young people is a real symptom of social failure that we have to confront before it overwhelms us as a people and destroys the possibility of *Brown* entirely.

These days, given the power of the critique of *Brown*, there is a temptation to surrender to despair, a temptation to say that *Brown* is a failed social experiment, that it was an excercise in romanticism, that different races cannot really live together. The best that we can hope is that they will live side-by-side without trying to kill each other, but that the true notion of a community of people who love one another despite the differences in their skin color and their religion and their ethnic background and their gender and their sexual orientation—that that type of community simply cannot be achieved. I cannot surrender to that despair. I will not surrender to that despair, and I hope the rest of you will not either.

It reminds me of a discussion I had when I was on sabbatical several years ago in Paris. I would get up each morning and I would go to work at the Sorbonne and I would be surrounded by a series of French professors who would take turns telling me what was wrong with American life. We would start at 9:30, we would end at 4:15 each day. We would stop for lunch—but I would be required to take the appropriate amount of notes and to eat an appropriate amount of crow each day. Monday, I think, was food, Tuesday was literature, Wednesday was something else—Friday was philosophy. Fridays, I would come to school and they would tell me that in France, philosophers were revered, they are public figures, you see them on television, they discuss all sorts of interesting things, they are treated as major figures, and they challenged me to name a single American philosopher who had attained prominence in American society.

So I went home that afternoon and I said to my wife, "They got me again. They nailed me again. How can I answer them? I have to have some answer for them after lunch." Then it occurred to me on the way back on the Metro that the dominant strain of French philosophy, at least since World War II, has been one or another strain of existentialism, dwelling on the difficulty of living a rational life in an irrational world. And I thought to myself, "What's the equivalent of that strain of thought on this side of the Atlantic?" And it struck me, in large part because of cultural differences in the two systems, that people in the United States who would have studied philosophy in France and would have gone on to speak in those terms, to debate in those terms, go into two professions: They become civil rights lawyers or they become teachers. And they carry out a desperate struggle to do rational things in an irrational world.

I know as a civil rights lawyer that it is impossible to do substantial justice in a society that is beset with economic inequality. It is impossible; it rationally cannot be done. And yet I know that if I am going to live in this society, if I am going to be a part of a legal system in this society, I can do one of two things. I can cynically surrender and simply go ahead and just carry out my career, make as much money as I can, and forget about the fact that I am operating in an unjust system. Or I can act as though justice were possible, and make a life knowing rationally that perfect justice is impossible but refusing to acknowledge in one's heart that it cannot be achieved, which of course is the ultimate definition of existentialism. So I said to my French colleagues when I got back that afternoon, "You're wrong. I'll show you philosophers in the United States that have more influence on public policy than any philosopher in France. You show me an American civil rights lawyer, you show me an American public school teacher in an urban public school, and I'll show you a practicing existentialist. I'll show you individuals who, in the recesses of the rational mind, know that what they're trying to do is impossible; but they keep doing it anyway—and they achieve miracles. Small and minor miracles through the triumph of the commitment of the heart over the despair of the mind."

My wife always says that I redouble my efforts whenever I lose sight of my goals. I think the definition of where I am at this point is yes, I acknowledge the critique of *Brown*; yes, I acknowledge how much we have failed, how far below we are from where I hoped we would be forty years after the opinion. But if we give in to despair, we betray all of the ideals of those years. This is the time to redouble our efforts, not because we have lost sight of our goals, but because we still know who we are. This is not a time to listen to the counsel of despair, or to listen to the counsel of cynicism, but to redouble a commitment to the ideals of *Brown*. And in that light, let me give you six visions of *Brown*.

I am going to suggest six visions of *Brown* that we have to keep in our minds at the same time if we are to have a real picture of the case. The first is a vision of triumph: *Brown* as achievement. Never lose sight of the fact that *Brown* began a series of cases that lasted for eleven years and that utterly and totally dismantled legally reinforced apartheid in every single aspect of American life. *Brown* is not just an education case. *Brown* is an apartheid case and as an achievement it is extraordinary. It is probably the only time in any culture, over a period of that time, that apartheid has been dismantled, root and branch, in eleven years. Never forget that the legal regime of apartheid was destroyed by *Brown* and destroyed effectively.

Just as an anecdote, when I began working on Wall Street as a lawyer in the early 1960s, there was not a black face, not in my firm, not in my building, not even on the subway train that went to Wall Street. When I set foot in that building for the first time, I was absolutely stunned. Today, when I go back to visit my firm, there are black partners, black associates; the multitextured hue of the culture was irrevocably changed by *Brown*. And so, let us not forget what a triumph *Brown* was in the dismantling of legally reinforced apartheid.

The second vision is also triumphant: *Brown* as aspiration. American law has never spoken with the moral fervor, with the moral authority—I will go further—with the moral prophecy that it attained in *Brown*. When the Supreme Court spoke in *Brown*, it spoke to the very best in us, to the very best that we could be, to the very best we could hope to be as a people. *Brown* succeeded in setting a benchmark for decency that we can aim for, that survives from generation to generation, and that is a luminous symbol of what we could be as a people if only we could learn to live that way. In that sense, *Brown* functions like moral prophecy in religion. There is to *Brown* a prophetic, almost religious call to decency that is part of its moral strength and that is one of the most successful aspects of the opinion and that is something precious that all the sociologists in the world cannot measure. How do you measure the effect of a decent thought? How do you measure the impact of a call to moral greatness on a people? Let us not forget that that's what *Brown* did.

The third vision of *Brown* is *Brown* as catalyst. *Brown* ushered in an idea of egalitarianism in this society that is still playing itself out. If it were not for *Brown*, there would not be a women's movement. There would not be a gay rights movement. There would not be a movement for the relief of oppression of group after group in American society that found its identity because it read *Brown* and realized that there was an aspiration for equality embedded in the Constitution that was the common property of every oppressed group. *Brown* as a catalyst moved us toward the political understanding of egalitarianism that underlies every single civil rights statute passed since that time and the enduring movement for equality that continues as the Rainbow Coalition and as the political movements for equality in American society today.

Now, the bleaker side: *Brown* as failure. *Brown* did not integrate the schools, especially in the North. *Brown* did not penetrate the consciousness of all white Americans. *Brown* did not bring about a brave new world of racial decency and fairness. The world is very different than it was before *Brown*; but if you measure *Brown* against its aspiration, against what we prayed and hoped it would achieve, *Brown* has not fully succeeded, not in the way we thought it could. And that is a sad thing that we have to acknowledge. We could have been better, so much better. *Brown* called us to it and we did not respond.

That leads me to the fifth vision of *Brown*: Brown as challenge, the name of this aptly named conference. For me, the challenge is to remember the difference between aspiration and failure; to insist that the role of the next generation is to close that gap as much as possible; to press forward on every front, legally, educationally, politically, socially, to make it possible, now that we no longer are bound by chains of law and chains of ignorance, to deal with the divisions of the society. We can learn to love one another in our separateness so that we can go forward and talk about being separate *and* equal, not separate *but* equal—separate and equal. To remember that we are both different and the same and to love both.

And finally, *Brown* as promise. *Brown* sets the standard of what a decent world could be if only we would learn to do it. When I think of many of you teaching in the public schools, the notion that we could help each child to understand that the world can be as *Brown* promised it could be, that the moral prophecy of *Brown* is not just words on a piece of paper, is not just law, but is a real promise of what America could be if we would only learn to listen to the voice of *Brown* v. *Board of Education*. So I think it is wonderful that the conference focuses on *Brown*. I think it is fitting that we acknowledge our losses and our failures, but I think it is even more fitting, indeed, wonderful, that we go forward with the notion of *Brown* as a commitment to decency over the years to come. I want to leave you with my favorite line from American poetry, a line that encapsulates my beliefs about *Brown*. I hope it encapsulates yours. It is by Robert Frost, in *The Black Cottage:* "Why abandon a belief merely because it ceases to be true?"[4] Frost was telling us that ideas come in and out of fashion. Sometimes, the academics like them, sometimes they do not. But there are some ideas that remain true whether or not academics like them, whether or not politicians embrace them, and one of those enduring truths is the promise of *Brown*.

## Notes

1   Gerald L. Rosenberg, *The Hollow Hope: Can Courts Bring about Social Change* (Chicago: University of Chicago Press, 1991).

2   Dred Scott v Sandford, 19 How. (60 U.S.) 393 (1857).

3   Rosenberg, *The Hollow Hope.*

4   Robert Frost, "The Black Cottage," from *The Poetry of Robert Frost*, ed. Edward C. Lathem (New York: Henry Holt, 1979), p. 55.

# About the Editors and Contributors

ELLEN CONDLIFFE LAGEMANN is professor of history and education and director of the Center for the Study of American Culture and Education at New York University. A member of the Teachers College faculty from 1978 until 1994, she was editor of the *Teachers College Record* from 1990 to 1995. Her last book, *The Politics of Knowledge: The Carnegie Corporation, Philanthropy, and Public Policy,* is available from the University of Chicago Press.

LAMAR P. MILLER is professor of education and executive director of the Metropolitan Center for Urban Education, New York University. He is the author of "School Desegregation and Early Childhood Education," *The Encyclopedia of Early Childhood Education* (Garland, 1992).

JOSHUA P. BOGIN is senior project associate, New York University's Equity Assistance Center.

KEVIN BROWN is professor of law, Indiana University, Bloomington.

ROBERT L. CARTER, former NAACP General Counsel, Special Assistant U.S. Attorney, and partner at Poletti, Friedin, Prashker, Feldman & Gartner, is presently U.S. District Judge in the Southern District of New York.

ROSA CASTRO FEINBERG is associate professor, College of Education, Florida International University, and a member of the Dade County School Board. She is the author of "Getting Your Act Together: The Use of Technology to Increase Your Effectiveness in Public Service," *The American School Board Journal* (forthcoming).

HOWARD A. GLICKSTEIN is dean and professor of law, Touro College, Jacob D. Fuchsberg Law Center. Dean Glickstein was the former General Counsel and Staff Director of the United States Commission for Civil Rights.

EDMUND W. GORDON is the John M. Musser Professor of Psychology, Emeritus, at Yale University. He is currently Distinguished Professor of Educational Psychology, City College and the Graduate School of the City University of New York.

CARL A. GRANT is Hoefs Bascom Professor, University of Wisconsin–Madison. He is the coauthor, with Mary L. Gomez of, *Campus and Classrooms: Making Schooling Multicultural* (Merrill/Macmillan 1995).

WILLIS D. HAWLEY is professor of education and public affairs and dean of the College of Education, University of Maryland, College Park.

JEFFREY R. HENIG is professor of political science and director of the Center for Washington Area Studies, George Washington University. He is the author of *Rethinking School Choice: Limits of the Market Metaphor* (Princeton University Press, 1994).

BRIAN K. LANDSBERG is professor of law, McGeorge School of Law, University of the Pacific, Sacramento, California. He is the author of "Equal Educational Opportunity: The Rehnquist Court Revisits *Green* and *Swann, 42 Emory Law Journal 821* (1993).

CONSTANCE BAKER MOTLEY is Senior U.S. District Judge, Southern District of New York. She is the author of "The Historical Setting of *Brown* and Its Impact on the Supreme Court's Decision," *61 Fordham L. Review* (1992).

JOHN A. MURPHY is superintendent of schools, Charlotte-Mecklenburg, North Carolina.

BURT NEUBORNE is professor law, New York University.

JEANNIE OAKES is professor and assistant dean in the Graduate School of Education and Information Studies, University of California, Los Angeles.

GARY ORFIELD is professor in the department of Administration, Planning and Social Policy, Harvard University.

DENNIS SAYERS directs the bilingual educational program, in the department of teaching and learning, School of Education New York University.

LISA A. TANNERS is a graduate student in the Ph.D. program in school psychology and works as a research assistant at the Metropolitan Center for Urban Education, New York University.

AMY STUART WELLS is assistant professor of educational policy, University of California, Los Angeles. She is author of *Time to Choose: America at the Crossroads of School Choice Policy* (Hill and Wang, 1993).

ROGER WILKINS is Robinson Professor of History, George Mason University. A lawyer, he has practiced law in New York, served in the federal government under Presidents Kennedy and Johnson, and worked as a journalist at the *Washington Star, New York Times*, and *Washington Post.*

JUDITH A. WINSTON is General Counsel, U. S. Department of Education, on leave as associate professor of law, Washington College of Law, American University.

# Index

in minority-majority schools, 45
poverty of, 12
in the Southwest, 50–51
tracking and, 81–90
trends regarding, 76
*Lau* v. *Nichols,* 11, 158, 165 n. 5, 167, 175, 187
Leake, D. O., 120 n. 22
Lee, V., 176, 181 n. 4
Lehrer, Dan, 173 n. 2
Lesbian and gay rights movement, 15
Levin, Henry M., 104 n. 3, 142 n. 1
Lewis, Samuel, 127–128
Lichter, D. T., 181 n. 13
Lieberman, Myron, 134 n. 11
Liebman, James, 51 n. 5, 175, 179, 180 n. 2, 194–195 n. 3
Lin, Nan, 100, 106 n. 31
Little Rock, Arkansas, desegregation of schools, 29, 40–41, 110, 112
Longshore, Douglas, 104 n. 4
Los Angeles riot, 61
Louisiana, 37, 39
Louisville, Kentucky, busing in, 63–64
Lucy, Autherine, 39–40

Madison, James, 14
Magnet schools, 67, 138, 158, 159
  goals of, 129
  in Montgomery County, Maryland, 129–134
  school choice and, 129–134
Magnet Schools Assistance Program, 158, 159
Mahard, Rita E., 95, 102, 105 n. 14, 106 n. 40
Malcolm X, 185
Marshall, Thurgood, 14, 107, 108, 185, 186, 196 n. 18
Maryland, 129–134, 149, 152, 160, 171
Massey, Douglas S., 1–2, 6 n. 3, 150
Maximum practicable desegregation, 188
McCammon, Holly J., 181 n. 9
McConahay, John B., 69 n. 29, 104–105 n. 6
McDonald, Stan, 69 n. 30
McIntosh, P., 111, 120 n. 19
McLeon, Jane D., 181 n. 14
McPartland, James M., 7 n. 15, 99, 102, 104

n. 3, 106 n. 26
Mehan, Hugh, 179, 181 n. 18
Menacker, James, 178, 181 n. 12
Meredith, James, 41–43
Metcalf, G. R., 120 n. 15
Metropolitan Center for Urban Education, 6, 9–10, 19
Miller, LaMar P., 6, 9–13, 71–80
Milliken II Programs, 149
*Milliken* v. *Bradley,* 32, 59
Mississippi, 39, 41–43, 162
Missouri, 97, 100
Moe, Terry M., 134 n. 11
Montgomery, James, 106 n. 31
Montgomery Bus Boycott (Alabama), 15, 39, 44
Montgomery County Public Schools (Maryland), 129–134
Moore, David C., 181 n. 15
Morality, racial equality and, 3–4
Morgan, Michael, 170, 174 n. 11
Morris, Aldon D., 195 n. 11
Motley, Constance Baker, 37–43
Multicultural perspective, 44–53, 118–119
  bilingual programs in, 75–77
  concept of, 72, 73
  and cultural deprivation paradigm, 51
  curriculum in, 78
  defined, 44
  global learning networks and, 172–173
  immigrants and, 72, 73, 78–79, 169
  as utopian vision, 46
Murphy, John A., 143–150
Murray, Charles, 1, 6 n. 1
Myrdal, Gunnar, 2–4, 7 n. 11

National Assessment of Educational Progress (NAEP), 151–152
National Association for the Advancement of Colored People (NAACP), 4–5, 14, 22, 39, 43, 92–93, 108, 110, 185
National Education Goals, 163–164
National Governors' Association, 90
National Opinion Research Center (NORC), 59, 60
National Urban League, 186
*Nation at Risk, A,* 124
Native Americans, trends regarding, 76